VINTAGE CARBERY

VINTAGE CARBERY

by P.D. Mehigan

edited by Sean Kilfeather

BEAVER ROW PRESS

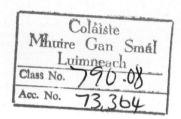
VINTAGE CARBERY
This selection first published in 1984 by
Beaver Row Press
9 Beaver Row, Donnybrook
Dublin 4, Ireland

ISBN 0946308 80 2 (paper)
      0946308 81 0 (cloth)

Cover design by Wendy Dunbar
Computerset in 11/12 Century Oldstyle by
Computext Ltd., Dublin
Printed and bound by Dublin University Press

Acknowledgments
The publishers and the editor are deeply grateful to the Mehigan family for
their unstinted co-operation in the production of this book. Thanks are also
due to all of the original publishers of Carbery's writings -- the *Cork Weekly
Examiner,* the *Kerryman,* the *Irish Times* and the *Cork Sportsman* (where he
first started to write under the Carbery name in 1909) and many others. The
Gaelic Athletic Association has also been supportive and enthusiastic about the
production and the co-operation of the President, Mr. Paddy Buggy, the
Director-General, Mr. Liam Mulvihill, and the PRO, Mr. Pat Quigley, is very
much appreciated. Many others, too numerous to mention, have contributed in
word and deed. *Buiochas doibh go leir.*

CONTENTS

A MEMOIR

By Peter Holohan

IT IS so long ago now since I first met Paddy Mehigan that I can't remember whether the purpose of his visit to Kilkenny was to cover Sevenhouses Coursing meeting or a hurling game in Nowlan Park for the *Irish Times.*
He had been a regular attender at Sevenhouses for many years. In his day, especially in Cork, Tipperary and Kilkenny there was a common bond between hurling men and coursing enthusiasts.

In the years that I knew him he never failed to attend Sevenhouses, then regarded as one of the best coursing meetings in the country. I think he liked coming to Kilkenny; he had many friends here. Jack Rochford, one of Kilkenny's greatest full backs, played against him in the 1904 All-Ireland hurling final and other Kilkenny hurlers who knew him well were Lory Meagher and Paddy Phelan. In fact it was established practice that Paddy and myself travelled from the city to the coursing in Paddy Phelan's car.

Whether his assignment was coursing or a hurling game he liked nothing better than to spend some time in Christy Bollard's licensed premises where he invariably met his friends.

On one occasion after the first day's coursing at Sevenhouses he was in the company of Barry Nolan of the *Irish Independent* and myself.

Barry was very keen to inveigle Paddy to the coursing dance held that night in the then Mayfair Ballroom. After inducing him to have one over his usual limited quota it was easy enough to do the rest and Paddy was unaware of his whereabouts until he met coursing club president, M.J. Mulhall in the ballroom. "Look what those fellows have done to me, Joe" he said; "they have brought me to a dance." Ballroom dancing wasn't Paddy's line of country but he took the joke in good part.

On another occasion the long standing friendly relations between Jack Rochford and himself were almost brought to an end. Paddy had told a story in the *Cork Weekly Examiner* about someone having remarked to Jack Rochford, "Easy for you to be a good full back, Jack; you met bad forwards." And Jack was alleged to have replied, "No, boy, I met the best of forwards, but I made them look bad."

Jack was infuriated when he read this and I had great difficulty in convincing him that Paddy didn't write this off his own bat; he was merely quoting someone else as having said it.

Only the older generation of coursing men and hurling followers in Kilkenny will remember Paddy Mehigan; they will remember him for the quiet dignity with which he carried himself; his affable, kindly and courteous manner. A great many of his friends have passed away since his death but those that remain will, like myself, feel happy that the valuable contribution he made to sport will not go unhonoured.

INTRODUCTION

A SERIES of coincidences, all of them happy, have contrived to bring this volume to the bookshelves. Chance meetings and telephone calls have played their part; ideas have come up quite suddenly in vague conversations; the typesetters, unaware of what was being planned, suggested "Century" as a type-face for the text and, happiest of all, March 17th 1984 is the 100th birthday of Carbery as well as being the official launch-day of the centenary celebrations of the Gaelic Athletic Association which he loved to the point of distraction.

For years the Mehigan family have toyed with the idea of republishing all or part of the vast amount of writing produced by P.D. Mehigan under his own name or that of Carbery or Pat O. From time to time old volumes of *Carbery's Annual* have come to light reviving these hopes but nothing concrete was done until the spirit of Carbery himself, or so it would seem, decided to take a hand.

The publishers, Beaver Row Press, had never ventured into the world of sport previously. Yet their association with the poet and sportsman Brendan Kennelly was to play a seminal role. The poet, Kevin Byrne, from the publishers and Sean Kilfeather discussed the possibility of a volume of essays on G.A.A. themes as a way to mark the G.A.A. centenary. Within the space of 24 hours Kilfeather had a chance meeting with Carbery's senior son, Denis Mehigan, a long-time acquaintance and, over a drink in one of Carbery's favourite haunts, The Palace Bar in Fleet Street, the subject of republication resurfaced and finally took control of everybody involved.

Soon Catherine Leyden, Carbery's grand-daughter, had lent her considerable enthusiasm to the search for the annuals. The other members of the Mehigan clan became involved and a set of the publications, dusty but complete, was cobbled together and became the source material for this book.

To give even a vague impression of the scope of the material contained within those pages would in itself be a huge task. Although Carbery will be remembered mainly for his writings about Gaelic games he also produced short stories, poetry, nature study, socio-political commentary, reflections on history, in short anything which took his fancy. He walked prodigious distances with a "stout ash plant" and a packet of cheese sandwiches covering on one occasion 100 miles in four days over the mountain roads and passes of Kerry and Cork. His work as a Customs officer took him to every county in Ireland. His descriptions of the scenery, the people he met on the way, his reflections on the history and folklore of the area, his constant concern for the condition of "the harvest," his fanaticism about wild life, his love of athletic prowess, step-dancing, coursing, music-making and everything which touched on the Irish life-style of his day provided him with ample inspiration for his writing, most of which appeared then in *Carbery's Column* in the *Cork Weekly Examiner.*

Born in Ardfield in County Cork on March 17th, 1884 — he liked to claim that he was older than the G.A.A. — he soon knew the pain of exile, first from Ardfield to the Civil Service in Dublin before the turn of the century and later to a post in London. He met Michael Cusack and admired him greatly. He had played hurling with a Rathmines team in Dublin and in London was good enough to be chosen to play against Cork in the 1902 All-Ireland final. London were beaten by his native Cork.

On his return to Ireland he joined the Blackrock club in Cork city and was a member of the Cork team which beat Kilkenny in the All-Ireland final of 1905. Kilkenny objected on the grounds that a former member of the British forces had played for Cork and in a replay, Kilkenny won and Carbery was deprived of his All-Ireland medal. He did however win an Irish title in the hop, step and jump and was a first-class athlete in many other events including the high jump and the sprints. It is also reported that he was an Irish champion step-dancer and an accomplished bowl player.

By 1926 he had been transferred to Dublin and became the first person to broadcast a running commentary on an outdoor sporting event in Europe. It is thought that he was second in the world only to an American boxing commentator. His first venture on to the airwaves is vividly described here.

He was now a national figure and, even though he had a family of six children to rear, he took the amazing step in 1934 of retiring from the Civil Service to devote his time to writing on a full-time basis. The fact that he reared and educated a big family on the proceeds is an indication of the determination and devotion he had to writing and gives rise to an amusing family anecdote. One of his favourite nephews, Michael Sullivan, noted that whenever Carbery was short of something to write about he had recourse to a description of the life of a thrush which had made its home in a tree outside his window in Dartmouth Square in Dublin. He wrote so often about the bird that the nephew once remarked: "Ye know, that ould thrush put the boys through college."

Carbery threw himself into journalism with great energy. He became Gaelic Games and coursing correspondent for the *Irish Times* and continued to write *Carbery's Column* in the *Cork Weekly Examiner* as well as contributing to many other papers, journals and magazines. He produced his first annual in 1939 and this publication became a firm favourite from then until his death in 1965. He also wrote histories of football, hurling and athletics.

Among his colleagues he was loved and respected. Mitchel Cogley, now the elder statesman of sports journalism, wrote on the occasion of Carbery's death: "(He was) a gentle man of innate culture, a lover of all that was best in life, a raconteur whose engrossing tales were never tinged with unkindness, a master of his craft whose knowledge, judgment and experience were at the disposal of all who worked with him.

"Words of praise from Pat O, and he didn't spare them, were an accolade to be treasured by his colleagues and rivals and if he had no praise to offer he gently steered the conversation into another channel. It was he who some years back coined a phrase which might have been his own epitaph: 'No better man'."

The reader who is already familiar with the Mehigan style and approach may well lament the absence here of this essay or that report. Some may say that there is too much hurling, too little poetry, not enough football, a scarcity of coursing, a lack of balance. The selection of the pieces included, however, are quite arbitrary and the editor's only regret is that there is not more of everything.

For those who have never come across Carbery before it is hoped that the choice of extracts may give an insight into the author's mind and whet the appetite for more.

Without doubt Carbery was a remarkable man. His writing today is as lively and evocative as when first penned and "penned" is the operative word. He wrote by hand with a steel nib on vast quantities of paper and, as his family recall, with many childish games and arguments going on around, about and under the dining-room table where he wrote, completely oblivious to the din. No better man indeed!

SEAN KILFEATHER is a native of Coolera in County Sligo. He has been working in journalism for more than 25 years including several years in the Middle East and in London. He has also worked in the newsroom at Radio Telefís Eireann and for the past ten years has been in the sports department of the Irish Times where he writes about GAA affairs and boxing.

No Better Man

A SALT SEA FISHERMAN

A POWERFUL wedge of a five-foot nine man was Topsey — back like a ball alley, shoulders wide, hips narrow, waist slim as the neck of a bottle, when I first saw him naked for all but an abbreviated pants and belt as he sculled his boat ashore. In broiling sunshine his back muscles rippled. He has thickened midriff now. His round red-brown face reminds me still of a summer sun setting behind Innis Cleire with a wee wisp of sheltering cloud on top to represent Topsey's hat — 'tis always the same hat — Neapolitan, wide rimmed, black; a soft battered felt with a laced cord as band; slim tassels hanging over the wearer's left ear. He has the true rolling gait of the sea.

To one born in an outpost peninsula on the south-west coast, deep-sea fishing was second nature — ling, hake, whiting, bream, cod, pollock, mackerel — each demands a different angle of attack. Accustomed from the leisured holidays of youth to haul in heavy fish or light fish with no long patience of waiting for the welcome "peck" that 'phoned your finger of a call coming through from a fish at the other end — I found fresh-water fly fishing and whipping a stream rather slow sport. I acquired some skill and patience in Kerry, Limerick and Cork streams, but always went back on holiday time to my old love of the salt — the boat, and the accompanying deep-sea fishermen — a race apart, in their astute knowledge of weather, tides, rocks, bays and fishing grounds. They knew their "sea" like an open book. They distinguished each vein of sea-bottom by Gaelic names born of long tradition. On our own coast we had ranges of fishing grounds from the cliffs out.

First came the sunken rocks — really a continuation of the headland broken by sea-action over aeons of time. Here was the pollock ground. Next outside was *An Triagh* — a purely sandy bottom where whiting abounded. Outside this was *An breac-thallav* — the broken, brekked sea-bottom where stout, heavy bream were found on the sunken rocks

Further to sea was a range of fertile deep-sea fishing known as *An Mig Mor,* the great main, where big liners crossed, and where trawlers from the Isle of Man, Arklow, Baltimore and Glandore operated. At that time every cove held its boats — 4, 5, or 6 oared craft who raised their lug sales in fine weather. On such occasions they went further afield than even the Big Main of the trans-atlantic lines. The further out they went, the heavier the fish they got on their long lines — hake, ling, codfish — their spillers, 60 fathom lines, carried a *nassal* and hook in every fathom.

Outside the Great Main was *Thallav-na-leac* (the slatey bottom) and away beyond the horizon was *an Slob* — the muddy bottom. These fishermen who shot their spillers and lines to sea bottom had traditional knowledge of the floor of the ocean by reason of touch and the particles found on their home-made anchors of stone and wood.

The fishermen spun their own handlines on rollers, attached to the kitchen roof. They sought much of their bait for long-lines and spillers on the ebb-tide flats. They called them *lugs*. A generation earlier, the spillers and long-lines were spun in rope-walks with flax and hemp as materials. These early fishing friends of mine spoke little but Gaelic. They were the sturdy and individualistic remnant of an ancient stock. Between them and my own time were a generation of young men who came in with the National School horror; they were bi-lingual. One of them, a master-linesman, I shall always remember — one Topsey Raegan, and it is of him I write.

Still hale and hearty, at seventy-seven, he was and is even now, the consummate fisherman of that coast — a coast of rocky inlet, deep-fishing banks and sheltered coves. Friend and foe, when it came to fishing, 'gave the palm' to Topsey Raegan — whether with shortline or longline, inshore or deep-sea.

His real name Paak Raegan. How he got the nickname Topsey I could never discover. Perhaps that he had spent his early life in a fisherman's cottage on "top" of the Hill, where it dips straight to the floodtide, facing the open ocean. Perhaps 'twas from that tousled mop of brown hair he carried as a crown in his all-too-brief schooldays.

Mrs. Harriet Stowe's best seller *Uncle Tom's Cabin* which freed the slaves, was a rage here in Paak Raegan's young days; emigrant relatives sent copies from America. The nigger child Topsey was an engaging character in *Uncle Tom's Cabin.* That may be the source of the incongruous nickname which sounded particularly strange in an Irish-speaking parish. His wife Mary, and no one else, called him Paak. Incidentally they reared a family of hefty sons, now scattered to the four winds of heaven — but that is neither here nor there in my relating.

A sound, thoughtful smoker of strong plug, he had a local reputation as a realistic yarn-spinner. His the *Dan-direach* touch; maybe futurist (say 1980) touch of brevity which will gap the shallow centuries of roundabout story telling. His yarns are short and sweet, like a donkey's gallop.

I recall one pleasant night with Topsey at a threshing. The harvest was complete; corn in the barn. There was a barrel of beer on tap in the kitchen. Topsey and a group of neighbouring fishermen had helped in the crowning harvest work. Between the ballads now, they swopped yarns of field and flood, land and sea. Topsey, who had learnt his first word of

English when whipped to a National School at the age of six, had picturesque, salty Bearla now; what matter that his metaphors were sadly mixed. We knew he had a story as he thoughtfully filled a blackened, wide-bowled briar which loaded a quarter ounce of plug. He was brief and dramatic as usual.

"One day I was out after pollock close under the Ladyswell cliff in Coos Cochlin where you can get a strong weighty fish. 'Twas the finest day of the year." He lit his pipe slowly. Between puffs he said: "And Darmuige, what did I see!" (puff, puff). One of the children at the fireside — they all loved Tops — said: "And what did you see Tops?" "What did I see boy! Tha'sa Dia, I saw a seal foaling on the rocks and she had a pup as big as a calf!!"

Often when fishing inshore in little yawls, fourteen feet overall, our lines were idle; one hundred yards outside, deftly working right and left-hand lines, Tops was standing in his boat, hauling in fish! Line fishermen, old as he, often had thin reward for their patience whilst the bottom of Topsey's boat was squirming with fish which Mary, basket on arm, sold to neighbouring farmers, teachers, shopkeepers, clergy and visitors before breakfast next morning. And a pollock fresh from the salt, scales glistening, makes a sweet summer breakfast. I liked it better than the stronger sea trout. And Topsey knew this. One week the weather broke whilst I was on holidays and I looked disconsolate at the waves on which no small boat could live. "Don't mind, Sir," said Tops, "I'll get you a fresh fish for breakfast." And he did!

The storm did not abate. Night was settling down quickly on the coast like a cloud of black wool on creek and cove. I saw Topsey in home-made oilskins heading for the cliffs. He carried a long light pole of ash. He went down-cliff at Lauravaun and landed three nice rock pollock in half an hour. He knew where to meet them even from the land side.

When getting into years he found the long pull to and from the fishing grounds a bit of a strain. One day at anchor fishing bream he was off deep sunken rocks where bream lie, on the brow of Carriga-Dhinn. Anchor-stones were light for quick hauling. When a basking shark took one man's line and bait, he swept boat anchor, man and all away — for 200 yards, before the line broke, as Tops knew it would. "Dar-muige," says Tops with Celtic imagery, "if we could train him!" The basking shark if trained (like a young horse) would take them to the deep-sea fishing grounds without strain or stress!!

I tried to fathom Topsey's consummate skill or consistent luck. I found it was a proverb's truth — "Trifles makes perfection, but perfection is no trifle." He knew the particular "ouvar" (timeliness) of every rock, bank and cove. He was painstaking with his lines and baits. He changed his length, weight and depth of lead and line, he changed the size, character and colour of his bait to every breeze that blew. He had what is known to deep-sea fishermen as a "light-finger" (sensitive to a fish's touch) — no fear of a hooked fish lying long on Tops' line, however deep. Fearless and daring in heavy weather he took no foolish risks with the undying power of the sea and its changing changelessness. He took a parent's care of boat and gear. A master artist if ever there was one, instinctively weatherwise.

When I saw him gaff a weighty fish — dead sure, in the firm centre of the back — and swing him into the boat, I thought him cruel. He was anything but that, as succeeding paragraphs will prove.

Topsey was superstitious, like all of his trade. He stood religiously by the Sabbath rule — no fishing from Saturday night at midnight until dawn on Monday. He had three great hatreds — "The Divil, the Hangman and *Faoileann-na-druime dhee.!* (the big Black-backed Gull)."

'Twas the "Divil" tempted him whenever Tops took the wrong turning in search of fish; the 'Divil' brought him every patch of bad luck in his way of life. And he forthwith examined his conscience.

He hated Hangmen from Fenian, Land League and later days. One day in the height of the Anglo-Irish War I was fishing with him. The execution of young Kevin Barry at Mountjoy that week had hurt Topsey to the depths. We had been discussing the boy-partriot's tragedy. Just then Topsey gaffed a weighty fish beside me with a vicious stroke. "Tops," said I, "would you hang a man for gold?" His look would poison a trout stream. 'Twas worse than a process-server's Summons. He was clearly shocked that I could ask such a vile question. Then his clouded face cleared with bright good humour: "I would," said he. "I'd hang one man for nothing." "Who?," I asked. "I'd hang the Hangman," said Tops and he drove the gaff into the ferrule in his next fish!

He loved and feared the sea. Solemnly he said to me one day after a local drowning — some "green" swimmer had taken liberties: "The sea wants to be left alone. He makes no friends, and wants no friends; he wants to be left alone!" And he was a fine ploughman in his youth. Often in the hush of dawn I heard him take a team of horses with their rattling chains across the meadow to the tillage fields. "I often kicked the larks out of their nests," he said truly. But the sea was his bride!

Topsey had his stated routes for solitary pollock-fishing when came the scarcity of crews for distant fishing grounds, high on the rim of the ocean. He clung close to the beetling cliffs; as tides and weather suited he went to left or right, but often got heavy fish in most unexpected places, where it was dead lonely as he trolled for hours. He had one little companion, a lone seabird called "Petereen" or *Peaderin.* He believed that Petereen was one of the weaklings of the Stormy Petrel tribe. Day after day Petereen would dally not far from the lone man's boat. Occasionally he got small scraps of discarded bait. Topsey loved him. Often Tops would range away on his westward beat and return at eve under Lauravaun Cliff where Petereen always awaited him.

One balmy summer evening the big Black-backed Gull was calling from the rock, savage for discarded bait-food. Tops gave him none. He hated him — the Black-backed Gull — *Faoileann-na-druime-dhee.* The gull hated Topsey's patronage of Petereen. At last the big fellow swooped down from his perch and seized poor Petereen in his long curved beak. That big gull was dominant and fierce — his tribe feared him. Before the fisherman's oar could wave its protest the big gull swept back to the rock, and in his hunger gulped down poor Petereen in one fell swallow! "I saw the big bulge in the divil's throat as he flew away," said Topsey bitterly. Tops fumed and mourned for the tragic fate of his little friend.

Next evening he was again under the Lauravaun when the big Black-backed Gull appeared roaring hungrily for bait. Tops was prepared. He threw three scraps of bait high in the sky. The gull swept on them and swallowed. He still circled around ravenously for food. Tops threw his lightest dark line high, bait and small hook attached, heavy mackerel bait; the big gull swallowed it hook and all. The fisherman struck. Viciously he hauled in the line — hook, gull and all. "His wings were the width of the boat," says Tops. "I gave him a lingering Hangman's death. I slit the gullet that swallowed poor Petereen!" Three things Topsey Raegan hated — The Devil, The Hangman and *Faoileann-na-druime-dhee!!*

DUBLIN IN THE BORDER CENTURIES

Still stands she; athwart the banks of Liffey.
Noble City; thou hast seen
Strange tides of stress.
Spears, swords, battleaxes, flashed across thy
fords,
And hordes of foreign knights
Sought thy caress.

Dane, Saxon, Norman built material fanes
In lanes of towering stone
And open square.
Till martyr blood and cleansing creed of Pearse,
In verse and holy fire
Laid thy heart bare -
                    'Twas Eire's.

SO small was I at fifteen, that the young man at the ticket office in Glanmire Station, Cork, never hesitated in giving me a single ticket to Dublin at half-fare. All impressions of that first journey in 1899 have vanished from my mind but one. At Limerick Junction five hard-bitten men got into the carriages, empty for all but me — I sat demurely in a corner next to the window.

"This will do fine," one of them said. There were no corridor carriages then. I'd have forgotten all about these men, except for the strange antics of one. They were all friendly and kind to me; asked how far I was going, where in Dublin I proposed to stay; they preferred me some of their rough sandwiches. I told them I had plenty in the bag. 'Twas a good train — four stops between Limerick Junction and Dublin. As we approached each stop, one of the five kept a careful look-out at the window, and immediately proceeded to stow himself under the seat. His four companions then placed themselves close together on the seat above him. This behaviour, strange and unexplainable to me, was repeated during each stop. Was he a fugitive from justice? Each time the man rolled out from under the seat as we left the station, his clothes were more dusty than before. Then it dawned on me — he was travelling without a ticket and he got clean away with it! His look-out was for the checker who could then only operate while the train was stationary. They were bookmakers of the poorer type, coming back from a race meeting — I saw their traps at the station.

The terminus had gloomy gas-lamps; so had the City but it looked a fairyland to me in the November night. A kindly cousin met me at the station. That first drive in a horsetram to O'Connell Bridge thrilled me; the red plush seats were luxurious. I feasted my eyes on the crowds and the lights and the tall buildings. Another horsetram took us to our destination in the southern suburb — there I was destined to stay and work and study for four years.

That relative of mine was a father to me. It was he who guided me to the Confraternity at Rathmines where I founded a comradeship with Dublin City youths — a comradeship that never was broken. They were budding intellectuals of the new movements — Gaelic League, Industrial Revival, National Theatre Revival, Gaelic Games Revival — just stirring some of the young pulses of Dublin, though by no means popular with mature folk of a workaday city, steeped in parliamentary politics.

Soon I was devoting all my leisure to the new movements. I had a good smattering of native Irish and had learned to read Father O'Growney and *Fainne-an-lae* at home. I was soon teaching O'Growney to a young class in the Rathmines Branch of the Gaelic League at Summer Hill South; later at Teach Laighean. A few of us started a hurling club of which they made me captain. We went to the Phoenix Park every week-end. We were at Celtic Literary Society lectures — Willie Rooney the leading light; we saw the birth of the Irish Literary revival — first at the Ancient Concert Rooms and then at the Abbey. With the opening of the twentieth century a new spirit was abroad in Dublin — a spirit that was to grow and prosper despite overwhelming difficulties; to change the whole history of the nation.

Dublin was and is, a kindly gracious city. My friends of the Confraternity and Gaelic League took me to their homes. I was a bit of a novelty then with my Southern brogue and a share of Gaelic, some hurling and step-dancing skill. I sought to develop them all. During the winter we had "at homes" galore in these hospitable houses. In summertime we had week-end outings into the Wicklow Hills or lower Dublin mountains; we hurled in competitions and travelled down the country with the Gaelic League — Keatings, Ard Craobh, Colmcille. In the little stone-flagged kitchen where our hurling club met, we had a hanging oil lamp and a turf fire in winter. There we read our monthly manuscript journals and had debates on national questions. We had fiddlers and pipers in. We sang and Dudley Digges recited, and we often step-danced. 'Twas probably the happiest time of my life, though I studied mighty hard and mighty late. I was lucky to do well at my exams.

I had close contact with many of the prominent men in the new movements. Outstanding amongst them was Dr. Douglas Hyde (*An Craoibhin Aoibhinn*), first Gaelic League President. This kindly Roscommon man was a remarkable personality. Able scholar, linguist, historian, poet. He was a charming platform speaker in either Irish or English — fluent, scholarly, sincere. His black, drooping moustache covered a strong mouth; his dark grey eyes were of wondrous brightness. But it was his kindliness that captivated us all. His addresses to the Oireachtas were inspiring. He read his annual odes; his *Preachaun Mor* was a masterpiece of invective. I saw his first play *Cassadh-an-tSugan* produced at the Rotunda in 1902. The North Parish (Cork) Branch created a bit of a sensation with *An Tobar Draoichta;* Hugh O'Neill of Limerick and his eight hand reels made another hit. So did Martin O'Reilly, master piper of Galway. Mrs Flanagan, famous Dublin street fiddler; 6 foot 2 Eamonn O'Neill of Kinsale, delightful tenor; Margaret Hannigan of Waterford, traditional singer; Owen Lloyd, magic harper of Dublin. I was in the heart of a great history-making revival and lived every hour of it. Even if we were called the *la breaghs* in the street as we smattered Irish, what did it matter.

Willie Rooney, poet and writer, was a delightful lecturer. A mystic too, but a supremely practical one. His lectures were on advanced national lines; he taught Irish, edited and wrote most of the "United Irishman" weekly newspaper. Arthur Griffith just back from South Africa, threw his lot in. He was ever calm, cool and staid. Greatest political journalist of his period. Mr. David Moran's weekly — "The Leader" was bursting with witty constructive (and destructive) thought. He fell foul of the United Irishman leaders and dubbed them the "tinpike party" and "hillsiders" with acid wit. We admired Moran's industrial campaign, but he lacked, I think, the brilliantly lucid and long-range vision of Griffith and Rooney. All did herculean work and there was room for all in the great awakening.

W.B. Yeats, tall dreamer of the thoroughfares, was a striking figure. He had not then reached international and Nobel Prize fame. He usually wore dark clothes, precisely tailored. He was thin then; his black bow-tie had long rakish tails. His hair was black and sleek, pulled over a lofty brow where stray locks of hair swung across his dark eyes. We thought him affected. His hands were ever nervously clasped behind his back in a perpetual kneading process. But there was no denying his brilliancy. People said he was in love with Miss Maud Gonne. To her and for her he wrote his plays *Countess Kathleen, Kathleen Ni h-Ualachain* and *Deirdre.*

What a sensation she caused when she walked on to the stage that "first night" in the Ancient Concert Rooms — centre of what is now call

Pearse St. Maud Gonne was no great actress but she had superb height, grace and majestic beauty. She looked the part in her striking Celtic dress. She was a forceful and incisive platform orator, preaching physical force everywhere and founding *Inghini-na-hEireann* — The Daughters of Erin — advance guard of the Revolution of 1916.

But the young brilliant actresses — Maire Quinn, Miss Walker and greatest of all, Sarah Allgood of the golden voice, were coming along. Yet, they played brilliantly to half-empty little halls in Camden Street and out of the way places. Meanwhile the big theatres of Dublin were packed to British travelling companies of tragedians, musical comedy and musical hall artistes — all from across the Channel.

But thinking folk realised even then that the "Abbey" plays and players were a coming force in cultural Eire. Lady Gregory of Coole, Galway, her neighbour Edward Martyn, Synge and Murray were blossoming and soon opened a phase of distinctive culture with their true-to-life peasant plays. I was a first-nighter to them all — *Riders to the Sea, Shadow of the Glen, Playboy of the Western World, Pot of Broth* with the Fay Brothers; Lady Gregory's *Rising of the Moon, Workhouse Ward, Spreading the News.* A new school of cultural revival was stirring the nation. Painful the process was, like the labour throes of a new dynasty.

And the young athletic men were throwing themselves into the G.A.A. Movement, which, after a sweeping opening in the eighties, had suffered through internal disunion and lax management. Young men with high spiritual outlook; young men of the Gaelic League and industrial revival, started their clubs everywhere. Order was now won from chaos; punctuality and discipline followed. Here too there was a rebirth of great potency. From that day to this the native games have gone on from success to overwhelming triumph.

Within the Gaelic League. the Literary Revival, the Industrial movement, the Gaelic Athletic movement, there were two schools of thought — the staid and safe, the young and revolutionary. First striking change was the election of young Padraig Pearse to editorship of *An Claoideamh Soluis,* the official organ of the Gaelic League. The English sculptor's son from Westland Row wrote in a strikingly fresh and intellectual way. He was soon President of the League. All Ireland, in a general way, was then politically behind John Redmond and his party. Later when hopes of Home Rule were brightest, Redmond was side-tracked by British politicians and Pearse, product of the Revival of the Border Centuries, got his chance to lead a chagrined nation on the thorny Calvary road where, as Yeats wrote, "a terrible beauty was born."

DAN FRAHER'S FAMOUS FIELD

THERE was a Gaelic atmosphere about Dungarvan that seized the visitor forthwith in its warm clasp — as all-embracing as the salt sea air that swept in from the famous Cunnigar. Gaelic was the tongue spoken by these big contingents from the coastline between Ardmore and Ring; and by the tall, shouldery men from the Comeraghs with the soft black hats, who paraded the wide Square. To all of them, their Mecca lay at the other side of the town — up the creek and beyond the railway — all were heading for Dan Fraher's Field, where the big Gaelic championships were played in the old days, and where Feiseanna and Aeriocht were common in pleasant summer time at "The Old Boro."

That beautifully laid-out Gaelic park was the finest in Ireland in the early century, outrivalling Jones' Road itself in smooth hurling turf and spaciousness. And that Gaelic Park, with its dressing rooms and equipment was the work of one man — Gael of Gaels — big-hearted Dan Fraher of Dungarvan.

Champion all-round athlete in the pioneer days of the G.A.A., Dan Fraher lived his own distinctive Irish life from cradle to grave — his locks were silvery when the grand old warrior suffered his last term of imprisonment in the Black and Tan days.

It was in fluent Gaelic he talked to most of the customers in his fine drapery shop at Dungarvan; his spacious home was open during G.A.A. weekends to hundreds of friends and officials — Dan himself was like some ancient Irish chief, talking rapid Gaelic in their midst and dishing out hospitality with a liberal hand!

But I must get on to my theme of Fraher's Gaelic Park, and the hurling finals I saw there, fifty or more years ago. The first was the All-Ireland home final of 1903, when Cork (Blackrock) beat Kilkenny (Three Castles).

That was the day Blackrock's diminutive forward, Andy Buckley, scored seven goals off his own ash — a broiling July day of 1905. This phenomenal score swung the game Cork's whirlwind way, with Steve Riordan (captain), Tom Coughlan and Jer and Jim Kelleher, Billy Mackesy, Billie O'Neill of Sarsfields, Pat O'Sullivan of The Barrs, and Daw McGrath of Redmonds — one of the finest teams that ever left Cork, before or after.

Kilkenny had their revenge a year later at Carrick-on-Suir when a powerful Tullaroan side won by a point from Cork and scored the first of their phenomenal seven championships in ten years.

Another year raced by in the tumult of youth and we were again back in Dan Fraher's Field with Kilkenny and Cork again battling for supremacy. Cork had won at Tipperary but we unwittingly had an illegal goalkeeper and a replay at Dungarvan was sportingly arranged.

I recall that well for I was one of four Blackrock men picked on the St. Finbarr's selection. I had a poor match, for I was marking big Dan Kennedy of Erin's Own, and he was at his great peak.

That was a wonderful Kilkenny side with Dan Stapleton as captain, the flashing Jack Anthony of Piltown on the wing; Mat Gargan and Sim Walton of later fame; Dick and Eddie Doyle, and Drug Walsh of Mooncoin, the Tullaroan Lawlors, and scoring machine, Jimmy Kelly. That time Kilkenny got seven goals against us and won well.

But the greatest All-Ireland ever played at Dungarvan (or perhaps anywhere else) was the one I next saw there — that final of swaying fortunes and brilliant hurling, won on the last puck of the ball by Jimmy Kelly, a doubled dropper from Anthony — the odd point of forty-one. Final score: Kilkenny (Tullaroan) 3-12; Cork (Dungourney) 4-8!

Dan Fraher's fine field was a picture on that June day of 1908, when the final of 1907 was played. The old Fenian himself had paid special personal attention to the pitch — 'twas like a billiard table, and every man on the field was a master hurler.

Old-timers will remember them — their names are worth recording here — seventeen men a side:

Kilkenny (Tullaroan) — R. Doyle, M. Doyle, E. Doyle, Drug Walsh, J. Kelly, R. Doherty, J. Kenny, M. Gargan, D. Stapleton, O. Kennedy, P.J. Keohane, J. Rochfort, D. Grace, J. Power, J. Anthony, Sim Walton.

Cork (Dungourney) — Jim Kelleher, J. Ronayne, J. Desmond, W. Hennessy, T. Mahony, P. Leahy, E. O'Shea, P. Lynch, A. Buckley, Jack Kelleher, T. Coughlan, S. Riordan, W. Parfrey, D. Kidney, D. O'Keeffe, J.A. Beckett, W. O'Neill.

From the opening sally, the pace was a cracker. Flying points at long range were a feature. Father James Dollard, a native of Mooncoin (poet, author and distinguished cleric of Toronto) threw in the ball and had to race for the line from the flying hurlers. Overhead hurling of rare beauty was enjoyed that day.

The four men, who were to win seven All-Ireland medals, shone that day — Drug Walsh and Dick Doyle of Mooncoin; Jack Rochfort of Three Castles and Sim Walton of Tullaroan.

The Dungourney men, strengthened by Rockies, Barrs, Reds and Sarsfields, were a team of giants — gloriously long hitters on ground and overhead.

Kilkenny's wristwork and tenacity balanced and the pulsating game proceeded. The cheering was continuous. They were playing a hectic patch of "lost time" when Jack Anthony of Piltown sent one sailing into the Cork area; Jimmy Kelly met it on the drop and drove it high and far above the crossbar — victory for Suir and Nore; but also a triumph for the men of Lee-Avondhu.

That was the last All-Ireland Final played at Dungarvan. I saw some great Munster Finals: Cork v. Limerick; Limerick v. Tipperary. But bigger issues claimed Princely Dan Fraher and Pax Whelan. But good days are coming for The Old Boro and Dan Fraher's famous field.

MIDNIGHT ADVENTURE

WE, inter-county players, had great fun and more than a few adventures in the old days. No petted favourites were those enthusiastic G.A.A. players of fifty years ago; no special dinners at choice hotels for inter-county men then! Generally we paid our own way and were glad to have the honour of representing our county. (Every word of this story is true).

Sometimes the secretary of the club to which we belonged would push a third class excursion return ticket into our hand at the railway station on Sunday morning. Gates were usually small then and profits of even the most attractive games were thin. But we enjoyed every minute of it, gladly paying our own expenses for we loved the games for the games' sake. Players often travelled long distances over bad roads and there were no motor-cars then! The players would arrive shortly before train time with a pair of boots strapped to their hurleys. Bright-eyed, eager men, who had worked hard all week — their best and only training.

That was how we gathered one August day away back in 1906 (or so). We were away to a distant town — a strong Cork hurling team to play a big inter-county game in aid of the Christian Brothers.

We won a fine match before a bumper crowd and the good Brother in charge, delighted with the gate, gave our club secretary the unusually large present of £5 — "to give the hurlers a feed and a drink," he said.

But our members waited on the field for a later match and we got scattered. To young folk like us there was much to be seen in a strange town; we met old hurling friends and opponents from Kilkenny and Tipperary. Time flew on angel wings and the little group of players with me were satisfied with bottles of Blackwater cider and some sandwiches in the way of food and drink for the day.

It was a late, slow return train, stopping at every station on the way to the junction, where we were to meet the night mail from Dublin to Cork. We made light of our hardships then. We sang all the way down.

When we — eighteen young, healthy hurlers — arrived at the Junction we all discovered that we were as hungry as hawks, for not one took a sit-down meal during the long day, no unusual thing with young glad-hearted hurlers.

To our dismay, the refreshment rooms at the station were closed for the night. We had some twenty minutes to wait before the down mail was due and then we heard, to our grief, that our train was held up for an hour and would not be in for almost one and a half hours! We were hungrier than ever then.

We made eager enquiries. Yes, there was a hotel some distance down the road where we could get sandwiches or a full feed and a drink. They were staying open, we were told, for the arrival of the mail train. A few groups of well-dressed folk were parading up and down the platform apparently expecting friends off the train.

The summer night was starry but moonless. It was midnight as, headed by our club secretary (with his five single notes still intact) we hurried down the dark road outside the station.

Soon we came to a big fully-lit hotel at the roadside. There was not a soul in sight; the halldoor was wide open. We rang and knocked — no response. We even looked through the windows into the dining-room and there we saw a sight to gladden the hearts of hungry men. Tables were laid for twenty guests — cold meats and all the trimmings. On the huge side-board were bottles of stout, beer and minerals galore. Our secretary moved through the hall, knocked and called; no response, all was silent as the grave. Patience was exhausted. The club secretary was human and an honest man. He looked at his watch for train time and he threw four single pounds on the table and said to the hungry hurlers: "Wear in, I'll pay." Such a meal was never enjoyed! It was immense; many of the players were tee-totallers but there was lemonade in bottles and syphons, openers with corkscrews, stout and beer. The dishes and sideboards were cleared! The cold beef and cold ham were delicious. We ate standing.

We expected that the night porter or proprietor would arrive any minute but as we were waiting on, we heard the distant whistle of the mail train far into the night and we hurried to the platform.

'Twas a heavy August train and a strong arriving party joined the waiting group on the platform. We sought carriages. We were happy; we had eaten and drunk delightfully; one or two sang a little; there was banter galore about our great feed. All that worried the poor club secretary (he is long since dead, God rest him) was whether he had paid enough.

Some of the tired hurlers were soon asleep but I kept thinking of that empty hotel and the absence of man, woman or child; no night porter or proprietor; no waiter or waitress! All had been silent as the grave. I eased the mind of the worried looking club secretary: "Look here, Pat, you'd get a great feed and all the drink you want for four shillings a head and they have more than that and a good tip for the waiter."

The tired men fell asleep then and, youngest of the lot, I must have dozed myself for we were soon at Glanmire. When we met next day we voted 'twas the best trip we ever had — and with a spice of adventure to crown it.

A few years afterwards, my duties in life took me in the direction of that junction (which must be left un-named) and I decided to explore the matter of the empty hotel for my own satisfaction. I discovered strange facts. The hotel to which we were directed was closed and locked at 12 o'clock that Sunday night long ago. We had gone in another direction and into a mansion. The inhabitants were well-off folk. That August night they were expecting, from across-Channel, a party of visitors coming for the opening of the grouse season on August 12th. The good people of the mansion which we had invaded — shooting and hunting country folk — had all preparations for a reception party made. They had heard the first train whistle, mistook it for the Dublin mail and rushed out to meet their friends. Good for hungry hurlers!

KERRY IN FOOTBALL AND HURLING HISTORY

"KERRY for a man, a horse, a dog or a boat" is an old saying in Irish sporting circles. Since the G.A.A. was founded in 1884, Kerrymen played a big part; their old hardy breed of clean-legged cobs and horses were noted for their speed and tenacity. Kerry greyhounds swept all the major trophies in Irish coursing over a long stretch of years; Kerry beagles are distinctive and traced back to ancient strains; Kerry Blue terriers have few peers and no superiors in their own line; whilst on the Killarney Lakes or the many picturesque creeks and harbours of the south and west Irish coasts, Kerry crews and skiffs were unrivalled in past generations.

It is not generally known that a very distinctive game of communal football flourished in Kerry long before the Gaelic Athletic Association was established. The game was known by the Gaelic name of *Caid* and was played with an oval ball between rival parishes and baronies. Very often, big games of *Caid* were played on spacious strands during ebb tides. I have met with and interviewed in my young days, many men who had taken part in this communal game. There was no limit to the number of men taking part; and the game finished whenever a fixed number of goals were scored.

Rules as we know them, there were none. The *Caid* or ball (cured skin stuffed with hay) was thrown up into the air between the rival teams whose aim was to bring, carry, kick or punch the ball over a stated line or boundary fence. The team that took the ball over such line had scored a goal, which often decided the game. Kicking and carrying were the principal means of transport; wrestling and running with the ball were permitted. It is recorded that these games were played, as one veteran told me, "with great good humour."

Skill with *An Caid* probably helped Kerry to take a prominent football part in the early days of the Gaelic Athletic Association. The Laune Rangers were the first great side. Hailing from Killorglin and its neighbourhood, the Rangers reached the All-Ireland final in 1892. Captained by J.P O'Sullivan, an all-round athletic champion of the period, the Laune Rangers swept through Munster and narrowly lost to the reigning champions — the Dublin Young Irelands — in the final. It was a fine game which Dublin won by 1-4 to 0-3.

New teams sprang up all over Kerry and the most skilled amongst them hailed from Tralee and Killarney. They were slow in reaching their ambition but when they became All-Ireland champions in 1903, they opened a prolific period of successes which made the name of Kerry the envy of the Gaelic football world.

Having reached the 1903 final they first met their famous rivals, the "All-Whites" of Kildare at Tipperary when a disputed score forced a replay. The return match at Cork opened a new standard in Gaelic football — a fast, open, clean game of catch and kick and diagonal ground passing — which delighted a record attendance for these days The second game was a draw — 7 points to 1 goal and 4 pts. for Kildare. Kerry won the replay decisively on a heavy pitch — 8 points to 2. Kerry's outstanding players of the period were Dick Fitzgerald of Killarney, estimated the greatest forward of his period if not of all time; the O'Gorman brothers, Austin Stack, Maurice McCarthy and Rody Kirwan. Kerry retained the championship in the following year when going clear through to the final where they beat Dublin Kickhams by 5 points to 2 in a thrilling contest.

Kerry teams of the period were of good physique; their fielding of the ball at all heights and angles was very secure and confident; they believed in long accurate kicking and ready shooting when within range of the goal. They were a delightful side to watch.

Kerry's greatest period may have been from 1909 to 1915 when the county sent out powerful sides of polished footballers; they won out-right in the 1909, 1913 and 1914 before losing to Wexford by a goal in the 1915 final. Kerry were the biggest attraction in Gaelic football of that vintage Gaelic period when gate attendances multiplied. Dick Fitzgerald continued as a great forward; John Skinner was right corner man and a scoring genius; Tom Costelloe, Jack Lawlor and Paddy Healy were great defenders; Pat O'Shea was a peerless midfield star.

Kerry did not again reach the final until a new team was built up around 1923 and from that day down to recent years, no county could compare with Kerry's phenomenal record — they won the 1924 title beating Dublin by a point (4 to 3); won in 1926 beating Kildare by a goal; lost to Kildare in the 1927 final (5-3) and came back again in 1929 to beat their old Kildare rivals by 1-8 to 1-5.

Then ensued a period of real Kerry dominance. They won four championships in a row — 1929, 1930, 1931 and 1932 and so equalling Wexford's great record from 1915 to 1918. In this prolific period Kerry seemed unbeatable. They played football without frills relying on superb fielding, kicking and shooting. Take their 1930 side — every man a star — J.J. Sheehy (capt.), J. Riordan (goal), D. O'Connor, J. Barrett, Jack Walsh; Jack Walsh, P. Russell, J. O'Sullivan, T. O'Donnell; C. Brosnan, R. Stack; J. Ryan, M. Doyle, E. Fitzgerald, P. Sweeney, J.J. Landers. That side is often referred to by critics as the greatest ever to adorn a Gaelic football field.

Many of the prominent players of that prolific period retired after 1932, but five years later with a comparatively new side, Kerry took the final from Cavan in a replay — the Munster side winning by 4 gls. 4 pts. to 1 gl. 7 pts. A year later Kerry lost to Galway on a final replay but came back like giants refreshed to take three successive championships in 1939, 1940 and 1941 with splendidly uniform teams. Dan O'Keeffe, Kerry's renowned goalie of that period was the only man in Ireland to have won seven All-Ireland medals. Joe Keohane, full-back, W. Dillon, W. Casey, Sean Brosnan, T. O'Connor and P.B. Brosnan were shining lights.

EUROPE'S FIRST GAMES BROADCAST

TO the Gaelic Athletic Association and to 2RN (as Radio Eireann was then called) belongs the honour of giving the first open-air games broadcast to Europe and to the Western World! An outdoor boxing championship had been put on the air by an American service in the summer of 1926, and it was the late Mr. P.S. O'Hegarty, then the Secretary to the Posts and Telegraphs Department, who conceived the idea of broadcasting a hurling match on the air service under his control.

Mr. O'Hegarty, a native of Cork City, was a hurling lover from his youth and played for a time with London Hibernians. He had some journalistic and other associations with me, and he asked me in August 1926 to call on him at the G.P.O, Dublin.

Broadcasting was in the swaddling clothes then. The crude cat's whiskers as reception medium, the high poles and aerials over many gardens, crystal sets and earphones were in many homes.

I was surprised when "P.S." (as we called the G.P.O. Chief) broached the subject of broadcasting a hurling match from Croke Park. In his blunt, direct way he slung the question at me: "Mehigan, will you help us by giving a running commentary — describe the match as you see it from the Hogan Stand?"

He was full of the possibilities of the project. He had examined the technical difficulties with his engineers. The thing could be done; they would make all arrangements. The G.A.A. had given them permission. "P.S." decided that I was the fitting commentator for the pioneer effort. He knew I had considerable inter-county hurling experience. I had been writing descriptions of matches in the papers and magazines for years. It was a novelty and the prospect of being "first on the air" appealed to me. Almost without thinking I said: "I'll try."

It was only when I had time to think over the matter that I realised how important to the success of the pioneer venture was my share of the work. I was doubtful of my ability to keep up the necessarily fluent commentary for an hour or more. Never venture, never win, indeed. My meeting with "P.S." was in mid-August, 1926, and though I broadcast hundreds of matches from 1926 to 1932, I suspect that the original game was the Kilkenny-Galway All-Ireland hurling semi-final of 1926.

I was at Croke Park half an hour before the match when the day came and was introduced to the engineer-in-chief. I inspected all the contraptions and wires and earphones in the office underneath the Hogan

Stand. A cable led up to a corner of the press stand. Then a big square mahogany box with wires and screws and gadgets galore was set out and, when the time came, I was asked to sit beside the box. A leather contraption was put around my neck with a yellow brass tube in front into which I was told to speak. It was all new to me; I had no voice test whatsoever. I had just my teams on a slip of paper in my hand.

The mysterious signal came that I was "on the air," and the engineer nodded to me to "fire away." Without more ado I "fired away" and found that I could spout freely enough, particularly as soon as the game, which I was so familiar with, started. At half-time I had to do a summary on the first half and so on to the end. I was very tired at the finish; they were beaming in the engineers' room below and clapped me on the back. They told me I had done fine; I didn't believe them. But I knew that I was only a raw recruit and had a lot to learn. Yet I got a great kick out of it all, and was glad to help to spread the light about the loved game of my boyhood.

I remember very little about the first game but the records say that Kilkenny won by 6 goals 2 points to 5 goals and 1 point.

Not everyone was happy about the new departure. Of course, it would never do to keep that mahogany box on the press seats of the Hogan Stand. My constant shouting greatly upset my press colleagues trying to take their notes beside me. That knowledge was upsetting to me right through the game. I was determined that I should shift the contraption to the sideline or elsewhere. My recommendation was carried out.

Then there was that very earnest G.A.A. man, a fine Gaelic footballer in his time, who loudly declared to all round him: "If they don't take that bl___dy box out of Croke Park they might as well close the gates." And the councils of the G.A.A. were doubtful — "would broadcasting reduce attendances?" they asked. Some officials looked on me with cold if not unfriendly eyes. Yet the far-seeing ones saw the light. Said G.A.A. President William Clifford of Limerick to me when he met me: "These broadcasts of yours, P.D., are worth a thousand pounds a year to the G.A.A. as publicity."

And so it proved. The fame of the games spread; the newspapers doubled and quadrupled their space for Gaelic games; and instead of keeping the public away, we brought them, eager to see with their own eyes, what they had heard over the air! And so I pursued the good work under difficult conditions, out in the open with roaring thousands shouting me down. And still the throngs doubled to see the games, so much so that accommodation was stormed.

I remember one day in Cork broadcasting a hurling final from the sideline. The crowd around me got out of hand. I could see nothing. Stewards were helpless. I stood on a chair and tried to keep the commentary going. I was hit on the poll, in the ear and on the shoulders with clods and grass sods, some of them hard enough. The crowd swarmed round me and swept the phones away; the match was abandoned and the broadcast broke down. I was blamed but it was not my fault. Four times too many were in the field; the gates were burst; over-popularity of games is a curse sometimes instead of a blessing.

These early difficulties brought reform. Special boxes are provided for broadcasting work now and all is smooth, but I have happy memories of these pioneer days, before my voice failed.

The greatest thrill I got was out of a scoop made by me when broadcasting the boxing championships of the 1928 Tailteann Games at Croke Park. I was doing pretty well and was in good mood when I saw a distinguished group being ushered in to the ringside seats at a lull between events. They were four in number and I recognised them. A blanket would cover the four great men — John Count McCormack, Eugene (Gene) Tunney, Col. Fitzmaurice and our own General Eoin O'Duffy, then Garda and N.A.C.A. chief.

Eugene Tunney had just won the world's heavyweight championship from Jack Dempsey. Here he was to see our Tailteann boxing championships!

A thought flashed through my mind — "what a scoop if I could get Tunney to the phone!" I got my friend, Eoin O'Duffy to introduce me. In a flash I had a word with Tunney. Would he do it? No. He pouted his lips. I persuaded; no good! "Who are you hooked up to?" he asked at last, curtly. 'Twas the first time I heard "hooked up." I tumbled. "We're hooked up to all Europe." No good. His face was still stoic. "We're hooked up to all America," I urged. No cord touched! Another brainwave came. I knew Tunney came specially to see his blood relations in Mayo and Cork. I spoke my tenderest: "We're hooked up" I said, "to every homestead in Mayo and every village in Co. Cork!" His fine eyes softened. Meekly, silently, he walked to the microphone. I introduced him in forty words and he was on the air!

A BALLAD

"LAMENT FOR ASHE"

(Air: Has sorrow thy young days shaded)

I.

I strayed down beside a lone river,
Where mountains kiss the sea;
A voice in the calm of the evening,
Came over the waves to me —
A maid sang with sad complaining,
In grief-stricken melody;
Oh! Tom Ashe shall your name be unspoken,
In Ireland from sea to sea?

II.

In the heart of a dark dreary prison,
They tortured your martyr soul;
But your name will be written by freemen,
One day, in the nation's roll.
"I carry my cross for dear Ireland,"
Your last prayer a *bhuachail achroidhe;*
Oh! Tom Ashe shall your name be unspoken,
In Ireland from sea to sea?

III.

You scattered the Sassanach foemen,
In storied old Fingal;
You raised Eire's banner of freedom,
Beneath it to conquer or fall.
We'll raise it again to the morning,
And rally by plain and lea;
Tom Ashe, your dear name shall be spoken,
In Ireland from sea to sea.

A CHILD'S CHRISTMAS

Young brothers three we rose at dawn
Adown the field we go
To wood beyond the meadows where
The holly-berries grow.
Tho' winter skies were dark and drear,
Thro' winding lanes we roam,
To pull the ruddy branches down
And bear them proudly home.

Then all day long with Liz. and Ju.
We deck each cosy scene,
Each giant Christmas candle had
A robe of emerald green.
Each window-niche a holly cross
Each pane an ivy spray,
For this was Christmas eventide
To-morrow: Christmas Day.

From under mother's hooded cloak
The brimming baskets came.
She'd just come down from yonder town
To set our hearts aflame.
Big barmbracks and children's toys
And whistles small to blow,
With cars and trains; they all come back
Those joys of long ago.

The afternoon was busy, too—
To share our store we went;
With farm gifts of meat and milk
Swift messengers were sent;
To every humble cottage home
Within the land tonight,
I mind how joyfully we tripped
To many a cabin bright.

The dusk descends, the good work done,
    Inside is joy and mirth,
Bright turf fires blaze, the lamps are trim'd
    Dad sits beside the hearth.
Wide is his back with blue-freize coat,
    I see him there to-day —
His feet up in the chimney nook,
    His hair a wavy grey.

He told us tales of Nazareth;
    Of Mary and the Child
Who came on earth to succour us —
    The Saviour undefiled.
Whilst mother brought the dinner in —
    Great fish caught down the bay,
Fat butter rolls and laughing spuds
    And jugs of new-made whey.

They we would climb in joyous line
    The hill behind the door,
To watch the myriad Xmas lights
    By vale and sea and shore.
For homeward bound, where Galley flashed,
    The Exiles forced to rove,
Were speeding now in starry ships
    Around the Heads to Cobh.

And supper was a sumptous feast,
    With cakes and fruit galore;
Whilst father drank his steaming punch
    We struck the old back-door;
With round brown cakes of wheaten bread
    Grown down beside the sea,
We wished "bad-end" to Erin's foes
    And swore to set her free.

In Gaelic came the call to pray —
We gathered near the hearth,
Responsive round of reverence
The Rosary of Earth.
And so to sleep with simple minds,
To rise at dawn's first ray,
For Christmas Mass was honoured then
And is, thank God, to-day.

That duty paid, we always trooped
To see the hurling men;
They gathered from the sloping hills
And goaled across the glen.
Then followed piper's tuning sweet
And fiddler's glancing bow,
To cheer the blithesome Xmas days
Of childhood, years ago.

THE HEDGE SCHOOLS OF IRELAND

AN ardent love for learning has been a characteristic of our Irish people young and old, down through the centuries. It lives today. From the coming of St. Patrick, historians can trace the uneven history of the Bardic Schools of Ireland which won international fame. Finished students from these schools took higher learning and the Faith of Patrick to Europe after the dark ages of the middle centuries.

The Bards, who were scholars first and poets after, held a place in the banquet halls of Tara next to royalty. Irish monasteries were the acknowledged world-leaders in the higher sciences. Then came their wholesale plunder by the Danes and their complete destruction in 1539 at the time of the "Reformation" of Henry VIII and the Edicts of William III. Religious institutions were outlawed and learning proscribed, under the Penal Laws.

The Ancient Bardic Professional Schools, under lay control, still continued to enjoy princely Gaelic patronage until the defeat at Kinsale (1601), the Rebellion of 1641 and the final (perhaps) clean sweep of the Irish Clans by Cromwell, the Boyne of 1690, Limerick, Aughrim and the Flight of the Earls, where all hopes of cultural Ireland vanished.

But despite rapine, plunder, fire and sword the deep love of learning remained and the courts of Gaelic Poetry flourished. But these were what Professor Corkery aptly called "hidden Ireland" — the teachers were outlaws and criminals according to British laws. Seeking to bring Ireland under complete subjection, all pains were taken by the government of the day to destroy native culture, history and tradition, of which the poets and fighting scholars were the most prolific medium.

Driven to the remote mountain fastnesses, the scholars still clung to their loved books. The people harboured them and soon (towards the end of the 17th century — around 1690) the hedge schools were born.

There, the earliest teachers had their learning handed down to them from the outcasts of the old bardic schools from the courts of poetry. Pupils were, for some time, taught privately at home — young men intended for the priesthood. These hedge school teachers sent out thousands of pupils, well grounded in Greek, Latin, Gaelic, English and higher mathematics and natural philosophy to man the Catholic universities at Louvain, Salamanca, Lisbon, Douai, Antwerp, Toulouse, Prague, and Paris. There is ample testimony from contemporary continental records that these pupils of the Irish hedge schools were heads of their classes. Many of their names live in the Catholic university archives of Europe. During all that time their old teachers in Ireland belonged to an outlawed trade, and risked life and freedom during every hour of their work. They became a vital force in the Catholic education of Ireland, right through the 18th century and down to 1831 when state schools, under the Commissioners of Education, were established as so-called National Schools.

The fact that during the Penal Days, the outlawed priests were secretly directed by their authorities not to leave the whole work of teaching the Christian Doctrine to the teachers, proves that the foundations of knowledge in Christian Doctrine formed a big part in the work of the hedge schools. So firmly were the hedge schools established that a British census taken for the purpose, perhaps, of securing teachers of what was called "good character" for the new schools then in contemplation, showed that we had 11,823 hedge schools in 1821; they taught 561,000 pupils, a figure which was probably a conservative estimate.

Though the British government had subsidised many anti-Catholic educational establishments from 1690 to 1782 — the Kildare Place Society Schools, the Chartered Schools, the Bible Society Schools and the Smith Schools — these proved utter failures and were abandoned one after another. Despite proscription and proselytism the Irish Catholic hedge schools flourished, commanding 95 per cent of the students.

The Kerry schools were famous in the early days. There learned men had to seek remote fastnesses where they taught in empty barns, in huts built of scraws and covered with rushes in winter time. In the summer they taught beside some sheltered hedge out of sight of their enemies; one boy always acted scout on the look-out for strangers. Soon "poor scholars" came on foot, drawn hither by the fame of the Kerry schools, to qualify for the precarious profession of teaching in their own locality.

Kerry poet-teachers like Owen Rua O'Sullivan, Thomas Rua O'Sullivan, Denis O'Sullivan (who went to Co. Kilkenny) had their counterparts in Brian Merriman of Clare and his countrymen Rua McNamara, who migrated to Waterford; Aindreas McGrath and Sean O'Tuama of Limerick; Michael O'Longain and Sean Clarach McDonnell of Cork. Other well-known teachers of the period — some of them later went in to the towns when the ban on education was eased in 1782 — were Patrick Lynch and Peter O'Connell of Clare; Paul Deignan of Ballina; Richard McElligott, Sean Fitzgibbon and T.M. O'Brien of Limerick; Humphrey Murphy, Francis Grace and John Kelly of Kilkenny; Donnacha Rua and Tadhg Gaelach O'Sullivan, Patrick Denn, James Nash of Waterford; James Fortune of Wexford; Peter Dorinn and Maurice O'Gorman of Armagh; Peter Galligan and Seamus Dall McCourt of Meath, and hundreds of hardly less distinguished scholars.

Hedge school tradition lived strongly in West Cork when I was a boy. My father and the neighbouring farmers had laid the rudiments of their education at the hedge schools, and the hollow behind a white-thorn fence where the boys sat in summer was well-known to me. Hedge schools went indoor in wintertime and I knew the tumbledown *coulachs* where they were held, and often explored the grass-grown crevices.

The pupils were wont to take two sods of turf each per day to heat the little school. A small stoneware ink-jar hung from each boy's coat button. The ink, I was told, was made from the crushed ashes of wheat straw diluted with water. The scholars made their own pens from goose-quills. Slates and slate pencils were secured locally. There were no seats or tables in the schools. Boards laid across big stones served as seats for the bigger boys who wrote on their knees. And yet their ardent love for learning overcame all obstacles.

A Latin, Irish and mathematics scholar, called Looney, who hailed from near Cork harbour, taught my father and our parishoners. These pupils of his wrote a beautiful hand. Native Irish speakers all, they learnt to read and write Irish and were soundly ground in mathematics, algebra and Euclid before Mr. Looney left the parish, and the boys went to the National School adjoining.

The first teacher in the parish under the new Board of Education was a profound mathematician, with good knowledge of history, geography astronomy and Latin, His gift for mathematics descended to his son, my first teacher, whose fame spread. Not alone did this zealous worker win the highest honour in Ireland for his school, under the Education Commissioners — he won the Carlisle and Blake Premium so often that he discontinued entering but he got scores and scores of boys through highly competitive Civil Service Examinations including Excise and Customs branches and was most remarkable in many ways — cultured, well-dressed, well-read, abstemious; with a rare genius for inducing industry and imparting knowledge. The name of Michael Madden, of Ardfield is still remembered and respected amongst the old school-teachers of Ireland. His father had been taught exclusively from the direct line of the bardic schools, courts of poetry and Irish hedge schools.

I am satisfied that the standard of education in the hedge schools was high. I have known some of their products intimately. The boys opened the day with religious instructions; reading, writing and arithmetic followed. The advanced boys, having had a lesson in higher mathematics in the early morning, helped to teach the younger pupils during the day. Readings aloud were encouraged. "Rehearsing" the teachers called it.

Books were scarce and dear, and pupils depended largely for their improvement on their phenomenal memories, exercised from youth by listening to the Fiannic tales recited by *seanachaidhe* at the fireside. One recital, and the whole tale was committed to memory in all its detail.

Many of the hedge schoolmasters copied borrowed books in beautiful script — English, Irish, Latin and even Greek. James Fenton, of South Kerry, the retired deputy chief inspector of schools, whose book of reminiscences *It all Happened* gives us much insight into the scholarship of one of the best known of Kerry teacher-poets, the hedge schoolmaster Tomás Rua O'Sullivan, of Caherdaniel, contemporary and friend of Daniel O'Connell, who took an interest in the young poet and sent him to school in Dublin.

Tomás Rua wrote many fine poems. A postman and fiddler he taught hedge schools in many parts of Iveragh. He collected and transcribed scores of rare books — he lost them all in one sad day when the boat conveying his belongings from Derrynane to a new adventure in Portmagee was lost in Kenmare Bay. His poem *The Lost Books* is well-known. Tomás Rhua led a blameless life. Born in 1785 he died a bachelor in the famine year of 1848 aged 83.

Donnaca Rhua MacConmara, born in Cratloe, Co. Clare, in 1715 was educated in Limerick and Rome, he travelled much of Europe and spent a season in Newfoundland where he wrote *Bán Cnuic Eireann O,* a song that will live forever. Donnaca was an independent character, taught school for many years at Slieve gCua and other parts of Waterford, not far from Kilmacthomas. He led a wayward life but sought God near the end, dying peacefully at 95 — a tall, flame red, shouldery man who revelled in defying authority.

His neighbour and friend, Tadg Gaolach O'Sullivan also taught in hedge schools and wrote many religious poems at the end of his life. Another remarkable man was Brian Merriman, author of that much debated, but brilliant poem *Cuirt-an-Mheadhon-Oidhche* (the Midnight Court). He was born near Ennis, Co. Clare and taught for some years in Feakle and Limerick where he died in 1805.

Eoghan Rua O'Sullivan, known amongst his contemporaries as *Eogan-na-beoil-binn* (Owen of the honeyed mouth) is perhaps the best known of the hedge schoolmasters. Born in Meentogues on that wonderful seat of bardic scholarship — Slieve Luachra, on the Cork-Kerry border, Eoghan Rhua, a disciple of the old culture, commanded Irish, English, Greek and Latin at 18 when he taught school in his native county.

But he was restless and as great a lover as Robert Burns, and he had to travel far afield — as labourer, private teacher (he taught in Donoughmore and Fermoy, Co. Cork) sailor, soldier and merriest of companions. Many of his *aislings* live on, songs came to him without effort and are still sung. Back at Knocknagree he once more taught school for a while. His love of jolly company cost him his life — gravely hurt at a brawl in Killarney and died in a few days at 36. His was the true gift of song.

Another product of the famous Kerry school was Daniel O'Sullivan who migrated to Kilkenny and taught for long at Callan where his son Humphrey succeeded him. Humphrey O'Sullivan's diary written whilst a hedge-school teacher at Callan, has been recently published and has attracted much literary attention.

Michael O'Longáin taught for many years in Carrignavar, Co. Cork. Like many of his kind he was a full-blooded rebel; he organised the Ninety-Eight men and led them to Slievenamon to help the Men of Wexford. Their leaders were missing as he told in his most famous song *Slievenamon*.

I have named some of the better known hedge school teachers earlier in this article and from close study and local tradition I am satisfied that their wonderful work for learning and religion during the penal years, has never been properly publicised. We are apt to lose sight of their thirst for learning; their love of country; their painstaking work in teaching the Christian Doctrine and keeping the Faith of Patrick alive when our priests were on the hills and the teachers themselves were every day risking life and limb. Cromwellian, Elizabethan and Williamite laws put their work under penalty of death. They were denounced in one edict as "Popish Schoolmasters, who taught Irish youth idolatry and superstition; we must rigorously enforce the laws against them."

Yet the faithful teachers taught on, flourishing tenaciously as the only medium, outside the hunted priests, of Catholic education in Ireland from 1680 to 1782. These laws hunted the teachers to the remote mountain fastnesses, pupils travelling long journeys to meet them. Poor scholars from distant counties, satchels of books hidden on their persons, sought the schools of higher learning.

English visitors to Killarney two hundred years ago were astonished to meet young men well versed in Greek and Latin. One youth who had held a visitor's horse discoursed Virgil and Homer with confident freedom. Young men straight from the Irish hedge schools swept the prizes at Louvain, Paris and Salamanca where they were forced to go under the Penal Laws to finish their religious studies.

Whilst the hedge schools concentrated on laying good foundations in reading, writing and arithmetic, they taught Greek and Latin well. But it is for their Christian Doctrine instruction of the young and for their deep patriotism that they will best be remembered. They were well-versed in land-surveying, conveyancing, will writing, translating; they inspired their pupils with a love of country and a hatred of their despoilers. They were sheltered faithfully by the people and were kept in the best houses. They were the life and soul of social company where their learning and historic story-telling were esteemed. Their remuneration was small but they got the best which the oppressed people could give.

Their teaching kept our faith and patriotism alive through the darkest days of our history, leaving the eternal embers behind which arose and sparkled in God's good time into a living flame. Our Irish hedge schoolmasters played a noble part and it is our duty to keep their memory fresh and green.

SPRING

THERE are buds on every tree. Even the laggard ash shows. When I pruned a young ash tree over the weekend my efforts were not directed towards beauty of form. Rather was my mind concentrated on a future day when I should cut it down and fashion a few lithe camáns for young hurlers. Not so long now; that sweep of root is thickening fast and it seems tough as the proverbial gad.

To induce this thickening of bole I nipped the lighter shoots that promised height and range, which I did not want. I was surprised to find the sap in strong circulation, proving that I had postponed my pruning plans too long. While my hand was in, and the unusual January sun still shining I set about a similar operation on a pear tree that gave a wonderful crop of luscious fruit in 1942, but altogether disappointed me last year — too much wood. That same pear tree intrigued many leisure hours last summer when a merry yellow-billed blackbird and his mate set about house-building in its branches. My first indication was the activities of the birds on the gutter-eaves at the back of the house. They splashed mud around in their many journeys to and fro when cementing the nests as blackbird architects always do. To make a long story short, they reared a brood of *gearcachs* big as themselves despite the attentions of a raiding cat. Must have been the same pair of birds that I saw busy amongst the bushes in recent weeks. They had clearly designs on their old home. When I climbed the tree and proceeded to lop off the branches that black and dark brown pair became wildly excited and scolded me no end with chattering bills and fanning tails. In acknowledging their loud-voiced protest I limited my clipping and left their section of the tree sacrosanct. I am hoping for their pleasant company as the days lengthen.

Wonderful seeding weather this. There are olive green tints over the mountain tops at dawn. The deep purple clouds change slowly to rise in infinitesimal alterations of shade, until they are as burnished gold as the sun tips the hill. Ploughmen with horse and tractor, are the men of the hour. Roads and streets dried miraculously under a thin sharp wind and within a week all soils will be awaiting the turning furrow. Watching the brown sods rolling over in easy rhythm is a fascinating pleasure. Every turned sod means an extra stone of flour and we need many.

Watching a batch of merry rural schoolboys with their satchels wending their way homeward under grey February skies last week, I took to wondering whether these boys of to-day work as hard on the land as we did in our youth. Boys growing up on tillage farms had no leisure at all so long as there was light, or even dusk in the sky.

No sooner were books put away than a hearty meal was consumed with healthy appetites — then heigh-ho for the countless jobs that awaited us. Mangolds and turnips — panniers filled with them had to be taken from their frost-proof pits, and sliced and pulped at lightning speed. Winter feed for horses, carrots and furze (mainly) had to be cleaned, prepared and dumped in mangers and stalls. Horses throve on carrots and crushed young furze that had succulent grass mingled with it. Working horses peeled their ears for such feed, and their coats shone like satin. As the spring evenings stretched we garsoons were "drilled" out to the tillage land clearing potatoes or root land of weeds and stalks in preparation for grain. Driving with long reins unsteady horses ploughing lealand with an elder brother between the handles. Helping the carting of farmyard manure — laborious work, or preparing wheat for the seeding. Mayhap helping to build up fences broken down after the winter storms or rains.

Proud was the day when I was entrusted with the handles of a plough myself. It was soft fallowland of course, with one steady horse in front of a light swing plough. I left the land too young to plough lea. Yet, even at eleven, I could plough a straight furrow of stubble — the height of my ambition. Most unpleasant job I ever found on the land was picking and clearing potatoes out of a pit on a wet, cold and frosty day. Christmas, winter or summer holidays were all alike to us, we had to work hard on the land. Long summer evenings after school brought no leisure — we had to "thin" roots, weed cornlands, and help with the hay. Handling hay or corn was delightful work in summer weather, but I shiver yet at the thought of clearing potato pits in cold, wet and bitter weather. Perhaps the hardships of youth proved a good university for the hard, rugged road of life, that all but the lucky few must needs face and conquer.

IRISH SONGBIRDS

DAWN was breaking over the eastern Irish hills one morning last May when I awoke to the dawn-chorus of the songbirds then in their glorious orchestral fullness. And I thought then, as I often thought before at different times of a fair Spring day, that if ever I were forced to leave Ireland for a living (which God forbid) what I should miss most would be the Irish songbirds. The dulcet thrushes at dawn, the blackbird's rich noting at dusk, the linnet's lilting, the finches of all kinds, the lark in his spacious element, the robin and wren warbling merrily through Winter's frost and snow!

Though the blackbird's bold and wayward habits, allied to his dusky coat and bright yellow bill, seem to have inspired our song writers and balladists in the past, I have always thought his meeker cousin, the thrush, his superior as a songster. There is more clear melody in his phrasing and more variety in his love messages to his mate in the well-hid adjacent nest. I have often studied the same brown bird's song at different hours of the day and been amazed at the different blending and variations; the accents and note-runs change as if he is telling a story of what a glad place the world is. Sometimes his song assumes a colourful bravado and his defiant notes tell his companion, that with him on guard, she is quite safe from all danger. But it is his joyous orisons to greet the sun in a Spring morning that best soothe the listener with their messages of purity and hope in God's world.

The thrush is common in every county in Ireland and they breed everywhere except in the treeless and shrubless regions of exposed coasts. The homebirds never leave our shores but the stocks are considerably increased in Winter time when migrating thrush flocks seek our milder climate from northern Europe. The bulk of these come through England and reach this country mainly by the coast of Wexford where many casualties are found in stormy weather at the foot of our outpost lighthouses.

The thrush opens his song in the mild days of December and I recall one "pet" day in November when cycling along a Limerick glen — Glenbrohane — I heard and saw a thrush sing tunefully low down on a bare elm. The bird comes to his full power in Spring and he sings on daily until well into June. On June 3rd, 1950, just a year ago, I heard a thrush break the silence with a gallant phrase of song at 3a.m. (sun-time). The usual hour in May and June is 4 o'clock or so. Like most other songbirds in these climes, the thrush is rarely heard or seen in July or August. Naturalists feel convinced that the migrants start their return journeys to North European countries in June or earlier. A big proportion remain faithful throughout the year. Nests are built in March and light blue eggs with dusky spots are hatched by April. By the time the birds first fly they look as big as their parents and can only be distinguished by their plump tailless bodies. When learning to fly, many young birds are caught by marauding cats and other creatures of the wild. A pair of thrushes once built in a pear tree at the end of the garden and I esteemed their presence, leaving steeped bread crumbs handy.

Then one day, the young birds fluttered amongst the branches for some time and their parents worked overtime bringing them food. All got clear away to the open park except one who flopped down amongst the cabbages in the garden. Just then a marauding cat stole into the scene. Soon the battle was on. That cat was hungry, but when he pounced the two parent birds attacked him with wild fury. The cat fought back with tooth and claw trying all he knew to seize either the angry birds or their plump progeny. The thrushes screamed and sought to pluck out the eyes of the equally angry cat with their beaks. It was a grim, noisy battle in nature's raw but the brave thrushes, with wings, legs and beaks, routed the cat who ran helter-skelter for cover. Only then did the birds tempt the fledgling by way of shrub branches to safety. I saw them no more. That next door cat was nursing his injured eyes and nose for a week.

On another occasion too when the thrushes had their nest in a great lilac tree down in the corner there was a weak fledgling left. To save him from the cat and give him time to gather flying strength, I caught him gingerly and, as the parents were missing, I put the young bird in a parrot-cage which I hung between the branches of the pear tree. Soon cock and hen thrush arrived and when I retired they proceeded to feed the fledgling liberally. After a day or two I opened the door of the cage and soon all three were away into the open fields.

The Mistle-thrush: bigger, longer and more lightly coloured than the song-thrush he is a wholly migrant bird which was first reported in Ireland in 1808 — a particularly severe winter when a flock of these birds arrived in Wexford from Northern Europe. They have been coming every November since then in larger numbers and are now very numerous in Winter and Spring. Called the Throstle by the poets, this beautiful bird sings from January to March from the top branches of bare larches and elms. His song is bold, defiant and of surprising power; he can be heard a full half-mile across the valley on still evenings.

Naturalists have observed that the nest of the chaffinch is frequently found close beside the throstle's home. When a hawk or other marauder attacks the chaffinch the mistle-thrush has been seen to attack the slayer fearlessly. A hawk was once seen so attacked and he was forced to drop the bird when the throstle alighted on his back with angry wings, beak and claw. The mistle-thrush says goodbye to Ireland as soon as the young are ready for flight. He defies weather — hence the name stormcock.

The Blackbird: a really lovable rogue and seems thoroughly at home in any surroundings. He is more widely distributed than the thrush and is a far hardier bird to resist severe winter weather. The blackbird is well and familiarly known in every county in Ireland and nests even in the treeless districts of remote coasts. In Lambay Island, in the Aran Islands, Rathlin, Achill and Connemara, this bold fellow with the mellow notes, will build in mossy banks or fences where there are no trees. The blackbird is disliked by orchard keepers for he is destructive on small fruit of all kinds and has been known to pick cherries through protecting nets.

Though many blackbirds remain in Ireland throughout the year, there is considerable migration in November when thousands come from colder Northern climes. Not such an early riser as the thrush, the blackbird's startled chuckle as he breaks covert can be heard right through the winter. He sings tunefully though rather meekly in the mild days of December but comes into his full song in April, May and early June. He is heard best on a sunny evening after rain when his velvety contralto notes are altogether charming and he has all the temperament of a colouroso for he can be grave, gay, tender, mocking or abusive. He is a skilful mimicker of other birds and in captivity can be taught to whistle many simple tunes. I remember having a blackbird in captivity. I found him wounded in the bushes when I was a barefoot schoolboy. He must have hit against wire when flying at night. One wing hung limply and a leg was broken beyond recovery, I thought. I brought him home and put him in a big open wicker cage. I spliced his broken leg carefully with a split match-stick and thread. I fed him and watered him regularly and he was soon flourishing. He was tuning meekly inside three weeks. Then I noticed a remarkable thing. He had made a plaster for his injured leg from the droppings in his cage. He sang gloriously by the middle of May; he would imitate my whistling call and could pipe every note in "wait a while and I'll be with you." One day in late April I found that his cage was empty. I missed him but was in a way glad that he had answered the call of the wild through a damaged bar in the cage where I found a feather he had left as he forced his way to freedom.

Finches of all kinds, are charming birds and are mainly Winter migrants, Goldfinch, Greenfinch, Bullfinch, Chaffinch are found everywhere where there are open fields and shrubs. Flocks have been found in the surrounding islands, rushing for mild climates from November to March. They sing early and the beautifully coloured Goldfinch is most esteemed as a songster. His enemies are many for trapping by birdlime and nets are general. The Irish laws have tightened against these offences and our wild Goldfinch stocks are recovering as a result. They live on "blackheads" and other seedling plants. The Chaffinches are homely, cheerful birds, though their song has little melody. The many finches that nest here between March and May, sing from February to June and they flock together in October before heading south for France and Spain, seeking warmer climes. Their nests are neat and elaborate — grass-roots, sheep's wool, vegetable down; their eggs are blue with tiny dark spots. The Goldfinch when well cared for thrives and sings happily in captivity.

The Skylark is familiar to all outdoor lovers and is found everywhere, even in bare mountain sides, moors and sandhills close to the coasts where he seems to be in his element. Flocks come hither from Scotland and overseas in Winter but the home stock never leave us. Their soaring, continuous song floods the countryside with melody. The lark has been known to sing at mid-night but strange to say he is not up with the dawn. He is far behind thrush, blackbird and linnet in that regard so "up with the lark" is somewhat of a fallacy.

I have seen larks sing gloriously in a spacious cage; bird lovers renew the essential green sod regularly; they are careful with their seed and water, but I should never dream of cageing a lark; there is something which calls to freedom in him and there is a tendency to soar as he sings in captivity. Once, through field-glasses I watched an adult male lark with his distinguished top-knot resting on a low briar near his nest. I could not help admiring the bold stand and build of him. For the lark is a gamebird as those who have shot much in the open can verify; keen Irish Setters if game is scarce will set a lark and disappoint the snipe fowler.

The Linnet: both grey and green are considered by many listeners, blessed (or cursed) by an over-sensitive musical ear, to be our sweetest songbirds. The linnet loves flocking and migration. He is a creature of the furzy bushes and the wilds, he shuns cultivation. His song in the open fields and moors gladdens the heart of the wanderer — delicate, tender, infinitely sweet — he sings from March to July and then hastens away.

The Robin and Wren are the most intimate of our songbirds. Their merry warbling all through the bleakest Winter days are refreshing. Both are sweet singers and closely related as their songs indicate. Bird lovers never forget the robins when snow and frost are about. Their nests are in most unexpected places — a discarded kettle or even the end of a broken-down hay-tedder will suffice. The wren is a master architect and his nest with a dozen tiny eggs is often roofed and adroitly hidden. Irish emigrants the world over miss these beautiful songbirds of home and cherish their memory with nostalgic affection.

THE OLD HURLER'S SONG TO HIS ASH

I'm eighty years come Michaelmas, and shaking is this hand of mine;
Your shape recalls the happy days when I was young and gay;
Last eve at dusk when stripping thatch, I found you on the rafter-line —
My old caman, that served me well,from Cork to Ballyhay.

'Twas coming from the Fair of Ross, I saw that bend of growing ash,
And swore I'd cut the makings true, before the night was done;
Tho' tyrants held the woodland then, close guarded by Black Tady Nash
I shouldered home the "soople" tree before the morning sun.

Right carefully we seasoned it, above the turf-fire's mellow smoke,
And waited till the moon was full to split the planks in twain;
One Seamus Og O'Leary, too, who came of good Tip'rary folk,
He helped me slope the handle-blade, and lanes of rugged grain.

It was upon this homely hearth I fashioned you most lovingly,
And planed your sides with patient hand, till every vein did shine;
Your sole was wide; your nose was slim; your graceful waist was
maidenly,
And sweetly balanced was the spring of beauty every line.

My love was there, that Christmas Day, I took you to the goaling field,
To try your steel against the might of camans stout galore;
She cheered your work, my nutbrown maid; when city stars were forced
to yield,
'Twas your broad boss that showed the way, and whipped the winning
score.

You made your name in championships, when Gaelic men ranged side by
side,
St. Finbarr's Reds, Dungourna men with Blackrock in the van;
Tip'rary fame, Kilkenny's pride, the fearless men from Shannon's tide —
But by my word, my honest ash, you never maimed a man!

'Till Mitchelstown, one Land League day, we stood with brave John Mandeville,
And in that first fierce baton fight, you cracked a peeler's head;
Blackthorn sticks they swept the square, of ashplants too, they had their fill,
Until they riddled down our ranks with Balfour's bloody lead.

Home-coming from a final match, and Mary on the car with me,
She held you in her loving lap, and told me she was mine.
Thro' all our joys and sorrows since, she never has been far from me,
And now we're slipping down the road with heart and hand atwine.

When we retired from playing fields, we sided with the Irish sort,
Near Padraig Pearse at Rossa's grave, we both remember well;
At Martyr's nights in Patrick Street; we held the gate at "Murphy's Fort,"
And often times we marched behind the sorrows of Parnell.

When Tans were raiding for our sons, my Mary there with me and you,
We faced them on the threshold stone, and gave ours time to clear;
That year I did my time in jail, with Turlough and Dan Fraher, too,
Whilst Mary hid you 'neath the thatch, with many a salty tear.

We're waiting now the final flag, and God's good home is on our view.
Two sons are gone — they nobly fought and died our land to save;
You're wrinkled too, my Mountain Ash, and few are left to fondle you,
When we're asleep, you'll rest with us and share a Fenian's grave.

FEBRUARY BREEZES

HIS stirrup was long, and he sat his horse in the easy way that only life-long usage knows. You see his like often in Kildare, Tipperary or the borders of Cork-Limerick, where they love a horse or a hurler.

I had the old bicycle, and a good man he is in these days of perishing winds and sleety showers that blow through you whilst waiting for a bus at the corner of the street. This time I was struggling against a strong head wind from W.N.W. when he hailed me.

"What brings you here? 'Twas a queer place your legs brought you. Did you hear that Christy Ryan, of Mitchelstown, is dead?" A feather would blow me off the bicycle then, and a kindly sign over a nearby doorway helped. He threw his leg over carelessly, and the horse was as agreeable as himself. Only his missing finger told the tale of that ambush at Drumkeen.

I'll come back to this tall, lean horseman (minus a finger) another day — he now fills one of the biggest posts in the country and is worth every pound of it. We were in the heart of Kildare — almost 200 miles from my native headlands and 130 from his own Limerick-Tipperary border. We talked of Christy Ryan, of Mitchelstown, for two hours. God rest him. Next day I had a letter from a well-known Glanworth man in Cork saying Christy was dead.

The Mitchelstown Blackthorns that "swept the square," in John Mandeville's days gave their name to the team of Gaelic footballers that flourished for a quarter of a century in that town where four counties meet beneath the Galtees. Some of you remember this song:

"Remember Mitchelstown" was a rallying cry in the Land League days —

> "Neath Galtees lofty mountains,
> Where breezes pure and keen
> Sweep like a gushing torrent down
> Through woodlands fresh and green.
> And by their verdant slopings,
> Where Funcheon's waters flow,
> The sprigs of stout blackthorn
> In rich profusion grow —
> 'Tis there you'll find that plant of fame
> Decked out by nature's hand,
> And stout hearts there to wield it
> To defend their native land."

I think Christy Ryan, of the Square, of Mitchelstown, was the kindliest and stoutest of men that braved all and suffered all. Forty years ago he was the best footballer in his countryside, and the Lees of Cork city sat up and took notice of this lively speedy youth from "Galtee's verdant slopings." Christy Ryan was soon called into Cork's inter-county team, and proved one of their best men in the 1909-1912 period.

Mitchelstown Feis was famous in these days and 'twas there I first saw Christy Ryan dance. He had the neat technique of the Cork City School — the school that gave us Willie Murray and Freddie Murray, Jack O'Brien, Curtin, Moore, Flanagan, Morley of Blackrock, Stephen Comerford, Monty Riordan and all. Christy Ryan too had some of the freedom of Waterford and Tipperary dancers in a happy blend with the Cork double-crosskey and rocking. He carried a lot of dancing with him to the grave. Coming of an old Fenian family, the Ryans of Mitchelstown were marked men in the Anglo-Irish struggle. Both Willie and Cristeór were raided time out of mind; they did their time in jail, and in the height of the agitation Christy Ryan kept a light heart. Whilst a price was on his head, I saw him dance *The Blackbird* in the flagged kitchen one night with all careless exuberance of a schoolboy — fit to take his place with Beresford of the Decies, Sean Nolan of Nenagh or Clune of Clare.

THE GREATEST HANDBALLER

THROUGH the schools and lecture halls of Munster, in many years of wandering, I have met no Shakesperean scholar more erudite than Father Tom Jones of Kerry, the versatile musician, scholar and litterateur.

But there was another Art, far removed from indoor study and culture, in which the saintly Sagart Paroiste of Glenbeigh, Co. Kerry, excelled all the men of Munster, aye, and outside Munster, Father Tom Jones, by general acclaim, was the greatest handballer of all time. One of the soundest authorities on modern handball — the late Mr. Geoffrey O'Herlihy (R.I.P.) of Cork city — father of champion Billie Herlihy, once gave me his opinion with emphatic conviction.

We had been adjacent spectators of a big handball "rubber" on the gallery of the Old Market Court, Cork, across the road from the Bells of Shandon. Mr. O'Herlihy senior, in a reminiscent mood, was running through the roll of World champions he had seen in action. He had more than one keen listener. Geoffrey O'Herlihy was a reliable witness; as Father Jones would himself quote Othello, he would "nothing extenuate, nor set aught down in malice."

Recounting in his critical way from long experience, the qualities and weaknesses of the different Handball stars of Ireland, America and Spain — Geoffrey gave his final verdict with expressive gesture:— "Father Tom Jones of Tralee was the greatest handballer that ever put foot inside a Court."

This was weighty evidence from a wise old admirer of the older schools of handball, and he had seen all the great ones perform from near and far — Phil Casey, Alderman Dunne, Michael Egan, Jim Kelly, John Lawlor, Oliver Drew, Billie Herlihy, Joe Leary, James Fitzgerald, David Browning, Tim Twohill, J.J. Bowles, Delaney, O'Shea, Coyne, Lyons, Pembroke and all, down to our own time. From personal contact over a stretch of forty years and close study of records, I am inclined to agree with Geoffrey O'Herlihy and others like him — Father Tom Jones was the "daddy of them all." He was ten years out of active handball when I saw him play. His impetuous speed and superb skill with left and right hands, his agility and judgment, his bubbling vivacity fairly took my breath away. He stood in a niche apart!

This remarkable man was born in Tralee in December, 1868 and grew into a sturdy sprightly youth who divided his leisure from studies between his violin and the ballcourt at Gas Terrace, Tralee, home of many great players. At seventeen he could beat single-handed any pair of visitors to the Court and quickly attracted attention. His earliest admirer and patron was a well-known Kerry sporting character, Mr. Jerry Casey — himself a fine jumper and handballer and judge of athletic talent. When a young Jones had beaten all and sundry — no local man could take a game off him — Jerry Casey sought further fields to conquer and issued the following public challenge in 1885 on behalf of the stripling of sixteen summers:—

"I Jeremiah Casey, of Bridge Street, Tralee do hereby challenge on behalf of Tom Jones, of Tralee, any boy or man handballer in Ireland of 8½ stone. An early reply will oblige." There were no acceptors; the name and fame of young Tom Jones had already spread abroad.

Handball in Ireland received a great impetus in 1886 when the world's champion John Lawlor of Dublin returned to Ireland unbeaten. He won through a championship tournament in Cork where his stoutest opponent was Joseph O'Leary of Fermoy. Messrs. Jerry Casey with Jones Major and Minor, visited Cork to see the champions play, and in the following summer, young Tom played his first big rubber — home and away at Tralee and Cork against O'Leary of Fermoy. The youngster's form astonished all the critics. His electric speed, his flashing accuracy with foot and hand, his boundless energy seemed to mesmerise his more seasoned opponent. O'Leary was beaten in each of the seven games at Gas Terrace and fared no better at the completion of the rubber in Cork.

Heavy side stakes were the rule at the time and the future Father Jones played matches in Tralee, Limerick, Kilrush and Cork before his challenge game for the Championship of Ireland (£200) against John Delaney of Athy, Co. Kildare, who was John Lawlor's successor on the Dublin man's return to America.

Of the ten games at Athy, Delaney won eight with a faster ball than Jones had used, against two for the Tralee boy. On his home court at Tralee, Tom Jones won game after game with astonishing ease and took the whole nine to win the rubber and championship.

Playing O'Shea of Carrick-on-Suir for a side stake of £400 and the Irish Championship, at the Racket Court, Cork in June, 1888, the Tralee youth won the rubber outright without conceding a game — a record in championship matches, where challengers had high credentials.

To say that this boyish clerical student created a sensation in handball circles was to put it mildly. He had a new conception of handball. Whilst earlier champions, like Casey and Lawlor, let an "impossible" ball pass and reserved their strength with cool judgment, the future Fr. Tom Jones "went for" every ball at lightning speed, from back wall to base-line. He had the heart of ten men; he would climb the wall for a ball and scoop one from all angles for a deadly kill; he went tearing after every ace, and usually got there. He would play an exhibition rally for his friends at home — his right hand against his left, starting with a brand-new alley cracker and crash it into bits before the rally was complete. He would bet that he could break the stoutest ball before his left hand would put out his right; and he usually won. 'Twas a revelation.

He challenged John Lawlor repeatedly, offering to play "ball and ball about" but Lawlor insisted on using the American ball only, and the pair, despite long newspaper arguments and many efforts by promoters, were never destined to meet in the same court.

As a result, a tournament was promoted in Cork in August, 1889, to decide the championship with a valuable inscribed gold medal associated. Lawlor had gone to America, and the entrants included: Thomas Jones (Tralee), Humphries (Cork), Herlihy (Cork), Murphy (Cork), Tobin (Fermoy), O'Leary (Fermoy), Doolan (Kilkenny), Roche (Kanturk), O'Brien (Tipperary), Beatty (Galway), Pervis (Galway), Murphy (Midleton).

Jones and O'Leary worked their way to the final — the first five games of 21 aces each. O'Leary gave his opponent a tremendous match winning three games against four scored by the Tralee boy. O'Leary refused to finish, and Jones was awarded the rubber, to become undisputed Champion of Ireland. Within recent weeks I have seen this unique Cork medal of 1889, and it appears in a photograph taken in California during Father Jones' mission abroad.

Before entering Maynooth college in 1890, Father Jones, unable to get a single opponent, played many double-handed matches in partnership with his townsman, James Fitzgerald. They were never defeated, and when taking up his sacred mission to bid good-bye to competitive handball for ever, the undefeated champion handed over his mantle to Fitzgerald — "the only man to give him a match."

Frequently, during summer holidays, the pair met at Tralee. Father Jones invariably won, and, though Fitzgerald had beaten Lawlor, Nolan, Twohill and Herlihy meanwhile, he was always ready to acknowledge modestly:— "I could never play Father Tom!"

Following ten years on the Australian mission, Father Jones, travelling through America in 1905 on his way back to Ireland, created a stir in Casey's famous Court.

Without disclosing his identity (he loves a joke) Father Tom had loads of fun with the Brooklyn "fans" before a brother cleric gave the show away. In an hour the word went around that Father Jones was here and the court was packed to see the phenomenon who, by popular rumour, was supposed to have died in the backwoods of Australia.

Most loved and devoted of priests, Father Jones came into prominence again in the early days of the European War when heroically rescuing eight Norwegian sailors whose destruction was threatened under Kerry's beetling cliffs. With the courageous peasants of Ballyferriter, the old athlete descended perpendicular cliffs on ropes and brought the unconscious men to safety. The King of Norway presented Father Jones with a Gold Memorial Cup which is amongst the most cherished of his many trophies.

During the National struggle from 1916 to 1922 Father Jones' intrepidity on the side of his people brought him into many dangerous places, with Black and Tan revolvers to his head, and a rifle muzzle to his back. The good priest, despite threats and vile abuse, never flinched in his high duty in defence of his flock. An illuminated address by the Nationalists of Killorglin, where he ministered for six years, is amongst Father Jones' most treasured possessions in his well-stocked library at Glenbeigh.

In his later years Father Jones has made some scholarly translations from famous French, German and Russian writers — beautiful, graceful translations into the Irish language, where he is a master of idiom. His work has attracted much attention in Irish periodicals, and we hope to see him again in book form, for he wields a powerful literary pen.

An accomplished musician and skilful interpreter of our native music on pipes, whistle or fiddle, Father Jones now quietly pursues his holy office with untiring zeal amongst Kerry's most rugged and picturesque glens. To see him as I did last autumn, stride across rocky fords, jump over swollen streams under Keel and Coomasharn, or trudge light-footed over Barnageeha to works of mercy in the wild fastnesses of Glencar, you would never suspect 'twas fifty odd years since he was World's Chamapion.

57

TO A CHILD — ON HER BIRTHDAY

Your face is fair as budding rose by June dews kissed,
Your cheeks the dawnlit skies that break thro' Maymorn mist,
Your ways the gentle breezes swaying brown autumn corn,
Your heart the pure and fragrant bloom of snow-white thorn.

P.D.M.

JIM STAPLETON OF THURLES TOWN

HATS off, Gaels and all you who love a grand old Hurler — eighty-five years gone, who still reads his newspapers without glasses, and one whose mild, open, honest eyes will sparkle when recalling the great days of his youth! Salute honest Jim Stapleton of Thurles, farmer and man, captain and only living representative of that powerful Tipperary team which won the First All-Ireland Championship (1887) — that history making final at Birr when Tipperary beat Galway 1 goal 1 point and 1 forfeit point to nil.

Born in Cathedral Street, Thurles, where his family carried on business, in May 1863, Jim grew into a stalwart youth — "a powerful bullet of a man," an old All-Ireland man told me — about five feet 10 inches with powerfully muscled shoulders and arms, of endless pluck and stamina, weighing around 12½ stone in his hearty prime. The bulk of his life was spent on the land and he still farms paternal acres half-a-mile from Thurles town. Next door was born Mr. William Dwan, well-known Thurles sportsman and G.A.A. patron, who has been a life-long admirer and friend.

"I am only anxious to give due honour to the fine team of men I captained in 1887 and 1888, for more than once, I have seen the wrong names in print. I can understand that, for we got very little notice in the Press in my day. We hurled for the honour of our country and wanted nothing more. I am anxious now," he told me, "that the full names of the men and their clubs, who played in that final should be published and here they are:-

Tipperary (winners of the First All-Ireland Hurling Championship held under the G.A.A.): James Stapleton (Captain), Martin McNamara, Edward Murphy, Thomas Burke, Jer. Dwyer, Matthew Maher, Thomas Maher, Andrew Maher (all of Thurles); Thomas Carroll (Moyne); John Dunne, Pat Leahy (Ferror); Edward Bowe (Leigh); John Mockler (New Hill); Thomas Healy (Coolcroo); Thomas Stapleton (Littleton); Dan Ryan, Jerh. Ryan (Ballybeg); Jerh. Dwyer (Ballyvinane); Pat Leamy, Pat Lambe, M. Carroll (Drombane).

So keen was this honourable old man, on having the full names of his team see the light of day, that he wrote to me a confirming letter and winding up: "Do not think I am stressing this unduly about the correct names of the team. I'll say no more. All I am concerned about now is to give honour where it is due and clear all doubts. I had the honour of captaining them, and I am the only survivor now of as fine a team of men as ever represented their county. I have only done my duty to my gallant team-mates who, each and every one, did a good man's part in giving to Tipperary the first All-Ireland Championship."

Yours very sincerely,
James Stapleton

What struck me most about Jim Stapleton was his sincerity and his tenacious memory of the historic final. James played in all the local Championship games and captained Thurles through the County final. Their next game was against Clare at Nenagh. Clare was represented by Smyth O'Brien's and put up a good show before losing to the sweeping Tipperary men — 1 goal 7 points to 2 points.

Next came a hard rugged game against Tullaroan, champions of Kilkenny, at Urlingford which Tipperary won by 4 goals and 7 points to nil. Galway, where Bishop Duggan had encouraged his men to hold fast to the ancient game, were supreme in the West, but found firm opposition from Castlebridge, the Champions of Wexford.

Thousands were thronging to local and inter-county tournaments since Michael Cusack of Clare and Dublin, with Maurice Davin of Clonmel, international athletic champion, had founded the Gaelic Athletic Association in a room of Hayes' Hotel, Thurles. It was in 1887 that the big scheme of promoting All-Ireland championships in hurling and football was underway. Galway and Tipperary had reached the final, which was fixed for Birr, on Easter Sunday 1888.

Teams at that time consisted of 21 men per side and they were as a rule big, stalwart men, fast and fearless. There were goalposts flanked by pointposts — a goal outscored any number of points. When a defending player put a ball over his own line a forfeit point was awarded instead of the present-day free puck from 70 yards.

Jim Stapleton tells me that there was a big crowd on the Birr field that day. The field was 200 yards by 100 yards and a friendly regiment of Scottish Highlanders, stationed in Birr at the time, volunteered to keep order and control the side-lines, for there were no railings then. Good order prevailed throughout; the field was level and not too grassy. Jim Stapleton says the ball was of good size and not so hard as the present; neither was it too heavy. The ball then used was of red leather with a worsted thread centre over a cork core.

These stalwart teams were well matched as the final scores indicated. The men played in their stockinged feet without boots. All the Tipperarymen except Jim Stapleton wore long pants. Jim Stapleton, at a vital stage of the game, helped to bring the ball down the field in a central rush of crowded men. The Tipperary Captain saw his chance of a score and passed the ball out to Tommy Healy of Coolcroo, father of the well-known cross-country runners — the Healys of Coolcroo.

Tommy was a fast runner and a sure, stylish striker — something of the type of Phil Cahill of Holycross in modern times. Healy caught the ball as it came towards him and drove it hard and low through the gap of the goal. That great score gave the first All-Ireland Championship to Jim Stapleton and his Tipperary men.

Galway had given Tipperary their hardest match of the Championship. The men of Meelick and Killiemore had a non-playing Captain (usual at that time) in Captain Lynam of Meelick, who had served with the American Army and directed hurling operations from the sideline. Capt. Lynam was later elected Parnellite M.P. for East Galway. Here is the Galway team as far as we can trace from the scant records of the period:-

Galway: Patrick Larkin of Kiltormer; John Cosgrave of Meelick, Arthur Cosgrave, Michael Mullen, Thomas Henly, Patrick Madden, Michael Kenny, Michael Mannion and two others all of Meelick; from Killiemore came John Mannion, Owen Griffin, John Saunders, Thomas Foley, Michael Conway, Michael Kirby, John Mannion, Patrick Haverty, James Haverty, Martin Griffin and Owen Griffin.

The teams dressed at the Cunningham Hotel and marched to and from the grounds in military formation, led by Captain Lynam. This was the forerunner of many All-Ireland Championships and many Tipperary victories.

Early in 1888 the rapidly spreading Gaelic Athletic movement conceived the idea of taking a team of fifty selected All-Ireland hurlers and athletes to America. Mr. Michael Davitt, founder of the Land League, gave his hearty approval to the project and Mr. Maurice Davin, President of the Association pushed forward the organisation of the tour. Mr. James Stapleton of Thurles was amongst the first of the selected hurlers. Here is the list of the hurlers who set sail from Cobh on board the Wisconsin on the 16th September 1888: James Stapleton, Thurles; Tom O'Grady, Moycarkey; J. O'Brien, do; T. Ryan Clonoulty; W. Prendergast, Clonmel; P.P. Sutton, Dublin; G. Burgess, do; J. Furlong, do; J. Hayes, do; Frank Coughlan, do; James Royce, Wexford; P.J. Molohan, Leix; P. Fox, Kilkenny; J. Grace, do; M. Curran, do; J. Dunne, Offaly; J. Nolan, do; P. Meleady, do; J. Cordial, do; P. Ryan and J. McEvoy, Leix; D. Godfrey, Limerick; J. Coughlan and J. Mooney, Cork; M. Hickey, Carrickbeg; and the Claremen, J. Rourke, J. Fitzgibbon, P. Minogue. Along with these many of the selected athletes were useful hurlers.

This "invasion" of the Irish Gaels created big sporting news in the American Press and the hurling exhibitions between two teams based on Tipperary and Dublin brought unbounded enthusiasm, not alone amongst the Irish in America, but in purely American circles where team games were then little practised. Here is what the New York Herald said about the New York exhibition between Tipperary and Dublin selected:-

"The great gathering enjoyed the hurling hugely, and cheered lustily as the stalwart Irish lads marched out, with the hurleys on their shoulders in military formation. They formed in lines in the centre, the ball was thrown up, and then the fun began. Such leaping, hitting, jumping, tumbling had never been seen on these grounds. Hardly a man missed a stroke and every man was ambidextrous. Once the ball was cornered amongst half-a-dozen on each side and heads, legs and hurlers were in inextricable confusion. To the stranger it seemed dangerous play, but the men from long practice never hit a head or injured an opponent."

Our venerable friend, James Stapleton, played in all these games at New York, Boston, Philadephia, Newark, Brooklyn, Providence, Lawrence, Lowell, Trenton and New Patterson, all in the Eastern States. Some of the hurlers remained and though lost to Ireland they laid the foundation of the Gaelic Athletic Association in America. Not one of the Tipperary hurlers remained and Jim Stapleton was amongst those who got a huge send-off when they sailed from New York on October the 31st.

James Stapleton was a hard worker all his life; he rarely missed a big hurling game, travelling many times far afield to cheer his successors of magnificent Tipperary. He looks like Oisin after all the Fianna had gone, returning from Tir-na-nÓg. A good citizen, upright in all his dealings, he is held in high repect by friends and neighbours. His sons farm with him and John was on Tipperary's All-Ireland side some years ago. The Gaelic Athletic Association owes much to such pioneers as this grand old Tipperaryman.

DAN DONNELLY'S GREAT BATTLES

WHERE the main Dublin Road to Kildare climbs into the open spaces of the Curragh a road on the left leads to the re-tiled military camp on the brow of the hill. Some distance down the road to the camp there is a quiet by-road on the left; and if you turn that way you soon reach a shaded, secluded country with a narrow opening on the right. You are in the famous Donnelly's Hollow of pugilistic history!

It can be approached from the Barrack Square, by the road dipping left into a deep dell. There before you are the round knolls, guarding the "Hollow," scene of many a sportman's pilgrimage in the 19th century. Here Dublin-born Dan Donnelly — "Sir Dan" he was affectionately called — beat two leading English prize-fighters, Tom Hall and George Cooper in 1814 and 1815 respectively.

When bare-knuckled prize-fighting was prohibited by law, no more secluded natural amphitheatre than "Donnelly's Hollow" could be found in the round of Ireland. One every side of the deep, grassy dell rise steep knolls, of considerable altitude. It is estimated that 30,000 people standing on these scrubby slopes could have a full view of the action. The "ringside seats" would carry many thousands more.

Contemporary writers lead us to believe that all available accommodation was necessary, for Dublin emptied itself on both historic occasions. All modes of conveyance, open and covered hack-cars, barouches, wagonettes, traps, saddle-horses, common and Scotch carts, streamed for miles along the road from Dublin. Thousands came on foot from all sides to see the free show. Dublin, Donnelly's home, sent far the biggest contingent. Twenty five thousand is a conservative estimate of the number of people, young and old, of both sexes, who saw Donnelly beat Cooper to subjection in eleven gory rounds on Monday December the 13th, 1815.

Who was this Dan Donnelly, of Dublin, whose heroic ring-battles made him the most famous man in Ireland at a time when prize-fighting with naked fists was one of the most popular sports and gambling medium attractions, both here and in England? These were the days of Jem Belcher and Tom Cribb, of Molineaux the negro; of Tom Spring and Jim Ward; of George Cooper and Tom Hall; of Carter, Gregson and Cannon.

Dan Donnelly was born in Townsend Street, Dublin where his father, Peter Donnelly, a respected citizen, kept a busy carpenter's shop. Peter, born on his father's farm in Cooley, Co. Louth, learnt his trade in Newry and worked at Dundalk where he married a Dublin girl. In Dublin they ultimately settled down. Dan followed his father's trade, and grew up into a fine upstanding, athletic youth, rather shy, though gay and witty in jovial company. When twenty years of age, Dan was six feet tall, and built in fine proportion. He took little or no interest in boxing, and never quarrelled. Boxing was forced upon him.

His father, then in failing health, was insulted one day in a tavern by a big burly sailor from the quays below. Dan was not far away; his fiery passion was roused and he made short work of the sailor. A challenge resulted, and the pair met the next day, when Dan, well backed in gold by a few friends, showed the sailor no mercy. He cut him to ribbons and cross-buttocked him to earth in double-jigtime. Dan's fame spread. He was induced to spar at boxing schools, at booths, common in Dublin then. He was soon "cock-of-the-walk."

A Dublin sporting gentleman, Captain Kelly, his sister, Miss Kelly, and the famous Captain Barclay were Dan Donnelly's most enthusiastic backers. Captain Kelly saw Dan box at booths and clubs. He challenged all comers, and Dan, never extended, was soon recognised as Irish champion.

At that time, a well-known English prize-fighter, Tom Hall, who had beaten George Cribb, (brother of the English champion, Tom Cribb) and had pretensions to the English title, was giving exhibitions and lessons in boxing in Dublin. Captain Kelly arranged a fight with Donnelly, then considered rather a crude boxer. The battleground was fixed for that secluded dell in the Curragh on September the 14th, 1814. The stake was £60 a side — only a small fraction of the bets laid.

When the men appeared in the ring before cheering thousands on the slopes, it was seen that the Irishman was some inches taller, with a big advantage in reach. He took the battle to his opponent in round after round, but Hall's skill and experience kept him out of serious trouble for a long period. Donnelly was surprisingly cool and never lost his head. Hall gradually weakened and a mighty onslaught by Donnelly in the 15th round finished the battle. Hall, sitting on his second's knee seemed dazed and unable to come to scratch when "Time, Time," was called for the next round.

This was Donnelly's first big fight and he was proclaimed a real champion. Bonfires blazed on the hills around Dublin and in the streets of the City. Dan had a royal reception.

Many challenges were sent out by Donnelly's backers but no reply was forthcoming, and the Townsend Street carpenter remained in popular seclusion for a twelve-month or more. In the autumn of 1815 the British near-champion, George Cooper, conqueror of the famous black champion, Molineaux, was giving boxing exhibitions in Dublin as well as lessons.

Cooper was born in Stone, Staffordshire and was a prize-fighter of much experience in first-class company. Standing 5 feet 10 inches and weighing just over 12 stone, he won a great reputation in Northern England, London and Scotland. His biggest claim to fame was his battle with Molineaux, the clever negro in Lancashire. Cooper knocked out the coloured man in the 14th round. He had nine wins to his credit and was on the way to the English title, when he came to earn more money in the Dublin halls.

Captain Kelly got busy at once; a side-stake for £400 was lodged, and the biggest bare-knuckled fight ever arranged in Ireland was fixed for "Donnelly's Hollow" on December the 13th 1815.

Although the venue was kept secret, Dublin sportsmen turned out in greater numbers than ever. The scenes of the Hall fight were repeated and surpassed in national interest. People came from across the Channel and from distant corners of Ireland. Probably owing to the big military interest in the contest, the police did not interfere, and to the cheering of the multitude the men took the ring at 10 a.m.

Donnelly showed evidence of being well-trained by Captain Kelly and Barclay, and Cooper, too was in excellent shape. An English sporting writer of the period, Mr. Henry Downes Mills, thus describes Dan Donnelly, the Irish champion, in his prime: "Six feet tall and weighing thirteen stone, he looked strong and bony, with no loose flesh. He was firmly muscular; his arms long and slingy; his shoulders uncommonly fine and of punishing quality in action; a hard-battling, determined face over a neck noble and bold. In a word he had a first-rate appearance for a boxer."

It must be remembered that under the old rules of prize-fighting, the rounds were not of regular length. Wrestling and cross-buttocking were permitted and in the latter Dan shone. Each round ended when a man went down to a blow or was thrown.

Round One: Dan, following his usual method, coolly took the battle to his more experienced and polished adversary. His raking left was well used; closing in after a sparring feeler, he wrestled Cooper to the ground.

Round Two: Fierce exchanges. After two minutes Dan drove Cooper to the ropes and bore him down.

Round Three: Tremendous in-fighting throughout. To wild cheers Dan forced the pace, his boxing improved and his weight and power bore Cooper down.

Round Four: A hard level battle of fierce milling. At the finish, both went down together with Cooper under.

Round Five: Dan was laughing, but Cooper shocked him with straight, powerful hits to face and body. Dan was floored, but was up at once. (Betting evens at this stage).

Round Six: A grand, clever round of dead even boxing; Cooper down cross-buttocked.

Round Seven: All Donnelly's; drove Cooper all over the ring. Donnelly's power telling; rangy left shots at body and face, a fierce wrestle in the close, and a strong cross-buttock by Dan. Cooper brought down heavily, Dan's full weight on top of him.

Round Eight: Donnelly well on top; showed fine judgement and timing of punches. At last a tremendous left-hander took Cooper off his feet and he went down heavily. "A guinea to a tenpenny bit on Donnelly!"

Round Nine: A gallant recovery by the Englishman produced the fiercest round of the lot. The boxers stood toe to toe exchanging telling blows. Both still strong; in attacking fiercely, Dan was ducked as Cooper stepped aside; his impetuous rush took him to the floor.

Round Ten: Dan's best round. Hard, determined blows, lefts to the head and one tremendous right to the body considerably weakened Cooper, who was floored in his own corner and looked distressed. He bled freely from the mouth. (No betting).

Round Eleven: Cooper recovered well and fought back with all his resources and bulldog courage. But Donnelly was fresh, punishing, and vigorous as when he began. Two tremendous blows, perfectly timed, followed in quick succession. A left hook to the mouth sent the blood down Cooper's chest, and a right to the body floored the Englishman, who lay bleeding in his corner. The game fellow could not come to scratch and Dan's green colours were flung high into the ring.

There was wild jubilation in Kildare and Dublin; every tavern on the road was open all night. Critics said Donnelly showed vast improvement in science and judgment since he fought Hall. He was unmarked and in splendid fettle. He was ranked first in Ireland and longed to try his hand in the classic boxing ranks in London, then headquarters of the fascinating sport. He had all Dublin at his feet.

GLAMOROUS GALWAY

AUGUST Bank Holiday week and Galway Races were synonomous terms to the Irish race-going community, and it was Galway Plate glamour that first drew me to "The City of the Tribes." All that I saw there only roused a thirst for more — for twenty-five years I have been retracing my footsteps and finding fresh charm in every pilgrimage.

From that first clear view of the Beanna Beola (The Twelve Bens) splitting the summer sunset that you get from the plateau of Clare, the West calls you. Every mile of the road makes the magnet stronger. Swinging down the cork-screw hill from Lisdoonvarna, the traveller's heart is singing; it sings past Kinvara and the head of the bay — the Aran Islands seem to move too and keep company with you all along the road — sentinels covering the left flank of your approach to the Gateway of the West.

People slept in the hay fields that Galway Race Week of cloudless sun. Farm prices were buoyant in that year when the great chestnut chaser — Golden Fleece, first appeared. She won my support out of her sheer beauty of form.

Galway City and Eyre Square were packed on race eve. We were lucky to have a "friend in camp" and a carload of us secured bed and breakfast in a comfortable drawing-room at a fair price. The breakfast itself was worth half the sum — trout, salmon, home-cured streaky bacon, fresh eggs, crisp toast, marmalade, bastible cake — that woman kept a great table.

We explored the Claddagh before breakfast and I swopped my Munster Irish with a Connemara fisherman. One of my doubting bedmates stayed behind and asked him:— "What kind of Irish has our friend?" "'Tis alright", says he, "but there's a bit of twist in it." That was the best explanation of dialects that I ever heard.

"Why is the Galway Plate so popular?" I once asked a well-known Co. Limerick breeder of thoroughbreds and hunters. His answer was satisfying and complete:— "Only a rale good horse can win it." And examination of the records from the Hill of Camus to St. Martin, bears out that theory — no bad horse, or middling horse, has ever won the Galway Plate!

When you walk the searching course the reasons are clear. The undulating surface, the formidable jumps, the fine galloping stretches, the steep fall and demanding rise with two firm leaps one behind the other when horses are tired; that pinch into the straight, the slope and fast finishing flat — all these test the best qualities of a true chaser. He must be a clever fencer, with speed and stamina to get home in front of a field that always includes the best horses in Ireland.

And Galway Races are unique in Irish sport. For this is a real Connaught holiday. Caravans and their picturesque owners are making the trek weeks ahead. Urgent farm work is abandoned for the hour. Business and professional men; regular racegoers, hunting folk, farmers of all ranges of acreage, holiday trippers from the Eastern cities; Connemara and Aran Island men and maids who speak Gaelic only, are here in colourful buoyant groups. All the fun of the fair; huge fields of beautiful horses; thrilling finishes and good priced winners — all lend glamour and life to this great outdoor Festival of the West.

Eyre Square on Race nights is a midnight bivouack. Taverns are open all night. Open turf fires everywhere. Dancing, singing, carousing everywhere — and all in the great good humour of glad holiday spirit — the hucksters harvest. The salt tang of the Atlantic fortifies us all against indispensable late hours. The morning brings no ill results that a dash to Salthill cannot dissolve. And the bright spirit of these mingling throngs is contagious. Even the bookmakers cease to grumble at Galway.

To the searcher after the picturesque, Galway City and County are a happy hunting ground. The labyrinth of cottages that make Claddagh with its feet bathed in green Atlantic waves; brightly coloured shawls of womanfolk with the soft hair and big brown eyes of Spain. Those huge warehouses by the Quay-side that once did a roaring trade with the Iberian Empire of Philip. Hardby, you pause awhile to mark the grim building known as Lynch's Castle. Away back in 1493, when James Fitzstephen Lynch of Norman and Celtic blood was Mayor of Galway, his wild son killed a distinguished foreign visitor. The Mayor sentenced him to death. When the executioners refused to carry out the sentence, this stern Chief Magistrate, to save the honour of his City, did the hanging himself. The hoary window from which the rope hung is still pointed out.

You visit the Church of St. Nicholas, founded by the Normans in 1320, where Christopher Columbus heard Mass while completing his crew for his epoch-making voyage which discovered America. The Franciscan Friary of William de Burgh, and the noble University Buildings of Tudor style are worth a visit.

Back by the Salmon Leap of the River Corrib the water was limpid clear one bright day and a wonderful sight the salmon made. For three hundred yards below the weir, the river was literally packed with glorious glistening fish — thousands of them swerving and swaying, noses up river, all urged by one instinctive call to the higher reaches of lake and stream in eternal law of propagation. Many of them will fall victim to the angler's line, many will return, when worn and weary; return to the sea to renew their youth in the depths of the mid-Atlantic.

Of all my journeys round Connemara, I best recall a leisurely one on a diminutive motor-cycle, familiar to many roads. We struck of course by the neat village of Moycullen, where the Twelve Bens again break into view; and so by the Angler's headquarters of Oughterard with Oough-Corrib fringes, away to the right.

Thus far the stone-walled roads are flat and bare; but at once the country changes in character and soon you learn that all Paul Henry's colours of blues and purples and reds and oranges, greens and gold — that they are not exaggerated. Moor bog, lake river, mountain all out-Henry, Henry. Maam Cross marks a low pathway over the rising hills, loved of rodmen. Shindilla and Oorid Loughs bring us to Recess itself of such rare and vivid beauty, where we are amidst the charming lake vistas — Loughs Garomin, Inagh, Ballinahinch and Derryclare — all have their thick and thin Waltonian disciples.

Past Cashel and Carna you hit the dark ridges of Urrisbeg and so to a lovely valley that ends in the glorious snow-white strand at Roundstone. The road swings in vistas of beauty until you hit the staggering seascapes of Connemara's capital — Clifden itself, of magnificent mountain and marine outlooks.

We next wound round the shallow valley of Monard to new loveliness at Letterfrack of the crimson fuchsia hedges. We were soon skirting the glorious pass of Kylemore, past Renvyle and the Norwegian fjord of Killary harbour and Leenane. Accustomed as I had been to Killarney, Glandore, Glengariffe, Lock Ine and the rest, I was staggered by the unfolding beauty of mountains rising sheer out of the water for 2,500 feet of variegated woodland and creek.

The hotels of Galway and Connemara are all good and hospitable; the roads sound and lively, especially close to the coast. From Maam Cross I struck south by entrancing turfland and mountain and moor to the territory of Padraig Pearse — the wilder, romantic, rock-strewn ruggedness of South Connemara. To Carraroe and Carna, to Rosmuck promontory, where thousands of young Leinster folk study the Gaelic at its pure fountainhead. The trip back to Galway along the south coast road past Carraroe, Costelloe, Tully, Spiddal and Barna gave us new glimpses of delight, dotted with cottages and the colourful life of the West — altogether the most entrancing trip that a leisurely cyclist ever explored.

Wondrous land where mystery is blended with vivid reality; where islands without number shimmer in the sea; where fish and wild fowl abound in the lake, river, sea and mountain; where the people retain their old world respect for matters of the spirit that cannot be weighed in modern scales; where the towering sublimity of Croagh Padraig is ever in the background of the picture — making little of immensity of time.

THE LASS THAT LOVES A HURLER

I.

I know a maid with sparkling eye,
She looks so sweet, she seems so shy —
But she smiled at me as she passed by,
    Going down to Mass last Sunday.
She's Irish too, both kith and kin,
I'm sure she's pure and free from sin,
But I'd like to tie her apron's pin —
    When she keeps house on Monday.

Chorus:-
Come fill your glasses to the brim,
We'll toast that maid so neat and trim,
Her step is light, her waist is slim —
    The lass that loves a Hurler.

II.

At last night's *Ceilidhe* down in Keel
I saw her dance an Irish reel,
Her dainty glance of toe and heel,
    Sent my poor senses storming.
She joined in chorus with the best,
Her voice was soft as thrush on nest,
I longed to press her to my breast —
    And keep her there 'till morning.

Chorus:-
Come fill your glasses to the brim,
We'll toast that maid so neat and trim,
Her step is light, her waist is slim —
    The lass that loves a Hurler.

III.

Her deep blue eyes and neck of snow,
Her breasts like billow soft below,
Her hips in easy numbers flow,
    Going to the well for water.
She cheers our team, her eyes aflame!
And after Sunday's final game,
I'll meet her in a glen I'll name —
    And ask her to the Altar.

Chorus:-
Come fill your glasses to the brim,
We'll toast that maid so neat and trim,
Her step is light, her waist is slim —
    The lass that loves a Hurler.
                P.D.M.

THE COUGHLANS OF BLACKROCK

MANY family groups adorn the records of G.A.A. champions down the years both in hurling and football; but I doubt if any group of brothers were so formidable as the great Coughlan brothers from the salmon-fishing village of Blackrock, two miles below Cork City.

One of my earliest introductions to Cork City hurling was through a photograph of the famous "Rockies" team — Cork County champions of the early nineties. That ancient photograph showed the father and five sons playing in the same senior team!

Mr. Coughlan senior had passed to his reward when I joined the Blackrock Hurling Club in 1904; but I had the pleasure of knowing all five sons and I played on the same teams as three of them. All were magnificent hurlers!

The Coughlan (pronounced Caalon in Cork) family were skilled salmon fishers in the Lee estuary, owning several (five or six oar) boats specially built for river work.

They lived in frugal comfort; they were quiet orderly men who led peaceful and industrious lives. They were held in high respect in their native village — upright, high principled, honest men.

Early in the G.A.A. history, the fame of the Coughlans of Blackrock had spread from Mizen Head to Innishowen and from the Skelligs Rocks to Ben Eadar. The eldest brother, Patrick ("Parson") Coughlan had retired from hurling when I came on the scene as a youth of 19. He was generally acknowledged as the greatest defender of this period.

When Redmonds were champions of Cork in 1892, Pat and Denis Coughlan were on the side that won the All-Ireland championship of that year. This was a vintage period for Cork hurling and the Coughlan brothers played a great part in the winning of three All-Ireland championships in a row — 1892, 1893 and 1894, just before the great sides from Limerick (Kilfinane) and Tubberadora (County Tipperary) loomed up. Blackrock as county champions selected the teams in 1893 and 1894.

The five Coughlan brothers: Pat, Denis, Jerh., Dan and Tom were all well-built stalwart men. Pat was 5ft. 11ins. and a master of strategy. A strong, fearless man, he revelled in the close hard clashes of his period.

All five were well-behaved even in the most exciting circumstances. Denis Coughlan stood over six feet tall — a magnificent figure of a man when training with Redmonds in the open Park (Cork) for the All-Ireland final of 1892.

Denis Coughlan, meekest of men, happened accidentally to hit a colleague and friend at a vital part behind his ear when both pulled on a falling ball. The injury proved fatal.

Denis ("Lyonsie") Coughlan took it to heart so seriously that he pined away and died shortly afterwards. Old hurling critics told me in my younger days that Denis Coughlan was the greatest hurler of the lot.

Big Dan Coughlan, the third of the famous brothers, was one of the finest wing full backs I have ever seen play. He was 6ft. ½in. tall and carried a huge chest and shoulders. His strength was immense yet he depended almost entirely on skilled ball-play.

In a championship match in Johny Butler's at Turner's Cross, Cork, I saw Dan Coughlan lift a ball on his own line; the wind and fall were with him and he let fly — that ball hopped over the far line 140 yards away!

When salmon fishing declined on the Lee estuary, Dan Coughlan emigrated at the height of his hurling career.

Next I remember was "big Jerh." another quiet and what is known as a harmless man. Jeremiah stood 6ft. 1in. in height. He did not hurl a lot in his young days, but when pressed into action with the Blackrock senior team, he made a fine hard-hitting centre forward — another stalwart hurler.

Youngest of the lot was Tom Coughlan who captained Blackrock during some of their most successful years early in the century.

Tom, known to all and sundry as "Honest Man" was a beautifully built man of about 5ft. 10½ins. and weighing close to 13 stone in his hurling togs. He usually played at centre back and there was tremendous relief in his pucks. Like all his brothers, Tom Coughlan was a masterly hurler.

He was one of three Blackrock men selected by Dungourney when they went on to win the All-Ireland final of 1902 and he figured prominently at centre back on a great Blackrock side which won the All-Ireland final of 1903 — one of the finest hurling sides that ever adorned the game.

Patrick Coughlan's sons, Eugene and John, grew to be very able hurlers. Eugene was perhaps the greatest winger that Cork county has ever sent out; he captained the famous 1931 Cork side that defeated Kilkenny in an epic final after two draws.

He won four championship finals and was never out of a Cork selection whilst he was playing. John Coughlan made his name as a goalkeeper and was in Cork's winning teams of 1926 and 1931.

Tom Coughlan's sons were also fine hurlers — one of them, before his ordination as a Capuchin, showed wonderful skill.

Many groups of hurling brothers have appeared in the club and county ranks of the G.A.A. But the five Coughlans made their mark on hurling history in a formative period of the game's development. They were magnificient physical men and all were master hurlers. Better still, they were sober, high-principled men honest and hard-working; they were spoken of by clergymen and laymen, as an example to the young men of what good Christian Irishmen should be.

CUSACK

AS long as lives the Gaelic Athletic Association, so long must live the name and story of its founder, and more than a founder — the man who conceived and wrote and planned with far-seeing mind and noble purpose — Michael Cusack of Clare. Though few live today who knew and appreciated that great man more affectionately than I did, it is with diffidence I approach this brief sketch. The fitness of the subject for the opening number of such a weekly paper as Cusack dreamed of, is my incentive.

Michael Cusack was born in the parish of Cairan in the Barony of Burren in North Clare on 20th September, 1847 — the 44th anniversary of Emmet's murder. His parents were hard-working, Irish-speaking farmers — as Michael himself said, "they only spoke English when a stranger who knew no Irish came to the house."

Young Michael grew into a sturdy, athletic youth and very bright at his books; his parents decided to send him forward for training as a national teacher. At Enniscorthy and Marlboro' Street, Dublin, he qualified as a trained teacher and from a long line of candidates he was selected by the manager to teach at Lough Cutra School on the County Galway side of the Clare border. He was a great success at Lough Cutra but was of restless energy and, on application, was appointed to teach Mathematics and English at the Diocesan College at Newry, County Down; here too he proved highly successful as an instructor and was appointed to Blackrock College, Dublin where he taught for three years. Michael Cusack once told me that he resolved to see as much of the land and people of Ireland as possible while he was young. He taught for some time at St. Kieran's College, Kilkenny and at Clongowes Wood Jesuit College, in County Kildare.

He was still youthful when appointed as principal teacher of English and Mathematics (the latter his favourite subject) at the widely known private college of Hamilton and Bell of North Great George's Street, Dublin. So popular was he with his pupils that Mr. Michael Cusack decided to found his own private school, opening first at Nelson Street and then transferring to bigger premises at Gardiner's Place which developed into a most successful private Academy with a national reputation.

Its owner, then happily married and blessed with a young family, had a steadily increasing income, for his fame as a teacher spread. But not on bread doth man live.

Michael Cusack was no ordinary man. Great thoughts were stirring inside that finely formed head. Ever since he came to the use of reason he was close to Ireland's pulse, her downtrodden wretchedness and her servility. He had seen all the sorrows and miseries which followed the famine of '47; he saw an alien race and civilisation ride high and hot-foot over the Irish people. He had read deeply of Irish history and literature. He quickly realised that the Irish people had a right to freedom.

A lover of the outdoor air and exercise and of nature's glories, he often took a class of his pupils out to the Phoenix Park where he taught them the art of hurling and interested his school in athletics generally.

Michael Cusack was a powerfully built man of 5ft. 8ins. He looked even shorter for his broad, square shoulders and muscular limbs suggested lack of height. He was amongst the first rank of shot putters of his period, but hurling was the game he loved. Without doubt, Ireland's woes and the possible remedy were ever in Cusack's innermost thoughts. In athletics as in all other things he saw Anglicisation in control. Irish nationality never touched a lower ebb than in the early 'eighties! Irish language, sports, culture, music, dancing and song — all were on their deathbed, while the coffin ships were crowded to the awnings with despairing, fleeing peasantry.

Courage and determination; clarity of vision; hatred of flattery and rhetoric; direct, clear-cut mind! These were some of the characteristics of Michael Cusack's dominant character. He saw his people were becoming serflike in soul and body. He almost despaired of them. He knew that the first step towards freedom was to restore national manliness and uprightness amongst young Irishmen.

Then his love for hurling and athletics inspired him with an ardent thought: "Why not unite the young people of Ireland into one great National Athletic Association for the development of all things Gaelic?" That was the foundation!

And it must never be forgotten, as too often it is, that though Cusack loved all forms of athletics and games, the great work of his life was not launched for games' sake — it was conceived, founded and planned for the regeneration of the Irish people, and as a road for the ultimate restoration of the full freedom of his country. It is from that viewpoint that any review, however brief, of Cusack's life must be approached.

Very early in his young manhood Michael Cusack was sworn into the Irish Republican Brotherhood in a village of his native Clare. From that day until the day of his death, on the 30th November, 1906, that upright, fearless and unbending man never deviated one iota from his rigid principles of Irish freedom — a gospel pure as MacSwiney wrote.

So soon as he conceived the idea of a Gaelic Athletic Association as a step to national resurgency, he set to work with tireless resolve. He had a weekly paper of his own called the *Gaelic Times* in connection with his teaching academy. It was in the columns of this paper that the concept of the G.A.A. was first presented.

Thenceforward Cusack pushed his case with succinct clarity. Public interest was aroused and Cusack's first great milestone was at that famous meeting at Hayes' Hotel, Thurles on November 1, 1884, when the greatest Amateur Athletic Association in the world was founded.

I was attracted to the carriage, figure and picturesque dress of Mr. Michael Cusack before I knew who he was. Every Saturday afternoon and Sunday forenoon, an upright, athletic figure of an elderly gentleman with a massive brow and manly expression, showing a magnificent steel-grey beard, could be seen walking the Dublin quays on the Arran Quay side on his way to the Phoenix Park.

He wore Irish frieze knee breeches and carried an Aberdeen coat on his shoulders. His destination was the Nine Acres on the stretches of land above the Gough statue — where the young hurlers used to play.

I soon made it my business to know who he was. He always carried a stout blackthorn. Though I was little more than a chap then, I knew much about Michael Cusack and his story. I knew that he had sacrificed a lucrative business and profession in the cause of Ireland a Nation and in the resuscitation of Gaelic games and Irish way of life.

It was the well-known Gaelic sports writer and essayist Mr. P.J. Devlin, who introduced us. My love of hurling and my knowledge of the Irish language drew us together — a new and attractive field of learning was opened to me.

Michael Cusack was a most unusual man. He was a man of singular dignity and independence. He was honest in thought and word. He hated long speeches and despised sychopants and their enervating trade. His voice was stentorian and commanding on occasions, but it was generally quiet and often bubbling with humour.

I often met Michael Cusack in social functions of Gaels — at Gaelic League rooms; at An Stad in North Frederick Street presided over by the balladist, Cahal McGarvey; at Citizen Michael Flanagan's behind the Four Courts. Then we would join in long walks together to the hurling grounds, speaking little but Gaelic, talking little but hurling.

He had thrown all his dynamic energy into the G.A.A. from 1884 onwards, to the neglect of all material things. He saw the G.A.A. spread like a prairie fire as he said himself. It spread to the four shores of Erin. Hundreds of men, flocking to the new limelight, were not so sincere of motive as Michael Cusack was. Some of them were petty designing men. The Association became a maelstrom of bickerings and jealousies for a few years and all unknowing, with no eye for petty things whilst holding fast to the great, Michael Cusack was swamped in the maelstrom. He had rough stormy passages in his life and more than one misfortune. He lost extensively on the *Celtic Times*, yet heroically bearing the blow of his beautiful young wife's early death, he reared a big family well. His son, John Cusack, is a well-known Dublin solicitor.

He never lost his serenity of soul. He was a reader deep and wide; Mitchel and Kickham were his Irish favourites. He often taught Gaelic classes and recited poems from the great works of the Clare poet, Brian Merriman. He was a realist and a dreamer at once. Gaelic songs and music were obsession in his leisure. I never knew a man so completely immersed in ancient Irish culture and national thought. He conceived a great and noble mission and sacrificed his all.

The G.A.A. have honoured his memory. Too bad he did not live to see more of his dreams realised.

A GREEN CHRISTMAS

VERY much surprised to find this morning (I'm writing on the eve of Christmas) that the currant bushes by the garden wall, with a southerly aspect, are showing long, light-green buds, proving that next Spring's growth has already started — the sap is on flow. Shy crocus blooms are showing in the city parks, and particularly mild days have given me a second crop of bright marigolds in the little flower-bed beside my window; a few yards away Christmas roses are in bloom on one spray, and budding in rich blushing red on another branch of a tree — that one of a half-a-dozen sent me many years ago from a friend in New York. Only one of the six carefully packed rose trees thrived in Irish conditions of soil and climate. But this one seems a miracle of continuous flowering — I have roses in every month of the year; and December is one of its best.

I write all this to tell what a "green" Christmas we had in Ireland — rain, yes, but not a trace of snow or frost or hail. The turkey flocks did well, my country cousins tell me. One thrifty farmer's wife realised £250 for 66 turkeys. The rearing of these rather delicate and susceptible birds demands endless pains, and indeed devotion. But reward sweetens labour, and one turkey feeder told me that half of the total sums realised from turkeys this year is clear profit to the farmer's wife who skilfully supplements table waste with shop "feed." But, my friend says, "They must run lucky with you."

Incoming boats at Dun Laoghaire were more crowded than ever I've seen them. Thousands of eager young men and women leaped gladly ashore when the gangway was slung. Their wanderlust is forgotten for the time being as they answer that imperative call of home and Christmas. Some looked rather worn and weary, but all were eager and smiling when their feet struck Irish soil again. To many it was their first visit home, and it is certain that they shall not return to cross-Channel work with the same anticipating thrill that marked their first adventure. Too bad that remunerative work cannot be secured for them in their native country. Gaeltacht development plans have not come a day too soon. To-day I learnt that a considerable number of the returned emigrants will be absorbed in turf and soil reclamation plans at home.

DECEMBER STORM

AMONG city dwellers it is only those born in rural places that have "fear reactions," if I may so call them, to gales and storms. Memories die hard. When the window sashes rattle ominously, the wind booms around the chimney tops and sighs in gusts through the silent night, recollections of destructive storms of early youth revive. People born on the coasts are particularly susceptible. Mounting waves breaking snow-white over rocks and cliffs, flying slates, battered hayricks, strawricks, lost sheep — all come back in vivid memory. City-born folk take little notice of gales beyond their own minor discomforts.

Since St. Stephens Day successive gales have swept Ireland and much damage has been done, particularly in coastal areas — boats battered on the rocks from breaking moorings, farmhouses stripped of their roofs, haybarns wrecked, lands flooded. The most serious results are in the complete hold-up in winter tillage, and to-day's official report on agriculture tells of minimum wheat sowing. So sodden are the countrysides that no plough can enter the land for weeks. We must hope for better February weather. New varieties of winter wheat will permit late sowings, and the increased guaranteed prices for wheat (67/6 to 75/-per barrel) should tempt farmers to increase substantially their wheat acreage.

I think the danger of "wheat midge" risk has been grossly exaggerated. I have discussed the matter very seriously with experts and am satisfied that a combination of the circustances under which the "midge" can do any harm is rare indeed. A recurrence of 1951 mid-summer conditions is most unlikely and deep ploughing is a further safeguard. The man who mentions wheat midge as a deterrent to extensive wheat growing is only looking for excuses. At its worst only small areas are involved, and timely spraying to cover the brief period where the grub can operate, will make the wheatear immune from attack. Wheat in 1952 looks like being a remunerative and attractive crop wherever the land is moderately suitable.

Emigration figures are still discouraging and we are still awaiting the Emigration Commission's report. The latest trend is organised effort by agents in all parts of the cities, towns and even villages, to induce young people (young girls in particular) to emigrate. Rosy promises of high wages and comfortable employment overseas are being offered. How many of these promises will be fulfilled! Too often the tempted ones find the work severe, the food bad and a big proportion of their wages held back for Income Tax. Intending emigrants should enquire carefully into the credentials of these "emigration agents."

Spring is the danger time and many untold dangers lie ahead of emigrants — morally and materially. Pulpit and platform must be used to tell the innocent young people the true story of what emigrants suffer and of the pitfalls in their path. Conditions of life, particularly cross-Channel, do not improve.

TOM KIELY OF BALLYNEALE,
WONDER ATHLETE

GREATEST athlete of Ireland's greatest athletic period, the name of Thomas Francis Kiely, of Ballyneale, at Suirside, will live on to inspire Irish youth for many generations. Twice he won the All-Round Championship of the World (1904 and 1906). He died recently in his 82nd year, full of memories and honours.

During the prolific period from 1885 to 1910 — Ireland's halcyon period in world athletics — Irishmen broke 28 world records, won eight out of ten international championships with Scotland, crossed to Stamford Bridge, London, year after year against the world's best athletes, bringing home title after title. From Athens to St. Louis a galaxy of talent was blazoning Ireland's name, proving our best silent ambassadors when international representation was denied us in other fields and platforms. Amongst that list of international champions, one name stands out for all-round excellence. A peerless athlete of lion heart who touched his peak performance whenever his country's honour was at stake. Kiely was never beaten in an all-round contest though he travelled to St. Louis and New York fearlessly to compete against the world's best. He was a man whom mother nature and a pure life endowed with generous gifts — a splendid specimen of manhood. When I first saw him — in 1899 at a Munster Athletic meeting — Tom Kiely of Tipperary looked a super Matt-the-Thresher come to life, straight out of Charles Kickham's *Knocknagow*. I had heard much of Kiely and I feasted my eyes on him then.

My first admiration came for his wide, square-turned shoulders and his trunk-like chest. He stood 6ft 2ins. in running shoes and weighed 14 stone in his athletic togs. When as a schoolboy I saw him in his prime, Tom Kiely was a lithe-limbed graceful athlete. His face was thin-spare with straight Grecian features and his body was of model symmetry — a beautifully modelled antelope of a man. In later years I learned to know him intimately for I frequently competed at the same meetings as Kiely with a fair measure of success. That was towards the end of his great career; I came to admire his quiet, easy manner full of cordiality. A man of high moral code, he entered wholeheartedly into the Irish way of life — outdoor sport, fiddle-playing, stepdancing and ballad music, he relished them all. A life-long lover of greyhounds and open coursing, he won many competitions even at Clounanna itself. He was a tremendous worker on the land and built up a properous career as progressive farmer, cattle breeder and fruit-grower.

Born on his father's comfortable farm at Ballyneale near Carrick-on-Suir, he came of a race of athletes from both sides. His neighbours and relatives, the Davin brothers, international champions, guided his early athletic ambitions. As a tall stripling of 18, Tom Kiely competed locally with abundant success and within a year he was going further afield winning prizes in running, jumping, weight-throwing and hurdle racing. At the age of twenty-two he had collected 150 trophies and his fame spread. Taking courage in both hands he entered for the All-Round Championships at Ballsbridge in 1892, and created a sensation by running away with the contest.

In September of the same year he swept the deck at the G.A.A. National Championships at Croke Park, winning no less than 7 titles in all — shot, hammer, 28lbs, 7 lbs., long-jump, hurdles and hop-step and leap. A new star had arisen on the world's athletic horizon.

In 1893 and 1894, Kiely again won the All-Round athletic title. This contest was held at irregular intervals but he won the honours once more in 1898. Crossing to London in 1897, Kiely proceeded to win the A.A.A. Hammer Throwing Championships 5 times and set up new records with the 7lbs. weight and the 56 lbs. He gave his service freely to struggling clubs. He won the unprecedented number of 50 championships and 2,000 prizes in a dozen years.

It was under the trumpet-blare of close international contests that T.F. Kiely found the unplumbed depths of his talent. I remember an occasion against Scotland at Glasgow, the countries were level at 5 events each and Kiely, having won two for Ireland, was dressing in his tent when news came that our long-jumper failed in the final event — the long jump. They rushed for Kiely. Not waiting to lace his shoes, Kiely came to the pit for action. In one mighty whole-hearted spring he broke the Scottish record for the event and won the day for Ireland! That was typical of the gallant-hearted Tipperaryman.

Kiely was 34 years old and about to hang up his atheltic shoes forever when he was called to compete for Ireland in the All-Round World Championships at St. Louis, U.S.A. Against four world-beaters, including E.H. Clarke, the holder, Kiely outshone them all and won the Gold Belt. There was tremendous excitement in Irish circles all the world over. He returned to America two years later and won for the second time — at 36 years of age; he was a man of steel and whale-bone. Irishmen of New York presented him with a gold cup. He had public receptions in Cobh, Cork, and Dublin. He retired in 1908.

Scotsmen will still speak of the great Donald Dinrice and England of

E.B. Fry but Tom Kiely of Carrick-on-Suir was the most enduring and versatile of them all. His last public appearance was when, along with his life-long friend, Mr. Peter O'Connor of Waterford, he led the *Tailteann* parade and carried the Flag at Croke Park — both looked straight and lithesome as when they were breaking records in their youth — a great tribute to a health giving and traditional Irish sport.

THE CUCKOO'S CALL

WHEN the cuckoo speaks early in April, one decides that Summer is on the wing, and our hearts lift a little in hope and joy. I saw the cuckoo this year before I heard him — it was in a defile, close to the granite quarries of Barnaculla on the slopes of the Dublin mountains. The date was April 17th. It was the sweep of the dark tail of this hawk-like bird that I recognised as he perched on a post below the wood. Then the soft, sweet "cuck-oo" note came clear and strong. Four times he called joyously and then he was away about his business. Any day now the dusky swifts will be slanting across the sky, for the wind has swung to the south. I can picture my colony of swifts resting somewhere in Southern France before the final thrust into their summer homes in Ireland's welcoming housetops!

I promised to write something of the hurling characteristics of Tom Semple of Thurles, Tipperary and James Kelleher of Cork, who captained their teams in the European tour of 1910, when they played exhibition matches at Brussels, Malines and Fontenoy. I played with and against them both, and was on the Cork team that lost by a disputed goal in a fast-scoring Munster Final between Cork and Tipperary at Fermoy in 1908. Tipp. won out the All-Ireland final readily in that memorable year. Tom Semple was a tall (6ft. 1in.) athletic man with a great stride and sweep of arm. In a prolific Tipperary period, Tom Semple usually played mid-wing on a 17-a-side team. He was a smooth, stylish hitter, with great ball control. His drives on the sod or in the air were of tremendous length and perfect in direction. He was a handsome, deer-like man. He always "played the ball" but when the battle was hottest, he could mix it with the best. Semple was a great leader of men and it was under him that the famous Thurles Sarsfields reached their peak. He was a charming companion.

In clubroom or Council chamber Tom Semple showed rare judgment and far-seeing wisdom. His love of hurling and hurlers was profound. For long he was the idol of Tipperary and played a noble part in the "troubled times." I often visited his grave at Thurles. Tom and his blackthorn were all-commanding on the crowded and excited sidelines in many a Munster final at the Thurles Gaelic Field.

James Kelleher, of Dungourney, Co. Cork, was considered by keen critics as the greatest hurler of his era — a hurling genius if ever there was one. I was asked more than once why I considered James Kelleher the greatest of them all. I replied: "I never saw him play a representative game in which he was not the outstanding hurler on the field." He was a broad-shouldered wedge of a man, about 5ft. 8ins. in height, but powerfully built, active and tireless. He was fast too. He had a perfect command of ash and was an artist with his caman and feet. He played with his brains and was artful in all situations. He usually played centre-half-back or full-back. The closer the crush, the better he liked it. By elusive skill, he worked round with the ball clung to his hurley — a lightning stroke and the ball was sailing upfield. A quiet, modest man, he was an outstanding horseman too, and won many races — Ocean Breeze, Red Mantle and all, the greatest hurling artist of my time!

THE GRACES OF TULLAROAN

FROM the pleasant Tullaroan country in West Kilkenny, and not too far from the Tipperary border, came many great hurlers and famous hurling families. None shed much lustre on the great game of hurling as the Grace family of stalwarts — Jack, Dick and Pierce. The Graces held spacious and fertile farms in the Tullaroan and Threecastles area and they farmed well.

First of the Graces that I knew and hurled against was Jack Grace, who was at that time attached to one of the big drapery houses in Dublin.

One of the strongest dual clubs in the whole G.A.A. range of the early century was the Dublin Kickhams, distinguished alike in hurling and football. As long ago as 1889, C.J. Kickhams won the Hurling All-Ireland and in 1897 they achieved like honours in football.

Jack Grace came to them early in the new century and whilst still under 20 represented Dublin in hurling and football.

Whatever club won the Dublin championship, the wonderful Jack Grace was certain to be selected either in hurling or football. He was in two hurling finals, where Dublin drew and lost the replays — one against Cork and one against Tipperary. Jack was luckier in the football championships, captaining the Kickhams in 1906, he led his men to many victories before winning the final from Cork (Fermoy selection) after a great game at Athy (0-5 to 0-4).

A year later the same two counties went through to the final and on a broiling summer's day in Tipperary town, Grace and his gallant band won through — 8 points to 2.

In 1908, Geraldines won the Dublin title from Kickhams, but Jack Grace was again selected with Dave Kelleher of Geraldines as Captain. That was one of Jack Grace's best games and he won his third title in a row when helping to beat Kerry (Tralee Mitchels). It was a tremendous game for 40 minutes but Dublin were the fitter side and won by the unexpected score of 10 points to 3.

I had often played with and against Jack Grace and I always place him side by side with Billie Mackesy of Cork, as the greatest dual players, which the G.A.A. has ever seen. Jack Grace was no more than 5ft. 9ins in height but he was beautifully built — 12½ stone of solid bone and muscle; he had the heart of a lion. He was an outstanding hurler and had few equals as wing half-back in his period — his ground drives off right and left were of surpassing length and his stamina seemed endless.

In football he showed rare judgment, was a sound fielder and an accurate kicker.

The "living-in" system prevailed in the drapery houses in Dublin at the time and poor Jack Grace's health failed unexpectedly. He died in the fullness of manhood — he was nature's gentleman, R.I.P.

No Kilkenny men who ever loved hurling can forget Dick Grace of Tullaroan. There was a first cousin of his, also D. Grace, of Threecastles who shone with Kilkenny winning teams of 1904, 1905 and 1907; but so far as my recollection goes young Dick Grace of Tullaroan made his first appearance with Kilkenny as a sub. in the great games of 1909. Thence forward to the All-Ireland final of 1922, Dick Grace played a noble part in the abundant Kilkenny victories.

He starred with the winning Kilkenny teams of 1909, 1911, 1912, 1913 and 1922, getting five All-Ireland championship medals and missing three more narrowly.

Dick Grace, a successful and progressive farmer, was almost six feet tall and of wiry, steely mould. He could hurl in the open with smooth masterly touch; in the close clashes he was rugged and fearless; he could use a legitimate shoulder or hip with devastating effect.

He had a great command of the ash both overhead and on the sod; his judgment of men was razor keen and he had all the hurling artistry which in later years distinguished his famous nephew, Lory Meagher.

Dick Grace loved hurling with a great love. He worked hard on the land and he trained hard of evenings and week-ends. He was loyal to his county and his comrades — a pillar of Kilkenny hurling to this day. Dick Grace, like brother Jack, usually shone as wing half back — a master hurler and as hard as nails.

The younger brother, Pierce Grace, went off to college at an early date, but he was quite as good a hurler as his more famous brothers. He was on the great Kilkenny sides that won the 1911 and 1912 All-Ireland Championships. He also played for Dublin teams before qualifying in his profession of medicine, where he became well-known — as much for his great humanity as for his medical skill.

Pierce Grace was, I think, the tallest of all the brothers and he was a grand striker with all the family love for the game. A good footballer, too, he helped his University during his student days, when Gaelic Games were introduced to the Colleges for the first time.

Now in retirement, Dr. Pierce Grace came to live near Kilkenny City, where his popularity is immense. Both Dick and Dr. Pierce take a lively interest in their native parish club at Tullaroan.

Somebody told me that another brother, Jim, was as good a hurler as any of the group; he loved his home and farm so much, however, that he could never be induced to train.

The fame of the Graces will live as long as there is hurling in Kilkenny. And to judge by recent results, that unique style and artistry is not likely to fade for many a day.

THE FABULOUS KERRY LANDERS

THREE of the Landers brothers of Tralee I knew in first-class football. There was Bill (or Liam) Landers, popularly called "Lang"; there was "John Joe" or "J.J."; and Tim Landers, known to all and sundry as "Roundy" Landers. What wonderful footballers they all were!

During a long and fertile period of Kerry supremacy, during which they won ten All-Ireland championships between 1924 and 1941, a Kerry team without one or more of the Landers was a rarity. No other county achieved anything approaching that Kerry record during "the Landers regime."

Before I develop my story about their football ability and records, let me write at once that the Landers brothers of Tralee were sincere and fearless patriots who suffered much for "the old cause" and who never allowed their football activities to interfere with their duty and devotion to the higher call.

Their All-Ireland records would have been greater had their attention to training for football been continuous. They were not alone in this matter amongst the patriotic footballers of Kerry who often saw the inside of English prisons because of political activities.

The year of 1924 was a year of re-organisation and closing of the Gaelic ranks which had been "split wide open" during the Civil Commotion of 1922 and 1923.

It was at that time that the G.A.A. achieved its greatest national success — in bringing the scattered ranks from opposite camps into one fold, doing much to quell the bitterness of the recent past. Through the healing medium of Gaelic football and Hurling, with their social amenities, estranged clubmates became unified again.

It was in that period that I first saw Liam Landers in action. Tall, square-shouldered, "Lang" had a fine reach and range; he had splendid ball control and played a big part in Kerry's victory of 1924. That was the year when Dublin's winning reign — three titles in a row, was broken.

I remember the day — 26 April 1925 — when Kerry and Dublin (holders) met in the final. Thirty players, many of whom had fought in different camps, stood to attention for the "Soldiers Song," at Croke Park before 30,000 spectators. Bill Landers, in attack, played shrewd polished football and Kerry won four points to three.

John Joe Landers looked a lanky, fair-haired youth, just out of his teens when I first saw him play with Kerry in the All-Ireland of 1927. Six feet tall and coolness personified, he was a fine fielder and once in possession he had superb ball-control, either in low ground dribbling or in swerving possession as he dropped or punted deadly accurate shots for the posts.

The old rivals, Kerry and Kildare, met in the 1927 final; though Kerry led 3 points to one at half-time, the Lily Whites played a grand finish and won 5 points to 3.

John Joe was on the untrained Kerry team that took Tipperary (home) too cheaply in 1928, — but he was at his peak in 1929 when he starred as wing for Kerry when they reversed their 1927 game with Kildare. John Joe contributed largely to Kerry's win by 1 goal 8 points to 1 goal 5 points.

Kerry were then at the crest of the wave in 1929, 1930, 1931 and 1932, breaking all records in scoring and equalling Wexford's wonderful record of 1915 to 1918 inclusive.

John Joe Landers was starring in one or other berth in attack in those golden years for Kerry football. Soon his younger brother Tim appeared on the scene.

Tim was of quite a different build to John Joe and Bill. The youngest of the Tralee stars, popularly called "Roundy," did not belie the title. He was stocky and rather low-sized; but he had all the football artistry of his older brothers. I think that it was in 1932 that his eternally sunny smile first figured above a Kerry jersey. And right well he wore it.

Tim had pace, swerve and tenacity. He was wonderfully strong for his size and could rough it with the best if needs be. But like his brothers, Roundy Landers relied largely on his football. On opposite wings the brothers shone in Kerry's great victory over Mayo in 1932 (2-7 to 2-4).

Kerry struck three lean championship years before they came back with a flourish; the Landers brothers were a big attraction and Kerry went through to the final where they beat a strong Cavan side (4-4 to 1-7).

John Joe Landers made a distinguished final appearance in a final when playing left wing for Kerry in the record breaking final with Galway in 1938. That was the day he kicked the winning point on the stroke of time. The whistle went as the ball was in its flight and a draw was declared before 71,000 spectators (new record then). Galway won the replay.

Tim Landers played right up to 1941 but his most brilliant season was in 1937 when the much publicised teams from Kerry and Galway toured America. The outstanding player of the tour and the darling of the American crowds was Roundy Landers who scored goals and points from all angles.

From the O'Gorman brothers down, Kerry has sent out many fine football families. But for pure skill and artistry the Landers brothers stand alone.

They were one hundred per cent sportsmen who played the game for the love of it. The much loved name of Landers will live long in the football memories of the Kingdom.

MARCH BREEZES

VEGETATION in the woods is tardy and forest trees are bare. The horse chestnut is the first bud to show signs of pressure from within and below — its long, podlike buds are swelling visibly; the flowering currant beside it is showing a delightful shade of green where the buds are breaking into leaf on the sunny side of the grove — a full week I reckon, before her sisters facing the Pole Star. Dry, hardy, breezy days are leaving their mark on every newly turned sod by the roadside. The sodden clay of February becomes more brittle and friable as March breezes sweep across the plain. Today I was surprised to find a thick layer of grass on a sheltered lawn where a pair of blackbird lovers were gaily playing hide and seek around the laurels. Mr. Yellowbill's bill is a brighter yellow and his glossy coat has a bridegroom sheen. Mistress Ciarseach is as demure and retiring as ever — though she lets her mate know where she is in her own warm-hearted call. They will be building presently close to the old haunts. The rookeries, where I passed yesterday were regular hives of noisy industry. The starling's tittering song was as bright as his new steel-grey uniform that heralds the spring.

There is a tall elm tree in the grove beyond and a bold throstle seems to occupy one of its highest branches throughout the winter. He was there last December and sang from the bare branches through the wonderfully mild Christmas week. Then I missed him for a session — during the wild, broken weeks. I was rather surprised at this, for it is characterestic of this brightly mottled branch of the thrush family that they give their loudest, boldest song in bleak, windy weather. In some countries he is known as the storm-cock for that reason.

Whenever I discover snails in my garden operations I have a habit of catching each one between finger and thumb and throwing him towards the elmgrove with arm-swing of a West Cork bowler. The result is that this section of the plantation just across the road is usually alive with bird life. I think the thrushes and blackbirds get the major portion and would have it so. But neither the blackbirds nor thrushes have resumed their song in that grove this year. I listen for them at every morn's dawn. It is the linnets and finches, with one robin that make my matins. The sweetest songster so far is a grey linnet that shelters beside the drooping seed-pods that still hang to the bare ash tree in the corner. That linnet's phrasing is as perfect as a Milan trained soprano. His notes are like the tinkling of a little silver altar bell that the priests used carry around to the Easter Stations at the farmhouses in West Cork when I was a boy.

JOHNY-THE-BALLADS

A Torn Coat Oft Hides A Golden Heart

MANY a song he sold me — good, bad and indifferent.

Johny-the-Ballads had struck the lowest depths of his misfortunes, at last. It was the foot and mouth disease that ruined him, he said.

Fairs were his main source of revenue — singing ballads in a thin, vibrant voice; holding horses for regular customers; running shopping messages for women-folk — old friends who loved Johny for his simple, half-witted ways; honest as the sun.

And now, many of his favourite West Cork fairs were banned. To-day's August fair (1941) at Ballineen was the latest. Early, too, he heard with sorrow that his best friend, Mrs Hugh Hartnett of Lackanagow, was seriously ill. Many a half-crown she gave him after selling the turkeys at Christmas. He took the bog road north-west to see her. Many the old suit she smuggled to him.

"Give me a pint, Mrs O'Neill," he said at the crossroad pub; "I'm a penny short, ma'am." He handed her his last stray coppers. She put the coins in the till without counting. Johny was always a penny short. Yet she loved his simple half-witted ways. He drank the pint in two rapid gulps. For drink was his besetting and only sin. He'd drink Lough Erne dry.

That terrible sunken wound on his temple he owed to drink; years ago, many years ago. You couldn't tell Johny's age. He might be forty, or a score more battered years for that matter. No one knew and no one cared. And yet (if they only knew), he came from good farming stock away inland on the Limerick-Tipperary border.

Home on holidays from a secondary school at 15, his besetting sin marked him for ever. Some foolish neighbour offered the thirsty boy a glass of porter. Lifting it to his lips he was when his hot-headed father walked the way. The sight of his own failing repeated, shocked the parent beyond control. The ash-plant blow on the temple fell fast and false, leaving Johny marked and maimed for life. A sore blow for donor and victim! Neither recovered from that blow. The father never did a taste of good after; he went to the bad; Johny was soon homeless on the waves of the wind. At first he would write brilliant openings to beautiful poems; then his hands would clutch his poor maimed forehead in pain, and vivid thoughts vanished into thin air. Poor Johny, witty for all in occasional bursts.

One day at a fair he was busy. A dashing Saggarth, who was "close" with his tips, hailed him. I told you the story before:-

"Hold my horse, Johny," he ordered.

"But — but father," stuttered Johny, "I'm busy, very busy to-day."

"If you don't mind my horse, I'll root you to the ground."

"Why — why then," says Johny, "Why don't you root the horse to the ground." Poor Johny had the perfect solution.

"I hear Mrs. Hartnett is bad, Mrs O'Neill," he said to the publican's wife, as he wiped his mouth now with a torn sleeve.

"She's dying, and a great loss with six young children. You'll miss her, Johny."

"That's the truest word you ever said, ma'am." His voice trembled and he was gone into the scorching August day.

In the farmyard at Lackanagow, the doctor and Hugh Hartnett were in earnest conversation. In his furtive, shy way, Johny-the-Ballads stopped behind a tree and couldn't help hearing. The doctor looked grave.

"Her temperature is back to normal, Hugh, but I'm sorry to say she's sinking. I never saw pneumonia to take such a turn in a young woman. The hot weather is against her. She has some strange longing on her. Her spirit is downcast. You must try and cheeer her; get her interested in the children. Don't worry her at all, I'll be around in four or five days. Oh, hallo, Johny, where did you rise out of! No fairs these days."

The good-natured doctor put his hand to pocket and slipped half-a-crown into the clutching palm. They all loved Johny for his simple, half-witted ways. But Hugh Hartnett was too worried just now to notice him.

Hugh's maiden sister was in the kitchen when Johny put his head over the half-door.

"God save ye, Miss Hartnett; how's herself," he said hoarsely.

"Yerra where did you come from! Is it Mrs Hartnett you mean? She's poor enough then; she's weak to-day; a terrible thirst on her, and talking now she is about her old home south at the say-side. She thinks if she had one drink of Lady's Well water from her native parish she'd be cured. Doting she is."

"And where is the Lady's Well?" says Johny simply.

"Yerra away south in the cliffs of Ardfield; in the townland of Dunowen I hear. 'Tis a holy well."

"And how far south is that Miss?" says Johny.

"Eighteen miles maybe; such a queer foolish notion for her to get. In the middle of harvest too, How could we get her that Lady's Well water! I'm afraid she won't last long anyway."

Johny-the-Ballads was crying. Tears running down his face like rain. He thought of the turkeys and Christmas and the white half-crowns.

"I'll be going, Miss Hartnett. Tell her she'll be better soon, with God's help. 'Tis often she helped me." The tears still coursed his withered face.

Down to the inn at the crossroads Johny again wended his way. The half-crown was burning his pocket.

"Would you have such thing as an empty half-gallon jar?" he asked Mrs O'Neill.

She opened her eyes wide. "I have," she said.

"Well fill me a pint first and rinse the jar after. You'll get it back."

Five minutes later, a refreshing pint of porter inside, Johny was swinging along the south road, the empty jar close under his arm. Though the half-crown was broken and the fairs off, a strange happiness came to him all at once. And yet there was a note of sorrow in the song he raised:-

"I came of honest parents, but now they're lying low,
  And 'twas many the happy day I spent in the Glen of Aherlow."

When he enquired the road, they told him keep straight into the sun. At 1 o'clock he crossed the Bandon at Manch Bridge and he counted his cash again when a tempting signboard showed under Ballinacarriga Castle. He resisted. 'Twas a long dusty road, thro' the green slopes of Rossmore and the empty jar was heavy indeed before Johny hit the crossroad inn at Lissavard. He had covered 12 Irish miles and footsore and weary.

But the innfolk were kindly. Two local farmers who knew Johny at fairs stood him creamy pints. The landlady cut him a loaf of fresh bread and butter. He sang them *The Bold Tenant Farmer* and *Cath Ceinineigh* with great life and feeling but a furious urge came to him again when he glanced at the empty jar. He got full directions and a short cut over the hills to Paroiste-na-Arda — south and still south to the sea.

Strange to say, Johny-the-Ballads had never seen the broad Atlantic. Heaven seemed open to his maimed poetic soul when he topped Curravalla Hill and saw the westering sun over that beautiful outpost territory of rich tillage land on the rim of the ocean — rocks and bays and headlands with the grey-blue horizon sweeping in a wide arc from Kinsale to Glandore. So this was Mrs Hartnett's native country. No wonder she pined for its wild open beauty of mountain and sea and wooded glen. That white low-roofed schoolhouse near the Chapel in the trees had sent hundreds of clever boys to good posts. An evening fleet of sail was leaving Glandore Harbour for the high fishing grounds. A big trans-Atlantic liner swung in from the Fastnett Rock and swept past the Galley Light. Johny was entranced.

But his poor feet were sore, and at the comfortable roomy inn on the roadside he had another long drink, enquiring his way south to the headland and Lady's Well. Late at eve he found it — a lovely lonely well; far out, near cliffs that dipped 200 feet sheer to the sea. The water sprang from gravel-rock, smothered in mosses and watercress. It was very cold and crystal clear. 'Twas on the eve of Lady's Day in August that Johny filled that precious jar on the Head of Dunowen. The kindly neighbours of the hamlet on the slope gave him meals and lodging; a pair of new darned woollen socks, that he needed sorely, was the gift of a Gaelic-speaking woman. They too loved poor Johny for his simple, half-witted ways. At dawn the urge to be on the move returned. He thought of that friend in the north country, far from her own sea; pining for a drink of this precious cold water.

He struck north. The jar was heavy. He changed it frequently from hand to hand. 'Twas a long, weary road now. Carefully he counted his "coaling stations" in relation to his remnants of half-a-crown. He was not short of food, for no house was inhospitable. But he was almost beat and was shifting the jar from shoulder to shoulder, when the thunder-storm broke on the open bog road four miles from home.

He refused to take the scant shelter. He was wet to the skin; a battered, worn body, staggering along as he crossed the Bandon River. A stabbing pain in his side grew worse. Pure spiritual courage kept him going to the bitter end. Yet it was a triumphal though bedraggled Johny that landed the jar on Hartnett's kitchen settle at sundown.

"There 'tis," said he. "Tell herself I brought it all the way from Lady's Well to-day, the 15th of August." Then he was gone into the dusk. Poor soul didn't want to trouble that sick house with his pains and his misfortunes.

"Wonderful, Hugh, wonderful," the doctor was saying. "Miraculous, I'd like to call it. The woman is splendid. She'll be out of bed in a week, hale and hearty. You can afford to give her a holiday south with her own folk."

"I will that same," said Hugh Hartnett. Then a reverent look came into his face. "Ever since she drank the spring water that Johny-the-Ballads brought from the south" — the Doctor interrupted him:-

"Poor Johny, he's gone. Double pneumonia swept him in four days. He died in the County Home this morning. The nuns say he was a saint. 'My friend is better,' was his last word. He closed his eyes and died 'like a child going to sleep.''

CHILDHOOD DAYS

"Cut me a hurl," says the sturdy youth,
His limbs were straight and strong;
I liked his eyes of budding truth
Alight to right some wrong.
"My mates play other games," he said —
I saw his proud lip curl;
"I'll play the game my grand-dad played,
— I want to hurl."

"Cut me a hurl," says the winsome lass, —
Her brown eyes smiled at me —
"For I can take a camog pass,
Too fast for you to see;
I hold my left hand down like all,
I strike without a turn,
I love to hit a flying ball
— Cut me a hurl!"

"Tut me a hudle," says the lisping boy,
Who climbed a weary knee;
My chain and medals were his joy —
"What are they, Dad?" said he.
The light of God was in his face;
His head had many a curl,
With pleading eyes he pressed his case
— "Tut me a hudle!"

So I cut the hurls in the ashen lane,
When Christmas fires burnt clear,
I shaped them true with serried grain
When Springtime days were near —
Mayhap in life's more serious play,
Or in some final's whirl,
We'll bless the hour the children say
— "Cut me a hurl."

BIRD SONG SILENT

A full fortnight earlier than usual, our blackbirds and thrushes seem to have forgotten their song. I do not blame them, for those leaden skies and chilly unseasonable nor' westers of July are not conducive to good cheer and buoyancy in any walk of life. We hear an occasional chuckle of a blackbird leaving covert at the dull dawn; but the glad songs of morning and evening are gone. The finches are still lilting a little and the chaffinch is a tough, cheerful fellow who still rattles out his chattering repeat from the invisibility of leafland.

Most likely I became a bird-lover because of my early life close to the woods and groves of the south-west, where all manner of birdlife flourished. And I had good early inspiration from my eldest brother, a young farmer, eleven years my senior. From my early toddling years, I watched him as he spent the winter nights building dove-cots and bird cages with devoted patience. The dove-cots were easy enough — plain boxes with doors on leather hinges sprigged on. The bird-cages were slower. He always set about them when his after-tea work of soling and heeling and patching the "boots of the household" was complete. He only left home on Sundays.

For the smaller bird-cages he bought great lengths of wire at the hardware shops and cut it into proper lengths. Then he built his square cages and planed out the little front laths and the perches. I remember his making one huge, wicker cage for thrush or black-bird — made it with peeled sally rods. He had a score of tame pigeons in the barn loft at the one time; there was consternation and tears when a neighbour shot them down, thinking they were wild birds as they circled over him, half a mile from home. He collected his birds with little or no cruelty. He loved larks and would await until a nest of larks in a quiet pasture was ready for flight. Then he would put the big wicker cage beside the place and shift the nest and young birds into it. The parents fed them through the bars. Later he would release all but the biggest, which was usually a male bird. One lark lived and sang with us for two years. I remember his proud walk like a game-bird and his soaring song out in the sun.

His birds were well-cared for night and day. We had linnets and finches. One fine cock blackbird he caught by a dexterous fleck of his long whip — the end of the lash circled round the legs of the bird and held him. One leg was fractured but it was soon carefully splintered with match sticks and hemp thread. The leg mended slowly, and I watched the blackbird constantly pecking at the droppings in the cage and fiddling at the injured leg. Soon he was sound in wind and limb, singing gloriously. I held him while my brother took off the matchwood splint — we were both astonished to discover that "Hoppie" (as we called him) had made a perfect plaster round the wounded limb — from the droppings in the cage. 'Twas one of the mysteries of my schoolboy days; hard, yet happy days!

BEAUTIOUS MAY

MAY in all its blue and gold, in all its balm and beauty, is here. I do not recall a Spring more nearly perfect, both to the nature lover and hard-thinking men of the land. From all corners of the four provinces, powerfully built bronzed men, well-dressed and happy looking, thronged to a record Dublin Spring Show.

I hit across more than a few of my friends, new and old — farmers, sportsmen of many branches but farmers first. All speak well of Ireland's most favourable Spring in their recollection. For once in a way there "were no complaints." All crops except roots were well laid in and promising; root land was rapidly yielding to cultivation and the improvement in artificial manure has given tillers new heart. I was much impressed by the comfortable confidence of these "men of the fields" who live so close to nature. Times have somewhat improved for them, and not before their time. Their main problem and a growing one is the shortage of labour.

The first week in May is their stated time and they are as regular as the tide's ebb and flow. Wonderful mystery of nature this! — how these birds find their way year after year — succeeding generations of them, to the same spot, where the older birds' nests were built, and where those younger birds, now pirouetting and tweeting above the greening trees of the square outside my window were hatched. But there it is, and no art or science can explain it.

MOUNTAIN MUTTON

"HOW can people live at all — mutton chops 4/- a lb. to-day." I have heard a lot of lament in that strain of late, and my mind turned back to the time when I could buy a weighty leg of mutton for the price of one man's dinner to-day. But I met a tall wiry, mountainy man of Wicklow whose step is light and his whistle bright as he calls his little black white collie to heel. Soaring prices of mutton are "Balm in Gilliard" to this happy man. He is an old friend. I often knock across him in my mountain tramps or cycle spins.

This time last year the poor man was in despair. His face looked worn and old; his forehead carried white beads of perspiration; he had lost eighty head of sheep in the snowdrifts that persisted far into the spring of 1947. But when I met him last week on the outskirts of his rangy teritory of commonage, he reminded me of Raftery's spring song, "the age will be gone from me, and I will be young again."

This is a great year for the sheep farmer of the hills. The ravages of last spring's severity thinned the stocks and many sheep farmers had to "go in the Bank" to replenish. But the courageous man soon doubled his capital. The 1947-'48 winter, just gone, was unusually mild. The lambing season was excellent and mortality low. At the moment spring lambs are fetching staggering prices in city markets. My friend has just sold 80 fat lambs in the Dublin market for what was a "small fortune." He is investing the money well. He is renting more land and will lay in young ewes when the season is ripe. The frost and snow are his deadly enemies. His house beside the winding road above Glencullen had a new golden coat of thatch and there was an air of frugal comfort about, the yard was covered with clean gravel from the river bed in the valley and scores of russet fowl had the blood red combs of brisk layers. Weather means much to the sheep farmers; they are deeply religious and I think their close communion with Nature is responsible.

The whole face of the countryside is changed this week. That soft drop of April rain that fell gently after a long stretch of sunshine had miraculous effects on wood and shrubbery, on lealand and cornland. The long avenues in the suburbs carry a wealth of flowering prunes and wild cherry. My cycle spin through the Dargle Valley was a sheer delight — snow-white cherry blossoms lined the winding road and the delicate emerald of early Spring was painted on tree and shrub and meadow with the Master's brush.

WHEN ENCLOSED COURSING BEGAN

AN IRISHMAN'S instinctive love of the chase traces back to the time of our extensive forests, when the welfare of a man's household depended on his skill as a hunter of game. Open coursing is as old as the green hills. In the days of Finn, the son of Cumhal, his hounds coursed the plains of Kildare, from his famous seat on the Hill of Allen to the Inches of Bourbawn. Finn's great dogs, Bran and Sceolan, hunted the Golden Vein of Limerick, between Seefinn above Ardpatrick, and Knockaney, on the Tipperary border, where the Fianna had their coursing camps, as told in the ancient Irish manuscripts.

Park coursing is modern. But it was not started in Ireland, as some people believe. No! Enclosed coursing was initiated sixty-six years ago in South-East England — Plumpton Park, near Brighton, was the scene of the first park meeting in "The New Departure."

Open coursing with beaters flourished in Ireland in the eighteenth and nineteenth centuries; its promoters and patrons were the Lords and landed gentry. Matches for big stakes were common in the Curragh of Kildare; the Lord Lieutenant and his train as distinguished guests.

The Province of Ulster was particularly strong in coursing clubs. With Belfast as centre, the counties of Antrim and Down, Derry and Tyrone, had regular coursing features.

Wexford, Kilkenny, Limerick, Tipperary and Cork had their fixtures where hares were beaten up and coursed in the open with gentlemen and ladies following on horseback.

England had strongly established open coursing clubs one hundred years ago. Of these Altcar, Essex, Sleaford, South of England, Ridgway, Northern England, West Cumberland, and Border Clubs were best known. Scotland had three flourishing Lowland Clubs as well as Netherby and Teeside near the Cheviot Hills on the Scottish border.

It was left for a well-known hare authority, Mr. T. H. Chase, of South-Eastern England, to first conceive and develop the idea of concentrating hares in enclosed parks.

Mr Chase knew all about the habits of the hare and visualised quick, succeeding trials.

He was the first man to use lattice wire, besides inventing hare-chutes and escapes and, at Plumpton Park (Brighton) he laid his first plans.

In the Autumn of 1876 Mr. Chase caught, enclosed, fed and trained his hares. He then formed a promoting company and organised the first enclosed coursing meeting. The venture was announced for the month of December in the year mentioned above and created something of a sensation in the coursing world at a time when the open Waterloo Cup on Lord Sefton's estate, at Altcar, was at its pinnacle of popularity.

The advertised events — one 32-dog stake, two 16-dog stakes and one 8-dog stake — at the Plumpton enclosed meeting were quickly filled.

At the Gloucester Hotel, Brighton, the initial dinner and call-over were held with great ceremony, special trains being run from London at suitable times on successive days.

There was a huge attendance and the novel departure was such a success that in March, 1877, the Southern Cup, for thirty-two all-ages at ten guineas each, was run. Several Waterloo dogs of distinction were entered, Dark Rustic, Kilkenny, Srapio, Huran, Sir Magnus and Hugh Gillespie being amongst the number. Whilst some of the thick-and-thin followers of the open sport held aloof, a goodly proportion of old coursers patronised the new sport. The first Southern Cup was divided between Dark Rustic (a Waterlooer) and Early Morn.

The great Southern Cup, for sixty-four all-aged at £12 10s. 0d. each, developed in 1878 and Irish coursing chiefs supported the meeting, Lord Lurgan (of Master McGrath fame), Captain Archdale, Messrs. F. Watson and J. Sandes having entries.

Though the old school of sport writers criticised the new sport severely and said that the dogs would be ruined, stamina and skill discounted for speed and cuteness, and while valuable dogs were killed at the escapes, the sport developed.

The Ground Game Act of 1880 thinned hares in the open. In September, 1884, a stake for 128 dogs was run at Plumpton Park — £6 per dog, winner £500 and a piece of plate. New stands were erected.

The North of England next fell into line. Gosforth Park was established, with its Gold Cup, where the Waterloo dogs, Burnaby and Mineral Water, ran.

Hot-foot on the Gosforth meet came the enclosed coursing on the racecourse at Haydock Park, near Liverpool, with its keen greyhound traditions. Great excitement followed the appearance of Fullerton, the Altcar champion, at Haydock Park, where he ran a series of brilliant trials on hard ground and divided the Champion Produce Stakes with the great greyhound, Herschel, who bred a line of Waterloo champions well-known to greyhound men. The distinguished Irish greyhound, Pinkerton, also won a big stake at Haydock Park.

Then came Wye Racecourse, Four Oaks Park, and Doncaster, for valuable stakes extending up to 1892.

Hare stock failed in quality and the sport became decadent. A "cruelty" outcry in England developed; open coursers rose in rebellion; and, finally, mismanagement killed park coursing in England, after a hectic reign of close on twenty years.

It was in the Autumn of 1879 that the first park meeting was held in Ireland. Mr. Chase (of Plumpton Park fame) came across to lay out the Mourne Park enclosure, hard by the Ulster Capital, in the demesne of the Earl of Kilmorney.

Hares were driven from a spinney through a park set in beautiful surroundings. Many English and Scottish coursers came across to support the meeting, which flourished for a dozen years.

Somehow or other hares died soft in Mourne Park and the critics agreed that it was suited for puppies only. Sound work behind a hare did not make up for loss of pace, and dogs got accustomed to the lie of the land, hanging away on the high ground instead of coursing honestly.

Purdystown Park, near Belfast, on Mr. R.N. Batt's demesne, had two meetings per season, and fine trials were enjoyed for some years at the meetings at Holestone Park, which was laid out by Mr. Chase in 1888.

Concentrated coursing in the South of Ireland was initiated on Lord Fermoy's famous demesne at Trabolgan, overlooking Cork Harbour, in the early eighties. This was indeed a very fine meeting.

Lord Fermoy had devoted much time and attention to the breeding, preserving and improvement of harestock and was a recognised authority. His meeting at Trabolgan had the dual advantages of park and open coursing. Hares were reared in the demesne and they were driven from two spinneys or shelters at either end of a big field. The hares at Trabolgan ran like open hares; they were never handled before or after coursing, and trials were of fine length.

Some of the veterans of present-day coursing remember Trabolgan and its picturesque situation above one of the most beautiful harbours in the world. Mr. Joe Shaw of Belfast, owner of Shane Barnagh, Shule Aroon and Salisbury was a regular visitor to Trabolgan. So popular did this meeting become that the Cork open coursing at Killeady and Coole died away and other enterprises followed on Trabolgan's lead in the South.

Later we had many cruel meetings with boxed hares before the Coursing Body intervened. But Park Coursing had come to Ireland and has there made its home.

BUSY BLACKBIRDS

TO me the loveliest sound in nature of a dewy May or early June morning is the chuckle of a blackbird in the bushes outside my window. Low-pitched and contented-like, comes the "chuck-chuck-chuck" of wondrous sweetness. The dusty yellow-billed fellow is just giving his message of confidence to his mate in the nest hard by, that all is well with his world. I do not see him at all as he calls quietly, his deep expressive notes cover the lower half of the octave. Suddenly he decides to break covert — probably in search of food for his young household, and his startling song soars to higher register in the seventh position of a violin.

Presently he will come back, his bill packed with juicy worms, dangling down untidily. And so sure as he does you can see the *dun ciarseach* burst forth from the thickly leaved pear tree on the same mission. Then if the air is still you will hear the expectant hissing call of the hungry fledglings — *gearcachs,* we call them in school-going days. All day long the parent birds will make shuttlecock flights to and from the feeding grounds, returning well-laden. Young birds grow to full size in a few weeks and are always ravenous.

Though the blackbird is supposed to be a bit of a rowdy and a braggard, I don't think he is so courageous in emergency as his cousin the thrush. Of all the concentrated bird-furies I ever saw it was a pair of thrushes defending their young from a marauding cat. The surrounding walls were high and one fledgling "failed to make it" when leaving the nest. He was being fed and sheltered in the potato stalks by the parent birds after the others had got clean away. Then Mistress Cat stalked up on its prey, striped and tiger-like. Soon the battle was on. Those thrushes roared and screamed and scolded and fought with feet and beaks and wings with fierce energy. They drove at the cat's eyes and nose. They put her back on defence against the wall, pawing the air, still mad to get her prey. They glanced and flashed at her like air fighters attacking a bomber. They drove terror into her heart and she ran for shelter in disgrace. Once before I saw two thrushes beat off a marauding sparrow-hawk — it was away back in Muintir-mhairle, beyond Kilcrohane, when I was on my O.A.P. rounds. These fierce thrushes were defending their home and their young. I almost cheered when they beat hawk off after a gory battle.

AT THE HANDBALL FINAL

DOWN through Leinster — Dublin, Kildare, Carlow into that lovely rolling North Kilkenny country we sped on our way to the All-Ireland senior handball final at Talbot Inch — biggest handball game of the year.

The gentle late autumn sun seems laggard to bid us farewell. Had he been half so kind last April and May we had our barns bursting. All that Master Sun can do now is to try to make good all the harm his absence in storm and frost and snow and cloud in our early year had done.

Handball — a great old Irish game of whose training values I am very conscious and very closely associated. Handball with either the rubber or alley-cracker, is a good game. I have seen many of the All-Ireland championships. They were mainly with the hard ball. I saw Father Tom Jones and James Fitzgerald play in competition. Living in Cork City then, a home of handball, I saw their successors, Billie Herlihy and Oliver Drew play forty or more years ago. Then came Tim Twohill, the footballer from Kanturk, and Joe O'Leary of Fermoy.

Later came John Joe Bowles of Limerick, a tall, graceful and stylish handballer with an easy style. Paddy Lyons of Dublin, a Cork man, was another stylist and an enduring handballer with great pace in his long legs and arms.

Hotfoot on the Bowles-Twohill-Drew-Herlihy and Lyons period came a handball revival in Dublin City, where memories of John Lawlor, the cab-owner, and players before his time still lived. Two young Dublin men, Morgan Pembroke and Jimmy Kelly shot to the limelight. Pembroke won his All-Ireland title in beating John Joe Bowles, our greatest stylist, in a home and home game at Limerick and Dublin. Agreed that Bowles was far past his best at the time he was soundly beaten by Pembroke — a strong and consistent handballer who trained well. So did his successor, a uniform striker left and right — a colleague of Pembroke's, Jimmy Kelly of Dublin City.

There were many cleavages in Irish handball, one of the games the G.A.A. sought to foster. There were considerable difficulties in control and examining the development of the game in a heartless fashion, one must conclude that the smallness of the space in which spectators could see the game, made it unprofitable to the promoters. The result was heavy wagers between men who had won their spurs. Professionalism is a ban. Any man who plays for a wager is a professional in the G.A.A. meaning of amateurism. We shall overlook all that, for men will bet and men will fight *secula seculorum*.

After Jimmy Kelly came T. Leahy, that powerful right-hand tosser from Ballymore-Eustace, Co. Kildare, who died in his twenties. He was strong and fast. After his time came a dandy handballer, Tom Soye of the Guards — light, fast, shrewd; he held the fort for many a year. But greatest of all the champions I have seen in recent years is the Kilkenny petrol van driver, John Joe Gilmartin. I have followed him through many of his best games. He was a past-master. Gilmartin had everything. When he went to England as a motor driver and mechanic, there was no handballer in this country to hold his coat. Austin Clarke of Dublin, a fast, fiery two-handed man, took the title in Gilmartin's absence. But the Dublin senior hardball and All-Ireland champion proved no close match for the Kilkenny wonder, when he returned from England.

So far as Irish handball is concerned the Kilkenny man is in a niche all his own. I decided to travel down to see the younger man, Austin Clarke, Dublin champion, play Gilmartin. The journey was pleasant in good handball company, recalling old scenes and old times. The morning fog lifted around Castledermot, Carlow's busy town was clear, and its tall sugar steeple towered over the plain.

Rich Kilkenny lands swung into the picture — a rolling emerald of grass and tillage. I was loath to leave Nowlan Park where Kilkenny and Waterford were to play. For that day handball claimed me and it was late in the afternoon when I heard that Waterford, battling well in the absence of Vincent Bastion, were beaten by a refreshed Kilkenny side, who now meet Tipperary in the League semi-final. Limerick awaits the winners.

Talbot Inch Court is not far from the troublesome Nore River that left its mark on Kilkenny city in last year's floods. I saw marks eight feet high on the riverside dwellings. Kilkenny is a beautiful city with all its old glory in situation, buildings and atmosphere.

This is probably the best handball court in the country — three and a half miles out. The gallery was packed to suffocation. Hundreds crowded outside despite the counter-attraction at Nowlan Park. We saw a delightful junior all-Ireland final in the soft-ball between Ryan of Wexford and Brogan of Dublin. Long, high rallies continued to the last game of five (two each) which Ryan won mainly through his easy, commanding style.

The Gilmartin-Clarke senior handball final opened to a hushed and tense court. Gilmartin tossing lightning balls to the Dublin man's left hand, shot out eight aces with no return that counted. There were few high rallies. In these Clarke was the champion's equal, but Gilmartin's low deadly tossing took the game 21 to 5.

The first game tells the complete story — Clarke rallied in the second game coming from 3-14 to 14 all. But Gilmartin stole away with fierce tossing which were so fast and consistent that no man could return them.

Games three, four and five all went the same road. Clarke was the champion's equal in all high open play. But Gilmartin's cracking tosses were winners every time. There was not a fault in his handball armour. Every branch is equally controlled. I haven't seen his like since Oliver Drew's days. He is coolness personified and we have no one that I know in Ireland to give him a game.

SCENIC GEMS FROM THE FOUR PROVINCES

My occupations in life, as well as my hobbies, gave me opportunity not presented to many, of seeing far more of Ireland, urban and rural, than the average man. Both by way of work and recreation I have travelled many roads, and more than a few boreens, in every one of the thirty-two counties. Often I had to travel in all sorts of weather; hail, sunshine, rain, fog and snow. But it is in the sunny days or rather the days when there is a blend of sun and cloud, that one sees Irish scenic beauty at its best.

And I travelled by all modes of conveyance — foot, cycle, motor-cycle, motor car, inside trap, back-to-back trap, side car, covered car, wagonette, tram, bus and train; by boat, lugger and river-steamer. I travelled on horse-carts without springs, in donkey cars, on horse-back, donkey's back and mule's back on occasion. I have yet to step inside a 'plane but I have ridden in a tinker's van.

Generally it was more by duty than wayward or reckless design that I travelled so much of the country. And it was hard to fail in developing a sense of the picturesque, had that sense not already been deeply ingrained in all lovers of rural life.

Much has been written of Irish scenery. I propose to add nothing new where tourist-blurbs cloy. To me Ireland holds such infinite variety of scenic charm that I never had the slightest desire to step outside her shores, for fresh fields and pastures new. Only last week I travelled through the easy rolling country between the quiet lakes of Westmeath, where I had never been before, between Lough Owel and Lough Lene. But I cannot attempt to compare Irish scenery with any other, having seen so little of the latter, beyond patches of England and corners of Scotland. But I have sense enough to know that Ireland is indeed very beautiful to one who seeks her charms with an open healthy mind.

So many gems have chained me in our four provinces that last night's brief survey of a battered map of Ireland left my mind smothered in memories — the inner eye's pictures of beauty spots down through the years. I made up my mind to select a few for a brief article, and ramblingly, I snatched the first seven impressions that formed themselves in the responsive photoplate of that most wonderful gift of God to man — human memory.

1. Over Belfast Lough

Away back in 1902, when I was eighteen years old and resident in Dublin, I had a golden chance of a free trip to Belfast. Playing fairly well (I suppose) for a junior hurling club in Dublin, I was selected on the Senior

County team to open the Sean's Gaelic Field in Belfast. I only remember hitting two balls for the hour; but both were points so I was in high feather when the promoting committee, after a meal, took us out on jaunting cars to see the sights. Of all places, they took us to Cave Hill on the Northern Ballymena Road and we climbed to the summit on a glorious summer's evening.

Stretched at our feet was the black smoky city of Belfast — factory chimneys everywhere, down the long quays. The Lough was crowded with shipping. I was enthralled. And then my eye wandered out over the grey-green Irish Sea. Visibility was extra good and what a thrill I got when pointed out the bright cliffs and green headlands of Scotland simmering in the evening sun! Then my guide swept his hand to the right where the dark mountains of Northern England loomed. But it was Scotland — land of Burns, Scott and Bonnie Prince Charlie — that fascinated me. I was speechless. In that dark cave at my back had sat three men in the long ago, in 1793, laying their plans for freeing Ireland. The Dublin man, of Belfast and Kildare associations, the bold Wolfe Tone; the Belfast man, Henry Joe McCracken was number two. And who was the third! — the soldierly man of European army experience; the man with the slouchy hat and the big roan mare; the man from "God knows where" — honest Tom Russell of Mallow, Co. Cork.

2. Connemara and Clew Bay

I found a neat little 2¾ motor cycle, a ready and independent way of seeing as much of Ireland as my fancy claimed and my leisure or duties permitted. I rode three of these machines for sport and business over a period of fifteen years in my young life. Nothing like a well-tuned and well-tyred motor-bike for taking you around. You have no ties; no clogging comrades to dispute your wishes. And early in my motor-cycling career I decided to see something of the Golden West, for historic Connaught was then a sealed book to me.

So from the Golden Vein I set out one early June morning, and so across the Shannon; I hugged the bold western coast of Clare of which much could be written. Aran Islands showed up dimly in the western sea as I hummed down the corkscrew hill beyond Lisdoonvarna in a low spark; so through Kinvara to hit Galway's old world city by lunch-hour. There was no Padraig O'Connaire in his leprachaun attitude perched on a stone in Eyre Square then. Poor, lovable Padraig — our greatest genius of a story-teller; many an hour we dallied together in pleasant places. His fame is international.

But I was hungry for the West where the sun called. I spun by Salthill and hugged the coast to Barna and Spiddal. I was in a new world! Stones and rock and crag abounded. Sweet pastures between. White, picturesque little dwellings; old world folk in their frieze and shawl and flannel. Gaelic galore.

Wilder grew the scene; more rocks and stones and rugged hillocks. On to Carraroe, Rosmuc and Carna — the heart of the Connacht Gaeltacht. The lights and the shades, the colouring were enchanting. Then came Clifden and Renvyle, Recess, Maam and the Scandinavian beauty of wood and creek and hill — of which reams had been written. The Beanna Beola in striking shades of purple and maroon and green crowning every turn of the road! I dallied a while here and there, but I swung away to the North on a rough switch back road and dipped over Clew Bay at last on my way to Westport — a lovely town well in from the coast — I slept deep that night.

Next morning I hit north for Mayo and Newport. 'Tis long ago now, but I was not far from there when I threw my bike against a stone wall and decided to climb a formidable peak on my right. It was one of the Nephen Range. They told me its Gaelic name was Carrig-a-binna. I loved a mountain climb then and I wanted a bird's eye view of famous Clew Bay and Achill while the sun was high. I wanted a higher view than that coast road gave. And the day way young.

'Twas a far harder climb than I suspected. Hills peeped o'er hills. The face of the brow was broken and irregular, with a multitude of loose stones everywhere. The ascent was steeper every step; but I was fit and wiry and held on. Past a waste of moss and shingle. Then stiff above me I saw a cairn of stones — it marked the top of the mountain. I stood on the pinnacle of the ridge. I was staggered at the superb view in all directions.

Clew Bay, a magnificent stretch of water, where once Grace O'Malley reigned was at my very feet; it was studded with a thousand emerald islets. Even distant Clare Island of my map looked within a stone's throw! The sharp peak of Dugort in Achill due west. Beyond Erris was the Northern Sea. And away east there were the rolling plains of Mayo of indescribable wild beauty — farms, pastures, rivers, ravines, lakes! To the South Croagh Patrick and the Twelve Bens of Connemara. Wonderful panorama that beggars description; a sight I shall never forget.

3. Killarney — Heaven's Reflex

Far different is my next scenic gem. All that has ever been written about Killarney's ravishing loveliness halts behind reality. For concentrated beauty in all its phases, Killarney stands alone. I have seen it from all angles and in every weather — didn't I live for long, just over the Reeks! But it was the first views of Loch Lein and Muckross from the Torc outlook that impressed me most in my young days. It was in such marked contrast I suppose with the stern naked beauty of the Gap of Dunloe I had just left, where rocks still look tumbling down.

That was on an April day of sun and shadow, when light came and went over lake, wood, hill and purple peak. There was just a faint ripple on the mountain — encompassed water kissed by tree and shrub. Then a great stillness came over it all; the fairies had passed and the restless spirit of O'Donoghue and his snow-white steed had sunk beneath the waters. Half-a-dozen times I had climbed Torc mountains; then one bright moonlit night, sojourning over a week-end in Killarney, I decided to see Innisfallen anew.

My friend knew the gate-lodge keeper at Torc Cascade. Our heels rattled off the hard dry road past Muckross. We climbed over the tumbling fall; at the second outlook we halted and lit our pipes. The serenity of lake, isle and wood; of mountain and creek was emotion provoking. The *driocht* was over it all. We climbed Torc Mount; the sound of the fall was now dim. The ripple of lake water made us drunk of peace. Then a boat with nightlines came out around the woods of Innisfallen. The sound of rowlocks came over Loch Lein. The high moon spilled its silver on the lakes. Behind us a fox vixen called to her marauding mate. Neither my friend nor I spoke all the way back to Killarney.

I thought of lonely Innisfallen, a queen in the bosom of the Lake — a lovely lonely woman with her dark tree-tresses and emerald gown, sitting aloof. The spilling moon-path trailed behind her in rippling lake-silver, like a bridal veil. Aloof, from her encircling sweethearts of mountains, particularly that tall commanding purple one with the Eagle's Nest for a plume, and the wavy heather-brown beard — eager to embrace his lonely love in the silence of the night.

4. Orchards in Blossom

Dewy May was in it — "twenty men from Dublin town" heading north by rail, fringing the low Eastern coast, past Malahide and Drogheda to the Gap of the North at Dandalgan. I forget the stations after that for it is many decades ago and I was neither a man nor a boy — just in between. Twenty Irish Ireland pioneers from the Dublin Gaelic League and G.A.A. Clubs, heading for St. Patrick's Cathedral town of the twin spires, on the hill, where we were to figure in an *Aereacht* and *Feis.*

Soon, in a bend of rail we came upon them — miles of rounded hillocks and gentle dells crowded with orchards in bloom. The May sun broke through filmy clouds. These orchards burst upon us — endless chains of carefully pruned trees with gnarled branches. All well spaced trees with mossy walls dividing the fields. What leaf was on each tree was smothered in glorious blossom giving back the young sun's light in a dazzling sea of beauty. Pink and white they were of infinite shades. Endless acres of them sitting on an emerald foundation. They had a strange emotional effect on a young mind that had never seen more apples in bloom than a few stray trees in a garden.

5. West Cork Jewels

Once more the little motor-bike, humming along, was my medium. I hit up the beauteous Lee Valley of which so much has been written, and never cried halt past Inniscarra, Coachford, Carrigadrohid's neat village with its stout castle splitting the noble stream, and so south by west through The Geragh to the long lake road at Inchigeela and Ballingeary to Gougane; 'twas a brave sunny day and I held on by Maura Bwee Ni Laoghaire's house to the source of the Lee in deep valley Desmond, and Gougane of St. Finnbarr. The little stone to Callanan the poet who made Gougane Barra immortal, was knocked to the ground that day — a gale, perhaps.

Even in that golden day, the lake was reverentially sombre. Sombriety in the western depths of the valley beyond where few sun hours reach. Due north, however, the midday sun shone on the bright green mountains torn with a hundred ravines worn by the rushing rivers of ageless storms, of rain and hail and snow. The streams trickled down now to feed the lake. Over the little causeway to the little church and the narrow stone cells of the holy monks, I thought of the Saint's wisdom in resting here for prayer and contemplation. Writes Callanan during his sojourn here:-

> "Was there ever a dwelling by valley or highland
> So meet for a bard as this lone little island."

A long journey was before me and I fled away after a decade of *Aves.* Out where the infant Lee tumbles through a narrow channel, I sped and broke sharply to the right on the sloping road to Ceim-an-eigh. If Gougane is a gem, an Ceim is a startling tiara. The mountain rift gathers depth and beauty as you climb. A silvery stream gurgles over the rocks beside the road. In gathering grandeur the rocks rise — clothed in all variety of shrubs and plants; gorse in bloom; rowan trees, hazel, willow, yew, ash, laurel, holly in abundance. In soft winds of the road each vista opens until the strikingly craggy double turn on top where the deer of legend jumped to freedom. I was to see much of Cork County that day. An Ceim was an old friend. I left it behind, not without a thrill, and I coasted down to Kaelkil, Ballylicky and the groves of Glengariffe. Though I like the northern approach from the Tunnels, best for rugged grandeur, this eastern approach was a new delight. The sheltered village of the winelike, balmy air, where summer dallies ever and winter never rests.

A right good meal I had beside Poulgorm. Then I climbed the Lady's Outlook of shady approach. I looked out on Bantry Bay as I never saw it before. The little islands crowd the secluded creek. Carefully every tree is placed to perfect purpose. They blend into a mosaic of riotous colour — flowers of Italy and Spain; luscious plants of the Indian seas. The sea blue as indigo; peace over all. Glengariffe grows yearly as an idyll of rest and beatitude.

Next serious stop of interest was beyond Skibbereen in my native Carbery. Turning to the right off the main Cork road I would round slowly until a steep well-wooded hill stood straight before me. Hidden behind it was Lough Ine of song and story:

> "I know a lake where the cool waves break
>   And softly fall on the silver sand
> No steps intrude on that solitude
>   And no voice but mine disturb the strand."

Lough Ine, wedged in between tumultous hills, is another jewel of the emerald pattern. That castled isle in front called in vain for my exploration; I didn't even see The Barlog where it roars with the spring tide from the Atlantic. I left lovely Lough Ine, and climbing out of it, I fled to the East for I had a resting place hard by Glandore. The tide was in right up to An Leim. The oakwood of Myross was mirrored in the water as I stole along at coasting pace. Round the bend of the road, Glandore's glories hit you in the eye. The steep open village clinging to the slope; the Castle and mansions overlooking the harbour where the fishing boats ride. Landlocked this beauty spot is, where violets bloom earliest in Northern Europe. I was soon at home in that big slate house of an uncle and godmother who were ever gracious to this rambling relative. I had *Cead Mile Failte.*

6 Depths of Wicklow

This time I saw Wicklow in a new guise — in a world of thin snow. Wicklow, the Garden of Ireland, deserves the name which however fails to describe its gripping variety — glens of staggering beauty yes; but mountain haunts of ever-changing vistas. Out of Dublin City we climbed in a sauntering car of high power, hidden in a spacious bonnet.

Up past the Three Rock Mountain into the rough hewn Scalp, which reminds one of Ceim-en-eigh though far briefer. I called a halt for the visitors as we reached that winding wall overlooking Enniskerry — an Alpine village of Christmas pines and shady elms, of spires and churches, slumbering at our feet — the Sugarloaf like a silver cone behind this, the loveliest village in Ireland. So rapidly down the Dargle where Bray's bold headland rises. Not a halt did we crave through the Glen of the Downs (and picnickers) till we hit Laragh of the towers and ruins that tell of Glendalough's ancient glories.

But it was the upper lake of Glendalough that touched our emotions. It looked black as ink with its walls of snow-clad mountains and St. Kevin's bed in that craggy rockface on the left.

"By that lake whose gloomy shore
Skylark never warbled o'er,"

said the white-haired old lady from the sunny South. Long we feasted on this unusual Wicklow scene. We dallied a while before taking the high road to town, by the Sally Gap, Lough Bray, Glencree, The Featherbed, over slumbering lake-strewn Glounnasmole. We left the charms of Avoca and Woodenbridge for the affinity of the long gracious summer's day.

7. Round Slea Head

The kiss of the soft, salt west wind caressed our faces as we headed towards the most westerly point in Europe, one day in July when the full-orbed sun rode high. The Dingle peninsula is a wonderful place, richer in archaeological remains than any like area in Ireland. Dingle, a substantial and prosperous town, that once did a roaring trade with Spain, is unique in that one hears far more Gaelic than English at mart, fair or tavern. That outpost territory west of the town is perhaps the richest Gaeltacht we own and prize. I was exploring new territory as our open car coasted past the long white strand of Ventry — Fionn-tra — of legend and story. On that strand Finn and his Fianna fought and conquered the invading King of the World — so the famous Fianna tale tells us. Dunbeg Fort, below us, now in battered ruin, was once a formidable stronghold high over the ocean. At Fahan, there are bevvies of conical stone huts of Ancient days and scores of ruins from early Christian times. The mountains and cliffs grow steeper in every mile; Eagle Mountain towers inside us; the open ocean, hundreds of feet below! Then as we rounded Slea Head the finest seascape panorama I have ever seen opened upon us as if by magic. On our left was Dingle's broad bay with the blue mountains of Iveragh beyond. On their seaward end, Valentia Island loomed high and bold at the Atlantic face and on the Southern horizon the sharp grey peak of Skellig Mhihil pierced the blue like a fairy castle. Over the hills at the head of Dingle Bay, the McGillicuddy Reeks with Cairn Tual's crooked top showed clearly though a far lighter blue — highest mountain in Ireland.

But we forgot our left hand where the road tunnels its rocky risky way on the face of Eagle Mountain. The day was calm, yet a gentle swell murmured far below us as we rounded the head. I stood on the sea wall high above the ocean. There, due West, three miles off Dunmore, was the Great Blasket with its attendant islands — Inisnabro, Inisvickillane, Beginish; hidden behind them were the Tereacht Lighthouse rock and the North Island.

So here at last were the famous Gaelic-speaking islands! — where the poet Dunleavy and the novelist O'Crohan lived; where Peig Sayers and Muiris O'Sullivan learnt their story-telling art; where Robin Flower amassed his Gaelic lore! The islands looked like a school of giant whales sleeping on the sea. One saw the snug houses of the Blaoscoid Mor with its range of upturned *naomhoges* (curragh) shining in the sun like beetles in slumber. The mind elevates on this stupendous outlook in nature's stern features. Profound natural grandeur unadorned, one calls it, loath to pass on. As we wind into Dunquin the northern headlands open — Sybil Head and the Three Sisters beyond Ballyferriter village, where I never heard a word of English spoken. We are in a new rich civilization; new though older than history. Kindly gracious sturdy folk; visitors galore round the village, seeking the pure front of native Gaelic. The Brandon's massive peak, broad and high, ranged into perspective. I sought Kilmaceader's 10th century church with its neddle gable and Ogham Stones — they abound here. Not content with all I had seen I walked half a mile across the field to see Gallarus Oratory — more ancient even than Kilmaceadar itself.

This is the loveliest and best preserved Ancient Church in Europe — so able authorities say. Its beautifully planned symmetry has defied the storms of thirteen centuries. All dry stone work from rock to ridge of roof — it fascinates one. Yes, that was one great day of sight-seeing for at eve we took the car to Connor Pass and the Padlar's Lake in the bosom of the mountains. One thousand feet below us in a valley of Alpine beauty, a chain of little lakes seemed to hold the sun of the day in their heart. Yes, Dingle Peninsula holds perhaps the noblest cluster of gems in Eire's crown.

Having completed my round of seven visits in fancy, I lounge and dream. But through them all, one placid picture tunes in as the others fade out gradually — it is — Moonlight in Innisfallen!

Hurling Highlights

Siar-Smaointe

Lá breáġ gréine
Ar bántaiḃ Éireann
Na sár-ḟear gléigeal, áluinn;
Mná seang réilteaċ,
Páistí mear pleiḃreaċ
Mo ġrá-neart éiḟeaċt—báire!

Faḋa síar mo smaointe. Na caoga bliaḋan! Lá nuair connaic mé mo ċéuḋ comórtas-báire i bParóisḋe-na-hárḋa, ar taoḃ síar-ó-ḋeas ḋe Conndae Corcaiġe. Mé i'm páisḋe aireaċ, súil-leatan ag féaċaint le hiongantas tar iongantais ar an raḋarc glionndaraċ mór tímċeall. Páirc faḋa réiḋ, leatan! Na hiománuiḋte ag rit is ag iomarscáil, ag taḃairt fé an liatróiḋ beag beoḋaċ!

Óg is aosta ar gaċ taoḃ, ina nésḋuiġ Domnaiġ, ag gáire is ag glaoḋaċ go sultṁar ceolṁar. Seanóir liat láṁ-maiḋeaċ baġaraċ; cailíní geala na gruaige casta, cnótaċ, rós-croiceannaċ. Na h-Óġánaiġ scópaṁail cróḋa ar taoḃ aistiġ; na cáirḋe páirteaċ béul-oscailte ar taoḃ amuiġ. Gaeḋilg flúirseaċ ann. Ó cliat go cliat an imirt tréun teagaraċ. Buaiḋ fé ḋeire ag mo ṗaróisḋe féin—Muintir na h-árḋa (na Mountaineers a glaotaí orra). Níor rugaḋar le puinn é; aċ bí mo ċroiḋe-se ag preabaḋ le h-átas an domain. Síuḋ aḃaile liom ar ḋeire na cluiċe ag triall ar mo Uncil ċun camán do ġearraḋ ḋom. Agus ġearr sé go cruinn é is é ag feaḋgail go haeraċ. Bí mo ċéaḋ camán gleoite agam! Agus ó'n lá san go dtí seo, ní raḃas aḃḟaḋ amuġa riaṁ ó ċeól agus gleó na gcamán!

'San ḃliain 1884 bí spórt ár sinnsear leagta; aċ ní raiḃ sé caillte. Tóg an G.A.A. é mar ḋo tóġfaḋ duine Críos taṁail crosa, naoṁta, ḃeaḋ leagta sa roilg. Do árḋaiġ arís é ós coṁair an tsaoġal go léir. Tá sé slán buanaċ againn anois, agus beiḋ ċó faḋa is mairḟiḋ Gaeḋil, gan baoġal gan eagla! Mar sgríobas in áit éigin ċeana-féin:
Hurling survives and is indestrubtible, because of its stern, naked grandeur.

"CAIRBRE."

CORK AGAIN

AFTER ten years, Cork are again hurling champions! And dual champions at that! Seniors and minors have gambolled through their 1941 games. Overwhelming margins left no doubt about their superiority. Two beautifully balanced sides, in their youth and prime, have treated spectators to model hurling — speed, science, daring, all were here, and not a cloud in the sky to dim the achievement. Last Sunday was a glamorous day for Leeside hurling — a triumph of perseverance, tenacity and painstaking skill. To the two score players concerned, to the officials from Liam Walsh, Sean McCarthy and Sean Murphy down, to Jim Barry, their buoyant trainer, the congratulations of Corkmen will be given with unanimous, unstinted voice. Fortune's wheel swings, *Bionn an roth ag casadh.* While the ball rolls, the game is fair, says the man at the wheel. You can't keep good men down, and the bad luck of yesteryears was forgotten in last Sunday's beaming Autumn sun!

When the green-drake rises over Lough Derg on a May morning, excited anglers shout "The fly is up, the fly is up." And it was like that in O'Connell Street, Dublin on Saturday night. "Cork are up, Cork are up" was the glad greeting everywhere. What matter if steampower was insufficient to bring the throngs along. Those that came were the thick and thin hurling enthusiasts of Leeside — the best few thousand of them. A sparkling talkative lot of men and maids bubbling over with enthusiasm. They painted the old Liffey town red, in the best sense of that much-abused term. When you asked them what their prospects were, they smiled a knowing smile and answered: "And the minors, too!"

Of course we missed the Sunday trains at King Brian's Bridge — for it was the Kincora King that bivouacked here in 1014 on the evening before Clontarf. And we missed the thousands from the provinces that would in normal times have packed the beautiful grounds over which our battle against the Danes was fought nine hundred years ago. The streams from O'Connell Bridge were thinned, but the spirit was the same — a glad, resurgent spirit which only needs peace to storm the capital next All-Ireland day — already visualised with Cork, Kilkenny and Tipperary dead level at the head of Ireland's hurling list — twelve championships all!

There was quiet confidence behind the Dublin hurlers. They had trained like dutiful men under skilled hands, conscious of the big task ahead. At the back of their minds was the day of 1927 when Cork's powerful champion side of 1926 were overwhelmed. And a great Dublin day five years earlier when the Faughs' selection shocked Midleton's hopes. Not a brilliant team, to be sure, this of 1941, but including seven of the 1938 champions and a lot of eager young colts — four of them born hard by the training grounds of The Phoenix Park. Yes, they would give those brilliant Munstermen a warm game. Even when Ned Wade won the toss, the Tipperary man pointed confidently into the wind and Cork faced the Railway goal.

Dublin opened at a fast pace. Wade and McDonnell were romping through. Allan Lotty held them and swung back. Lynch and Sullivan tested Forde, who cleared safely. Soon Gray, the tall Leix blacksmith, swung a ball that just missed the posts. A huge thrill followed. Big Liam Murphy, of Ballincollig, shook his black locks as he swung the puck-out. The like of it was never seen since Andy Fitz days. The crowd roared as the ball sailed in the breeze and dropped 140 yards away — on the 21 yards' line. John Quirke was on it in a flash. Ted Sullivan cleared the way and Quirk's ash swept the ball to the meshes — two strokes from net to net.

Jim Young next whipped one up and pulled just in time as Gill's hurley crashed on his — a grand ball, well above the bar. Cork four points up and hurling like a machine in tune. Sean Barrett was in his element, and his free was deadly accurate for Cork's second point. Dublin hurled splendidly in the next bout of open play, and Wade put a perfect curl in a ball into the wind which opened Dublin's register.

Barrett's huge shoulders hunched behind a seventy that he drove clean and fair for a point; but in a sparkling burst of Dublin hurling, where McDonnell shone, Thornhill and Lotty cleared only for Harry Gray to hit a typical ball for Dublin's second minor. Ring, the schoolboy, countered with a grand sailing point, but Dublin showed pace and power when McDonnell ranged up their right wing and gave a grand centre which Glynn should have crashed to the net. The Eoghan Ruadh man missed a glorious chance for a goal that would have given Dublin the heart that would make us a real final. Dublin never really recovered from that lost goal, for Cork took the game into both hands. Left and right those master craftsmen hit first-time balls with a delightful freedom. Every man of the backs was rock-like. Barrett and Lynch were playing exhibition hurling around midfield, and Cork's front lines soon had winning flags flying round the Railway goal.

John Quirke whipped a grounder in and Ted from Ballinacurra tapped it safely above the bar. That oak trunk of the O'Sullivan clan, arms and legs like gate-pillars, again tore in from Campbell's sweet-hit ball and crashed Cork's second goal to the net. Sailing along on the crest of the wave, Sean Lynch and Ring drove perfect balls high in the rigging and the half-hour was almost spent when Dublin burst upfield for Charlie Downes to double Dublin's third point home — 2 goals 8 points to 3 points sounded a safe margin, though Dublin were still a force with wind, sun and favoured goal to brighten their hopes.

Ring and Wade exchanged minors, but Cork's decisive score soon came. Cottrell was proving his worth; Phil Farrell was steadiest of Dublin's backs, but O'Sullivan tore his way through from an opening built up by the Buckley brothers. Ted turned the leather goal-wards and John Quirke flashed in to double securely to the net. White and Byrne had promising minors for Dublin and Wade still persevered with a reshuffled side. Mika Brennan next had a session, and he nipped in for two grand Cork scores — above and below.

All honour to Dublin for playing on gallantly to the end. They never ceased to persevere, though outplayed and outmanoeuvred at every vital point. Con Buckley, the Glen Rovers Captain, clinched a keen hour's play with Cork's eleventh point, and the Championship was played and won. Rarely have we watched a more polished display. The new champions are speedy as light. Every man hits with equal freedom from left and right. Their swing has the rhythm of the master artist. Their backs are cool, safe and long hitters. Ring and Young are dapper wingsmen, and if Quirke and Sullivan took the main honours of attacks they had uniform and well applied support from rank to rank. Just one cheer for Sean Barrett of Kinsale. In League, Railway Cup and Championship he has been a modest hero. Last Sunday was his big day, his best match, and his first Celtic Cross medal. *Tu slán a Seáin glegeal!*

Cork Minors are a darling lot of hurlers. No mistaking the fact that they learned their smooth-swinging art in the same Leeside school that has sent out so many champion sides since 1884. Young Condon's fair locks shone in the sun as he drove three 70-yard pucks in quick succession far above the cross-bar. He was symbolic of the side of which little O'Leary on the left wing was the dandy who "got" the crowd, with his wizard little hurley that charmed the ball. Kennefick, son of a great hurler, was another; Kelly, Morrison, Twomey and the Looney lad fairly bewitched the ball. Galway lads put up a sturdy battle, but their hurling was of the rugged, earnest type in contrast with the lightning hits of the young lads from the South. High up in the Hogan Stand I saw big Jim Hurley — seventeen stone of beaming manhood. Not far away were the evergreen pair of Cork sportsmen — Bill Mackesy and Michael Roche. J.J. Walsh's thin face looked happy. Dan Hobbs kept up his eternal humour; but not a smile out of those weighty leaders behind the throne — Liam Walsh and Sean Og Murphy.

We pressmen were rather isolated on the Cusack Stand. Though our view of the game was ideal, we missed the association of the kindred in the Hogan Stand and sideline, so necessary to the scribe. Mr. P.J. O'Keeffe's arrangements were of clock-like regularity. Our only regret is that the disastrous foot-and-mouth disease had kept our old rivals, Kilkenny and Tipperary out of the competition. We shall cross blades with them, please God, again in the glad years ahead. And, I think Cork have assumed only their legitimate place beside the leaders, with twelve titles all!

And since then, Tipperary hurlers — ever a surprise packet, came along in the postponed Munster final and trounced the Champions. Truly is hurling a great and absorbing game!

THURLES 1944

ONE missed the long ranges of petrol-driven cars from the spacious square of Dr. Croke. One missed them on the highroad and was glad of their absence on the byeways. One missed too, the thousands of eager enthusiasts from the cities that flowed out of Thurles Railway Station from the special trains in the days that are gone — days that will come again, and the sooner the better! Yet it was always a gallant and typical Thurles final day. All the brightness and good cheer of the hospitable Cathedral town were there. Hundreds of well-known faces, hero-hurlers of past decades and generations. On the roads from Cork, Limerick and Kilkenny perspiring cyclists were plugging their way in. From the top of a low hill outside Thurles town I saw them coming in happy droves along the straight roads like ants on the move. Big Jim Hurley had cycled all the way from Cork and stayed overnight threshing out hurling history with the famous Leahy family of Boherlahan. Too bad I missed that *seanacaidheacht* on the eve of the final!

And such a final! A final that had a heart-throbbing pulsating finish that took people's breath away, and yet was no final at all; for these sparkling hurlers live to fight another day — July 30th, at the same ideal venue steeped in hurling history. Rural Ireland looked well on the way there and back — a day of soft, fleecy clouds that lent light and shade and colour to the mid-summer hills — a faint sprinkle of rain to lay the dust; the Galtees a study in blues and emeralds rising nobly over the fertile Golden Vein. Grass-lands not so luxuriant as usual; corn and potatoes doing fine; beet and other roots recovering slowly from the drought; hay well saved in fair measure of yield. An air of peace and comfort over all.

Pleasant it was meeting the genial priests, always associated with hurling finals in Thurles: Fr. Hamilton of Clare, Fathers Lee, Fogarty and Meagher of Thurles, Fr. Punch of Limerick; the G.A.A. chiefs led in his Grace, Archbishop Kinnane, of the See of Cashel and Emly — typical athletic son of Tipperary. Many All-Ireland Captains living in the past: Willie Gleeson of Fedamore, Tim Gleeson of Drumbane, Denis Barry Murphy, Pat Collins, Liam Walsh of Cork, Denis Lanigan, Jim Humphries of the great Limerick sides, John Joe Sheehy, the Kerry star; Christy Leehy of Aherlow Glen; Chris Ryan of Mitchelstown; John Rochford of Kilkenny, who is the holder of seven All-Ireland medals; Jim (Hawk) O' Brien of Thurles, Hugh Shelly, James Maher and John Joe Callanan, the peerless forward; Phil Purcell, John Joe Hayes — hurlers champion hurlers all!

The game was beautifully controlled, the pitch a picture and the hurling hearty clean and fair.

I thought the first half somewhat subdued. Good sweet hitting on both sides; close marking, polished movement of swinging ash, fit, well-matched men. We had to wait for the second half for the fireworks, the heavy thud of crashing body to body and splintering ash — winding up in a crescendo of excitement. "Was it the best second half ever?" people asked me after the game. I was silent; I could only smile inwardly; it was good and very good, dramatic and a wondrous sporting finish, fit to take its place among the greatest of out-door sporting spectacles that any land can boast! And memory tracked back to many such finals on this same pitch, perhaps more long-sustained and gripping yet never one that more completely gladdened the hurler's heart. We don't love drawn games, yet here was one that left no doubting Thomases — it was a truly played and glorious finish carrying all the fire and brilliancy of the great Munster hurling finals of the past.

They broke at lightning pace, and Archbishop Kinnane, who threw the ball in, was scarcely on the sideline when Cork raced in and Quirke placed Morrison, a tall bony youth — smacked a grand ball past Walsh — Cork one goal up. Breasting the ball well, Cottrell and Donovan sent Cork away again and John Quirke's eye was dead in — he pulled on a hard ground ball that gave Mickie Walsh no chance at all. Limerick woke up and Tim Ryan hit a lovely ball that reached Mick Mackey. That veteran player trapped it well and doubled carefully to the net for Limerick's opening goal.

Cork forwards again sparkled. Kelly and Ring were moving fast and once more John Quirke's experience told — he dummied fast and pulled hard and low — net. Cork two goals clear and going well. Mulcahy next shone in beating back a Limerick bombardment. John Power was holding John Lynch well. Then young McCarthy, a tall rangy boy, landed a perfect point for Limerick from a free. Clohessy and Stokes raised sailing points but Cork were again two goals clear when Sean Condon pointed a beauty score. Cork 3-1; Limerick 1-3.

Cottrell lifted and slipped through to hit a great point from the 50 line but M. Mackey was back and hit a perfect point from a fast moving ground pass. Cork were again away and a regular storm of men swept in on Walsh before he was bundled into the net — Cork's fourth goal. Stokes was deadly accurate with a free for Limerick but they were seven points behind at half-way — 4-3 to 1-5 and the game looked all over for Cork with the wind, sun and way to aid. Christy Ring and Stokes exchanged minor scores in delightful hurling. Mick Mackey had another, but that speedy Farranferris youth, Kelly, sprinted past and drove home, Cork's fifth goal

— John Lynch's free set the score 19 to 11 — Limerick fighting hard against heavy odds.

Again these green jerseyed boys stormed in on Mulcahy and Thornhill's lines. John Power, Tim Ryan and McCarthy were rising to a great occasion. Power hit a long one — Dick Stokes trapped it and raced clear before letting fly for a smashing goal that set the crowd roaring. Kelly had another lovely point, but Stokes' goal had electrified Limerick. They moved like mowers in a meadow. Mackey was in his element now and when he dodged through and whipped a goal home, hats, coats, umbrellas and all went sky high — Score 21-19. Kelly and Stokes swopped points in a scintillating finish. Clohessy fastened on one and crashed it home for Limerick's lead, and pandemonium outside the lines — 20,000 swaying.

John Mackey set the score 24 — 22 in Limerick's favour. Broken time now. Then came John Quirke's greatest goal of his long career. Ring swung a pass to the old Rockie, Lynch helped to guard him. Quirke dummied twice and then shot. He knew a goal was the only rescue — he hit a beauty dead on the net for a goal and Cork's lead. Dead on time Stokes, cool as cold steel, landed above the bar for the balancing score — 25 all. And they meet again!

A FORTNIGHT LATER

AN HOUR after the drawn game of July 16th, I met John Quirke and Christy Ring. We thrashed out the pros and cons of a startling finish, and I told them of my friendly sporting bet with an old Limerick friend.

"Double it next time," said John Quirke.

"Carbery boy," says fair-haired Christy Ring of the beaming, ruddy face, "Quirky and I won't let you down," and the flashing Glen Rovers' winger shook my hand heartily.

Last Sunday, another glamorous day in Thurles town — same lighthearted, good tempered, 20,000 crowd. Same brisk air in the stately square. There seemed a smile of pride and triumph on the bronze face of Dr. Croke as the glad throngs of young vigorous folk — and old men too! — trooped past for the Gaelic Park over the bridge. Our transport scheme worked out difficult and slow; we were late for the opening scenes of the games which will rank with the classic Munster finals of the past in its stern, naked grandeur; in its hearty, manly spirit where rival surging bloods swung ash with freedom and abandon; where scores were level three times in the hour; where Mick Mackey treated us all to his wizard artistry; where Malone (from the Hill of Fedamore) proved almost the equal of Scanlon himself in the Limerick goal; where Limerick's flag was in the ascendant through 55 pulsating minutes until they were sailing home five points in front with only broken time to play. Cork's desperate final rally, whilst the clock ticked its last fateful minutes — a rally which every man in the field from Mulcahy out seemed to share — a rally which the spearheads (Morrison and Quirke) clinched with balancing scores that sent the comparatively small but virile Cork contingent shouting hoarsely.

Then came as dramatic and brilliant a score as ever Thurles finals have recorded. Christy Ring (of the Glen) still bounding with life and energy, nosed a rolling ball to the "boss" of his hurley, raced through on Cork's right wing and let fly a daisy-clipper — dead on the post. Five stout Limerick backs pulled and parried. That ball's pace deceived one and all. Malone shadowed in, made a despairing effort to arrest its flight, and all but succeeded. Young Kelly (the sheet-lightning boy-sprinter) sped to the ball's aid — 'twas over the line; the great game was lost and won!

John Lynch, playing confidently in his old, new and favourite place, broke away for a long-range point shortly after Mr. Seamus Gardiner had led in Most Rev. Dr. O'Dwyer, Superior General of Maynooth's Mission, an old All-Ireland and Tipperary hurler, to set the boys under way. In a crack Dick Stokes had balanced and McCarthy's score gave Limerick the lead. Cork were quickly downfield, and Morrison pulled hard and low for a ball to the net which gave Malone no chance.

Cork's lead was short-lived. McCarthy and Ryan were breasting the ball well and Mick Mackey was away on one of his specialities — a swerving, dodging solo run — he flashed the ball to his brother John close on the square: a deft tap and the ball was through. Limerick led now and played with abundant confidence.

Hurling on both sides was sweet and true. Sean Condon hit a beauty point, but Limerick were soon surging up and Mick Mackey was again on the job. The Ahane leader was in irresistible mood as he crashed a goal and a point home in effortless fashion — Limerick leading nine points to five and a third of the hour gone.

Alan Lotty (of "Sars") was holding Stokes well, but Cork's tall centre-half was limping badly. That old knee had let him down again. Cork's sideline brain-trust now got busy. Mick Mackey must be held or the day was lost to the triple champions! And so the brain-wave brought a rapid switch — Din Joe Buckley down to mark Limerick's star attacker; Curly Murphy in Lotty's place and big Pat Donovan of the Glen at right-half. Stokes swung a glorious shot for a point but Condon and Lynch were dead on the mark with high drives above the bar leaving Limerick a goal clear after a gallant first half: 2-4 to 1-4.

Malone had brought down many hot shots and continued to play well. At the other net Mulcahy was watchful as a lynx between the branches of a tree. Dick Stokes, from accurate frees, put Limerick five points clear. When Lynch and Cottrell — both hurling well now — opened up Cork fireworks, Malone stopped one from 10 yards out. Ash clashed; strong men pulled hard and fierce — there was a brief flare-up by lusty bloods. 'Twas quelled at once and the great game swung on. Joe Kelly again streaked in from Cork's left wing and pulled hard and true to whip a Cork goal home. Once again the scene changed to the other goal. Mick Kennedy, brought back after several years had been doing right well in front of Malone. He cleared again; Johny Power helped the good work; Limerick were away in a Shannon flood; young Clohessy raced past, and John Mackey made no mistake with a glorious swerve and shot — net — Limerick still five points clear and time running on.

Another wave from the Cork brain-trust. John Quirke who saved the game last time came in to the 40 mark. He had a sweet point in a tick. Cork were now staging a most determined final assault. John Lynch and Con Cottrell were bringing down every ball and feeding their front lines. Power and Cregan swung long balls back. Limerick's big contingent roared in one voice as Mick Mackey got possession — fouled on the way as he netted after the whistle had gone. Dick Stokes missed the free for once. Young, Buckley, the Murphys, Lynch and Cottrell were all moving fast — Morrison on the ball, a lightning swing — net — Cork one point behind and broken time being played.

John Quirke's cool skill again to the aid. A lovely neat swing — ball sails over the bar for the equaliser. Referee looks at his watch — we make it one minute to go — Christy Ring gets the ball; it glues to his hurley as he sprints up the wing like a shadow — away she goes — dead straight, fast and true to the Limerick net for so sensational a win that we are silent until the whistle blows. The 1940 final, when Limerick won the replay, was reversed. Limerick had led for the bulk of the hour and may have had the rough end of the day's fortunes. But there is no mistaking Cork's determined final stand and rousing rally. Christy Ring had prophesied truly — his goal will live in hurling history.

1944 FINAL

CORK hurlers have broken all records! Four All-Ireland Championships in a string and room for more! Fifteen titles to date — three clear of their greatest rivals, Kilkenny and Tipperary. Never before did any county win four All-Ireland Championships in a row; so young are many members of this crack Cork team, and so sturdy their veterans that one keeps saying: "What county will have the honour of lowering the Leeside flag?". That Sunday these fifteen Corkmen were a real champion side. From goal to goal every man played trojan hurling against the wind in the second half at Croke Park.

It was a numbing crushing exhibition of graceful, natural, I might almost say, instinctive hurling. Numbing and crushing to all but those enthusiastic bands of Corkmen with red and white favours, who had made the long journey on Saturday or on the unexpected train Special on Sunday morning. Dublin had made a thorough and efficient preparation. Their training was in skilled hands, and when I saw them wind up their preparation at mid-week they were a fit and confident side. Mr. Jim Barry, the famous Cork trainer, was not disturbed when I met him on Sunday morning. "My lads are good and very good — an obedient, honest lot of boys, who did everything I told them; we'll win all right."

Weather conditions halved the crowd. Thousands of Dubliners, more in hope than in confidence of a Dublin win, contented themselves with their fire-sides and a wireless set. Beyond sodden patches around goal the pitch looked fine; the curtain-raiser match was wisely abandoned to save the sod. Yet when the big game opened, players were slipping about as on a skating rink. The clouds lifted and Croke Park's clinker subsoil responded. So much so that we enjoyed some grand bouts of hurling on a rapidly drying sod.

Dublin won the spin of the coin and decided to face the wind and the Canal goal. So well did Mick Butler and his backs play for a quarter-hour that Cork had not raised a flag, even with a sweeping wind to aid. As the minutes sped and the breeze strengthened some Cork colleens' faces near us in the Cusack Stand looked anxious. Seamus Donegan was playing gallantly in a muddy goal; Jim O'Neill, son of a famous Sarsfield hurler of the past, was holding Joe Kelly safe; Butler, McCormack, White, Flanagan and Egan were playing such solid defensive hurling that Dublin hopes were soaring. When Ned Wade, Terry Leahy and Hassett ranged upfield the crowd roared. Jim Byrne was just wide of the Cork posts from thirty yards out.

Just then Con Cottrell got busy. Playing a gritty, eager game in the close and loose, he drove ball after ball "in around the house"; Dublin backs cleared again and again. Lynch's 70's were going wide of the mark, but he collared one and double-turned swiftly to hit a darling ball off the left — sixty yards out — it travelled all the way above the bar and Cork's procession of scores was under way.

Dublin defence was still very sound, and Donegan saved many shots. So Cork went for minor scores! They came in a steady stream — Cottrell, Lynch (2), Condon (2) and Christy Ring, before Dublin burst past and Terry Leahy, from Michael Hassett drove home a rattling point for Dublin — 0-6 to 0-1 after twenty minutes play — Dublin doing handsomely and Cork just opening their shoulders.

Con Murphy at centre-half, and indeed all Cork's back lines were playing confidently and Dr. Jim Young, in his long association with Cork hurling, was never seen to better purpose. He proved a handful for that fine Midland hurler, Frank White. John Lynch was again on the mark for Cork's number seven. Dublin played back in just wide of Mulcahy's lines, but Terry Leahy, the old Kilkenny star, was dead on the mark from 50 yards out. Mulcahy got his stick to it and tipped it over the bar. Condon's point from a free set the score — Cork 0-8, Dublin 0-2 at half time.

Even then Dublin followers were full of hope. "What was two goals with a wind like that." Cork had a few easy chances and Dublin's camp was still confident. But it was a different Cork side they had to face in the second half. I must confess I was not prepared for such a transformation. Defying wind and weather, this speedy and still youthful side treated the spectators to the most uniform and sustained hurling that sodden pitch has known. It was not that Dublin were so bad — their shuffling round of players was no great success. Cork had clearly made up their minds to win this "Fourth-title-in-a-row."

'Twas then we saw Tom Mulcahy's wizardry in Cork's goal — he was unbeatable. Batt Thornhill was never better; Willie Murphy and Din Joe Buckley hurled a glorious hour. Cork's half-line was a powerful breakwater — Pat Donovan in his true position, Con Murphy also in his best place and Alan Lotty of Sars, were on their toes — a real machine.

Sean Lynch and Con Cottrell hit up the perfect partnership at midfield — Jim Young, Sean Condon and Chris Ring — where was there a more brilliant "forty-line"; then streak-lightning Kelly, Morrison and craftsman Quirke as spearhead. Looking back on their polished exhibitions in their second half hour, despite difficult conditions, I keep wondering whether even our greatest Cork sides were a whole lot better — heavier and more dour under pressure, but hardly more uniform and never faster.

Good as Cork forwards were, it was crack sprinter Joe Kelly that captivated the crowd. His pace, his ball control, his judgment in crossing his deadly low shots, all mark him as a young forward of rare attributes. Shortly after half-time, he raced past and drove a grand ball into the wind. Cottrell placed him, and Young plied balls upwing to the Farranferris student. He used them all. Quirke shifted to the mark now, gave Joe another, and a smashing shot brought Cork's first and decisive goal after 40 minutes' play.

Dublin did recover and hurl gallantly for an exciting ten minutes. Harry Gray sent a 70 sailing and Downes helped it to the net from close range. Mulcahy saved Cork repeatedly. It was Dublin's last grand rally. Cork were soon racing upfield and swinging ash with precision and freedom. They gave a delightful exhibition of their skill with ash and ball. Kelly placed Morrison for No. 10 and another grand run of slim boy Joe ended in a sailing point. He slipped one to Quirke and a deft swing brought the Blackrock veteran's first score of a well played hour. 'Twas all Cork now, and the crowd was leaving the field when streak-lightning Kelly broke through again; he flashed up that left wing like a swallow skimming Gurranebraher. He swerved to centre and shot a further goal and point to wind up a rare hour's play of pace and skill.

TIPP'S 1945 WIN

"When I think of Matt the Thrasher's strength
And Nora Leahy's grace,
I love you Tipperary though
I never saw your face."

Brian O'Higgins

MANY an exile has repeated these words of the Dublin balladist, when far from home. Many an exile born of Tipperary parents far across the sea re-echo the words. And, perhaps through the charm of Kickham's mind and pen, many a man and maid with no connection at all with the wide county of Tipp. have a soft corner in their hearts for its blue mountains and emerald vales not to speak of what Thomas Davis calls — "the matchless men of Tipperary."

All this was running through my mind as I watched that splendid phalanx of Tipperary's six tall backs at Croke Park last Sunday in the 1945 All-Ireland Hurling Final against Kilkenny, led by John Maher — a cool and brilliant leader, we had Devitt, Cornally, Flor Coffey and the wing halves — Murphy and young Purcell. From end to end they stood straight as lances — averaging 5 feet 11 high — wiry, square-turned whippy men ready to do or die. And these Tipperary backs are first-class hurlers, everyone. I have always admired the distinctive swing of Tipperary backs when they meet or whip a ball. They favour ground play, they like it "on the floor," a dying hurling art much to be regretted. Off left and right hand every one of the six named above, can drive a ball with power and accuracy — they can hit the leather an inch outside their toes. And the present lot are as good as Arthur Donnelly, Johny Leahy, Widger Maher, Frank McGrath or Stephen Hackett at their best. Behind them, Jimmy Maher is a goalie, almost as good although not quite so "commanding" as "Skinny" Meara of Toomevara.

Lt. Gouldsboro and Tommy Wall held their own at centre but the surprise to me was the improvement in Tipp's attack. In the Munster games and against Antrim, Tipp's front line was so poor that I did not think they would pull through against such clever hurlers as Kilkenny invariably holds. But the "light behind the throne" shone brilliantly when James Maher and his colleagues, Capt. John Leahy, John Joe Callanan, Joe Loughney, T. Semple (junr.) and Tommy Butler put their wise heads

together. Young Gleeson was a real success as wing; Tommy Doyle and
"Mutt" Ryan made a fast moving and shrewd attack, whilst Anthony
Brennan, Sweeper Ryan and young Coffey, put in quite a creditable lot of
finishing work which brought very few wides. But it was the elfin art of
little Jimmy Maher in goal, and his stately fearless backs in front that
brought a grand All-Ireland to Tipperary, marking successive wins over
such stalwart counties as Waterford, Cork (holders), Limerick and
Kilkenny. Well done Tipp.

Kilkenny showed flashes of all their Leinster brilliancy and recovery.
Yet their backs were wide open as an empty barn door before the corn is
threshed. This was particularly true in the second quarter when Gleeson
(2), Coffey and "Mutt" Ryan flashed in for goals that paved the way to
victory. Kilkenny's half-back line was never happy or confident, and
Walsh, though he saved some good shots in the Noreside goal, was at
fault in that disastrous Kilkenny spell approaching the half-hour — for
they had a brilliant opening when T. Maher (a great collegian winger),
Mulcahy and Langton gave them flying opening points.

'Twas a gallant second half of close sabre work and sword play
between well-matched men. Kilkenny were not yet beaten, and they
treated us to some delightful wristwork. Grace, Kelly and Blanchfield
were holding up every dangerous Tipp. move with skilful ash; Dan
Kennery and Tommy Murphy opened their shoulders and it was only the
straight steel of Tipperary's backs that held those weaving forwards.
Mulcahy came outfield; Walton and Wall exchanged minors with well-hit
cuts. Kilkenny's weaving forwards at last got an opening. T. Maher raced
to centre, swung a deadly ball to the net for Kilkenny's first major. In a
bout of grand weaving hurling, the ball glanced from wing to wing for
Walton to shoot a lightning ball to the net. When Shawny O'Brien
fastened on another and rammed it home for Kilkenny's third goal the
70,000 crowd surged and swayed and roared.

Then it was that Tipperary's grand backs girded their loins in deadly
earnest and set about stemming the tide of these wasp-like and elusive
Kilkenny forwards, now busy as bees round a hive. Cool and straight and
strong was Tipp's tackling and straight, honest hitting. Once again they
took control. Brennan pointed and when "Mutt" Ryan whipped a perfect
ball to the square the tall Clonoulty spearpoint, though well covered by
Kelly of Mooncoin, turned the ball to the net. That was the clinching
score. Kilkenny staged a grand finish, but Cornally, Devitt, Purcell, (who
put in a great hour's work in mastering Gargan) and the two Mahers were
rock-like in defence. Tipperary had weathered the last autumn gale and
were worthy winners of a clean, hard-fought and honest game against
gallant losers. A long time ago I wrote this sentence: "Hurling lives on

and is indestructible because of its stern, naked grandeur" — as true in 1945 as when I first penned it in early manhood.

A thousand congratulations to Mr. P. O'Keeffe, G.A.A. Secretary and General Manager, and his efficient staff. I have no hesitation in saying that last Sunday's programme was the greatest triumph of organisation in the whole progressive history of our national games. The perfection of detail and masterly production of a brilliant national spectacle, was the talk of every spectator with an open mind. Here we had all the dignatories of State and Church in active participation. We had capable stewarding and courtesy; we had a magnificently impressive display by Artane boys; national music and ceremony alike touching and inspiring. We had bright minor hurling by Dublin Christian Brothers' boys ending in a late and unavailing rally by the unbeaten Tipperary striplings, and we had all the evidence of a reawakened Nation scenting and thriving in its recently won though partial freedom. It was a great national and heartening day in Dublin's capital, that had a gay cavalier air, with clean, wide streets, rattling outside cars, badges galore, wit and humour, flowers on the lamp-posts, and joy in the hearts of our people that God has brought us safely through a searching period in world history.

One of seventy thousand spectators at Croke Park last Sunday was a keen-eyed wiry man in the high sixties. He doesn't look his age, as sound a hurling critic as ever was — John Rochford, of Three Castles, Co. Kilkenny who holds the honour of playing a masterly full-back for his county, and took a good man's part in winning seven All-Ireland Championships within nine years! It is a record never surpassed, nor likely in our time.

He is one of four select men — all from Kilkenny, who hold seven All-Ireland medals — four only amidst hundreds of thousands of crack hurlers — John Rochford of Three Castles; Sim Walton of Tullaroan; Drug Walsh and Dick Doyle of Mooncoin.

John Rochford, here of the 1904, '05, '07, '09, '11, '12 and '13 finals is as good-humoured and merry-eyed as ever, and we love to "rise" him. "You met bad forwards, Jack in your time; easy for you to hurl well," a wag ventured.

"No boy," said Jack; "I met the best of forwards — only I made them look bad!"

As last Sunday's great game developed at Croke Park, I thought of the old Three Castle's man beneath me in the sunshine dreaming of his past triumphs, to be sure. Kilkenny forwards were good; it was Tipperary's high-grade backs, cool and resolute and strong, confident, accurate, ambidextrous hurlers, that made these stocky Noreside speed merchants look moderate betimes. Not all the time of course; for we saw the most brilliant diagonal pattern-weaving of the hour when Kilkenny staged the rousing rally in the second half; when college boy Tim Maher of St. Kieran's and soon of Maynooth, Shawney O'Brien and young Walton (name to conjure with in Kilkenny hurling) crashed home three lightning goals to get within four points of the leaders as Black and Amber followers in the packed stands, terraces and sidelines were losing heart at the end of the third quarter. The crowds cheered and swayed in their excitement.

Then the fur flew. Splintering ash crashed round the Tipperary goalie, Jimmy Maher, who had radar eyes on his wee hurley; "five feet nothing" of the best, coolest and most fearless stuff that ever crouched, eagle-eyed, between hurling posts. Jer. Cornally crowded round; Devitt, Flor Coffey and Captain Maher swarmed in to help. Full-blooded pulling of ash fair and free. Fit bodies crashed together with resounding thud; Kilkenny "black and amber" boys like wasps at a hive; heads went in where hurls should be. And what Thomas Davis called "the matchless men of Tipperary" weathered the autumn storm that battered down, but did not destroy, their plenteous harvest, won with so much pains and care in Munster and Leinster fields last spring and summer.

Soon the sweeping ashen scythes of these tall, wiry Tipperary backs swept the field. The forwards tore in with right good will. "Mutt" Ryan (no mutt with ash in his hand), Tommy Doyle, the boxer; Gleeson and six-foot-one spearhead "Antsy" Brennan of Clonoulty, were "in about" Kilkenny's house for a last vital and decisive Tipperary goal. Tipperary 5-6, Kilkenny 3-6.

It was immense. No wonder Lord Wellington, who once had a hurling team of his own Meath men among his tenants, C.B. Fry, Cambridge champion all-round athlete, and many a visitor described hurling as the best training for hand-to-hand fighting between armies when war was more "human" than it is today, when hurling-trained Irishmen made their name under foreign suns as the greatest soldiers in the world.

Hurling and Croke Park have changed out of all knowledge. Though still fast and fierce enough to please that war lust which appears to be innate in all humans, in hurling the G.A.A. have evolved a fine, manly, open-air spectacle, clean, sportsmanlike and honest. Last Sunday's programme was particularly fine; the young Dublin schoolboys, trained by the Christian Brothers at Marino and elsewhere, crashed the unbeaten Munster minor champions from Tipperary. The huge crowds were well and skilfully handled; Church and State were represented in the opening features and the Artane boys, with their easy rhythm and living script won all hearts. Their Young Ireland feature should have been photographed from the air.

Very different from the old days of my youth, when Croke Park was a rough dump, without stands or sidelines. I recall one day — a day of dark November fog and drizzle with a dun red leather ball, battered and sodden. Let the full-back tell the story:

"The fog was terrible, with mist and rain. We were winning easily and only an occasional ball came to me out of the mist. Then I saw it soaring in; I jumped up and caught with my left hand, a great catch; then I let fly ash. I hit, and the next thing I was covered with feathers — I'd caught a Croke Park pigeon."

They say that Skinny O'Meara, of Toomevara, Tipperary's greatest goalie, trained in the summer time standing in an open barn-door and stopping swallows. Jimmy Maher, of Tipperary, last Sunday could catch swallows and maybe the old story is right. But where would you leave the Clareman in last Sunday evening's (or night's) yarns.

"You know a goal is three points, P.D." he said to me, "and no-one should know better. Well I was playing centre forward for Feakle against O'Callaghan's Mills in the county final." They never met in the county final, but that doesn't matter. I sang dumb as the old-timer yarned on.

"Well P.D., we were three points behind in the last minute and I had a 'drink for the house' on the match down at Healy's of Bodyke. The goal-bar was a sharp spur of a tree that I had helped to cut that morning; it had a sharp edge. The ball was bad and I got it into my left hand. I took careful aim at the edge of the cross bar and let fly. The ball hit the edge and split in two — one half went in for a goal and the other went over for a point. He stood the drinks."

These American and Canadian officers in uniform beside me were captivated last Sunday.

"Nearest thing to ice-hockey I ever saw," says the Canadian.

"Faster than American football," says the rather meek and silent American. An English Army officer in mufti, speaking fourteen to the dozen (contrast in tradition of the respective races), wore Tipperary colours and roared hell for leather in an Oxford accent, when Antsy Brennan sped the final goal.

It was a good-humoured and buoyant crowd who smoothed away in quiet profusion. There was much good-humoured crushing and party-cries, but all went merry as a marriage bell. Dublin hacks did a roaring trade.

Tipperary's steel-like backs, resilient as whalebone sprung back to position from every assault. The Tipperary barber, operating with an equally keen blade last Saturday morning in a bye-street in Dublin, was not so cocksure, or was he!

"Who'll win tomorrow's match," he asked a client in the chair, who was half-shaved.

"Kilkenny, of course," said the poor man, with a roguish eye.

"Wouldn't you give Tipperary a chance?" says the blade swinger.

"No more chance than a snowball in h__ll," said the man in the chair.

"You wouldn't, so you wouldn't, put up your chin till I shave your neck; you wouldn't give Tipperary a chance; of course you wouldn't."

He pulled three strokes dead close to the chin with waving blade.

"I was only joking," says the shaking customer.

The jarvey rushed the American officer, just arrived, and his friend from Croke Park to the Pillar.

"How much?" says the officer.

"A crown, Sir."

"How much is a crown?" says the officer as he produced a fistful of silver.

"Oh, only seven shillings, sur."

FINAL AT CORK

THERE IS a certain distinction about Cork City, whatever the road of the wanderer's approach. Its surrounding hills and wooded terraces, with fine houses peeping between the trees; its graceful placid river, its open swinging central thoroughfare of tall, stately shops, and Patrick Street's unique bend, which adds to its charm with some of the whimsical mysticism of Cork's lilting accent. Cork City looks well-kept, prosperous and cheerful. Last week's soft heavy rain, so welcome after a long drought seemed to freshen up everything. The people of Cork, so much a part of its distinct personality, appeared to me more buoyant and confident than ever.

And Cork City again carried itself proudly on Monday morning after the smooth conclusion within its liberties of exciting Munster Hurling Championships. There had been much just criticism of recent unwelcome "incidents" in Gaelic Championships both in Leinster and Munster, where excited spectators and highly-strung players had overstepped the bounds of sportsmanship and discipline.

Cork City and Munster Council officials knew that they were custodians of a trust at the most critical time. Let it be written forthwith that they achieved a wonderful triumph of organisation. Press critics are often blamed for being over-severe on occasion but such criticism gives pain to the writer, as much pain as the writing-up of a well-controlled sporting programme gives pleasure. The weather too, smiled through its tears and favoured the pitch at Cork Athletic Grounds, where much banking had been done. I learn that a depth of a further fifty yards has been allowed to the field trustees for terraces and stands. Recent thorough draining had served the pitch well and the week's soft rains had induced a rich growth of clover, giving an essential lift to the sod. Indeed, the grass had such a mushroom growth overnight that it was the smallest shade holding on the pace of the ball.

Mr. Con Murphy, Cork's All-Ireland full back, was the ideal man to select as referee. His name for rigid and quick ruling played its part. Indeed, so severe was he on the slightest infringements that players seemed at times to hold themselves on a tight rein. Yet, for all, though I did not envy the job of the Herculean man (an All-Ireland hurler of great Cork hurling) who had control of the crowd from 10.30 a.m. onwards — a crowd clamouring from 11.30 on to get a place on the all-too-insufficient stand, where four thousand were struggling to occupy four hundred places. I learn that new stands are planned in the immediate future.

Clare minors put up a grand challenge to Tipperary's all-conquering boys. Indeed, these past and present pupils of St. Flannan's College, and youths from the outposts of Clare, fairly and squarely confined the game to Tipperary territory for the better part of the hour. But that indefinable something, known to hurlers as "Tipperary steel" prevailed near the end, and in an exhilarating finish, the blue-and-gold prevailed over the gold-and-blue by the narrowest of margins — 5-6 to 5-5.

Throughout a fast, open and beautifully clean first half-hour of senior hurling, Limerick gave a most attractive exhibition, and more than deserved their 4 point lead. Flor Coffey looked a big loss to Tipperary as they filed in but there was a compensating absentee on the Limerick side, where Creamer was called on to fill Bill Collopy's place. After Tipperary's lightning opening — two points in two minutes — Limerick showed fine dash and ball control. Dr. Dick Stokes levelled up from frees and the well-set crowd of thirty thousand, comfortably placed, were at once enthused with some skilful, cut-thrust-and-parry hurling.

Hurling veteran Jackie Power, of Ahane, made a Limerick opening after Kennedy and T. Ryan doubled Tipp's score. Mulcahy sent well in, and Maher trapped the ball skilfully to drive to the net for a grand Limerick goal.

Limerick, at this stage, were hurling with confidence, speed and precision. They outsped Tipperary, for whom Kennedy's superb markmanship from placed balls swung over the crossbar from all distances and angles. During the hour, the tall, lathy North Tipperary man landed nine points from frees and one from play. That he played a mighty part in Tipperary's win is far from exaggeration.

The Stokes brothers, Martin, Sadlier, the Cregans, Herberts, Power and Creamer (in goal) shone in a fine first half, where Limerick looked the buoyant side. Indeed, Tipperary in the opening session, appeared not to have fully recovered from their gruelling marathon contests with Cork's grim and resolute fifteen. As Captain John Leahy said, "Though we have the hay saved and Cork bate, if 'twas aisy to save the hay it was not aisy to bate Cork. Ye gave us enough of it," added Johny to me, as if he was ever so much surprised, in Tipperary humour.

But back to the gripping game, now so heartily being enjoyed by all, where genuine Gaelic sportsmanship and mutual respect of players for each other, and the game they play, had made us forget recent spasmodic outbursts which had threatened to smear our finely burnished Gaelic shield, wrought by long and skilfully executed workmanship from crude foundations.

Jackie Power, thundering man, tore in his 13½ stone of dynamic energy and crashed a beauty ball to the Tipperary net. Limerick 2-3 to 0-5 at the quarter hour. Kennedy's sailing and fruitful frees balanced points from Power and the Stokes brothers. Kennedy, Stokes, Boland and Ryan kept up a bewildering wealth of alternate points to the end of a glorious half-hour of honest hurling. Score: Limerick 2-8 (14 points); Tipperary 10 points.

The second half was not quite so uniform or fruitful of charming, flashing hurling. Tipperary set themselves grimly to their task, giving not a shade away. Midfield work by both pairs was hesitant at times under falling balls, but here Kenny rather dominated the Limerick City stylist, Paddy Fitzgerald, and Shanahan's weight was telling. My most vivid impression of this period was the dour, stolid, grim defence of the Limerick backs, whose set faces seem to say "This is our citadel and we sell our charge dearly." Bedad! they stood like Trojans and weathered the storm of flashing hurleys, and fit, eager, relentless attackers again and again. Reddan, in Tipperary's goal, showed a cool ball control that was a delight to watch, and to my mind, shared honours with Jimmy Kennedy in a great triumph. Yet, somehow, I thought Limerick a shade unlucky. They lacked their early sparkle, and Tipperary's hurleys were sweeping the field like scythe-blades of old. Dr. Stokes who had hurled brilliantly, failed on two vital frees, whilst Kennedy's eagle eye never erred. After further exchange of points, Jackie Power came outfield, and secured possession. In a storming, swerving run, he bore his mighty way through to within close range, when he crashed the ball to the net. The referee deemed he had over-run and disallowed the score.

Even then Limerick still battled on. Alternate points decided nothing. Limerick tore in time and again. Reddan held a charmed goal, and stopped one shot at bullet pace. Dick Stokes had a free on the "21" mark and shot low for the balancing goal, but Tipperary's backs hurled heroically. Tom Ryan, a good "Tipp" find, finished the hour with a flying point. Tipp's steel had won again!

HURLING FINAL 1946

CORK hurlers, returning this year to the limelight after four years' brilliant session and one year of reaction and rest, played with much of their old commanding skill at Croke Park last Sunday. This — their tenth meeting with Killkenny in All-Ireland finals (they have now won five each) gave Cork a wide margin of titles at the head of the hurling list — sixteen wins against thirteen for Tipperary and twelve for Kilkenny.

The 1946 final, patchy at times, gave us many thrilling passages, with rousing clashes of ash around either goal. But it is to the forwards on either side that "the greater praise belongs." Those goals of Ring, the Riordans, Connie Murphy (Bride Rovers), and Joe Kelly were all high-grade. Christy Ring, the Cork skipper, excelled himself — his tireless elusiveness, his artistry, his bright good humour, his rapid, unselfish passes to a pal well placed — all make the Glen Rovers man an ideal leader, of whom I have often written in praise. That solo goal of his near the end of the first half, following hot on Jerry Riordan's smashing "netter" will live long in hurling memory, for it inspired his men and sent them to the dressing tent at half-time with bubbling confidence.

'Twas at the thirtieth minute of actual play, Paddy Donovan was struggling strongly with Reidy on the Cork right-half backline and Christy Ring, ever watching for a chance, sailed down to the halfway line to pick up Donovan's clearance. He had the ball on his hurley in a flash and raced with it at sprinter's pace. As he dodged past man after man without losing speed, he kept the leather in perfect control. The huge crowd were roaring now. Coming to Mulcahy, he swerved, cut on inside Walsh and reaching the twenty-one yards line, drove a smashing shot shoulder-high to the net corner! It proved the key score to the Championship golden gate.

A limited number of special trains brought thousands of enthusiasts along. Ulster, disheartened for the moment by recent disappointments, was not as strongly represented as usual. All the other provinces were here in pre-war numbers, the use of private and hired cars streamed in to the heart of the city — every parking ground was black with cars over the weekend. Croke Park arrangements nearing perfection every year, were at their best. Mr. P.J. O'Keeffe was on his rounds of inspection from 10 a.m. on. Stewarding was so efficient that the 65,000 came and left in easy comfort aided by good Garda control of traffic.

I was on my feet on the Hogan Stand by noon, enjoying the happy gathering of the clans that streamed in. Banners of black-and-amber contrasted well with Cork's red-white — a great hurling colour to help rapid passes to a colleague, I thought. Then Artane's band took the field centre and kept us in good cheer. I put my glasses on the Cusack Stand, filling slowly — 'twas packed before the senior game opened. Sidelines were filled to capacity, and gates closed at 2.30 p.m. Despite broken weather, the streams of people flowed on steadily. Earlier, on the Hogan Stand were P. O'Sullivan and party of Cork City. Next came Michael Moore, Kilkenny's Treasurer. Both reported a clean bill of health. Mr. Bob O'Keeffe, retired President of the G.A.A., and one of its greatest administrators, next filed in — Bob, champion hurler, is now farming in Leix, after forty-five years of teaching. Mr. Frank McGrath, of Nenagh, and party were in my section. Soon Mr. Jim Hurley and party trooped in, and the usual cavalcade of Cork City boys — led by Mr. Tom Barry, just back from the U.S.A., Mr. Roche, W. Mackesy, Ned and John Buckley — Dan Hobbs not long behind. Below us on the sideline was sixty-eight years old Jack Rochford, of Kilkenny, holder of seven All-Ireland hurling medals. Soon the crowd was so dense with Lowry Meagher edging his way through the queue, that you could see nobody in particular until the dignitaries of Church and State took up their reserved seats.

Two well-known visitors who had flown over recently from the U.S.A. — Mr. Pat Cahill and party from Holy Cross, Tipperary and Chicago; Mr. Jim Breslane of Duhallow and Manhattan — came up to see me — both having seen every possible game since they came across, were confident that Cork would win after Thurles and Birr. Kilkenny men had a different opinion. Paddy Phelan, Michael Kenny of Comer; Dan O'Connell, Jimmy O'Connell; Fr. R. Carroll of Mooncoin and West Cork; his brother, Tommy O'Carroll, the old All-Ireland Captain — all thought that Kilkenny would win, and so we waited patiently for "the big hour" in Ireland's sporting calendar, set in all its ancient splendour. Croke Park's velvet, well-cared pitch, is probably the best in the world — it seemed to smile in defiance of the rain and retained its native firmness through three hard hours, from 1.45 to 4.45 p.m.

Strange to relate, yet good to relate for the sake of the future of hurling that the minor final between Dublin and Tipperary afforded far the greater thrills, though not of quite the same individual feats of brilliancy. Dublin's newly won school of native hurling promises even now to turn out from the Christian Brothers and Primary National Schools of Dublin City senior All-Ireland champions one day, and that not too far afield. Last year they shocked a powerful Tipperary side. This year Tipperary took the final more seriously.

They had to hurl "hip to hip." Hard pulling of senior tensity marked the whole exciting hour. Donnelly and Fingleton, for Dublin; Kenny,

Shanahan and McGrath for Tipperary, shone in a score for score game. When Tipperary boys, in blue-and-gold, rallied and led at the fifty-ninth minute it, it looked as if the minor final would go to Tipperary. Then from beneath the Cusack Stand the tall masterly St. Vincent Schools boy drove a powerful ball to the Tipperary net where O'Brien held a good goal though outshone perhaps by Sutton, the Dublin genius, guarding his net like a young Cuchullan.

My own impression (and it may be wrong) is that Dublin's forward charged O'Brien before the ball reached him. After deep consultation with the goal umpires, the referee awarded the goal and Dublin minors retained the title they won last year.

The Senior game opened on a quieter note. The sun shone brightly on the Tricolour over "Hill 16" and the tall apex of the Cusack Stand. Cork and Kilkenny seniors had rousing cheers and hectic waving of flags, banners and favours as they appeared. The Orphan Boys played martial music and then Peader Kearney's 1916 song, as only they and the 69th Regiment of New York can play it, giving a certain stately dignity to an air of moderate attributes that is retained because of history as a rallying song of the early Volunteers.

Mr. Dan O'Rourke, the new G.A.A. President, who helped to build the Association in Roscommon, himself an inter-county footballer of power and weight threw in the ball. Cork backed the Railway Wall, both sides saluted the Tricolour, and the game was under way. I will only deal with significant incidents in a game described at length already.

Kilkenny opened like a winning side — all on their toes. Walton, in the third minute, shot from the left corner and Kilkenny had first blood — one point. Both goals were visited in speedy succession. Backs stood up well. At the tenth minute Langton pointed a free from thirty yards. Jim Young, hurling well, was holding Gargan at bay and drove long "seventies" just wide of the posts. Then Christy Ring lobbed a free safe. Cork's next free was on the halfway line. Billie Murphy, who hurled his best match for two years and never gave Sean O'Brien an opening, lifted and hit a perfect ball into the wind. It sailed far over the posts for the equaliser — as good a free from midfield as I have seen since Bob-Mockler's days.

Langton, always an opportunist, landed three points for Kilkenny, and S. O'Brien one — score: Kilkenny 0-5; Cork 0-2; before Christy Ring, now finding his range, pointed a free. Ring was again in the story. He placed Mossy Riordan, who crossed sharp to brother Jerry, and a great bound ball beat Donegan to the net — Cork were one point in front, Then, in broken time, Ring "ran rings" round Kilkenny's defenders before shooting a miracle goal. Half-time: Cork 2-3; Kilkenny 5.

A point by Ring and a fine slashing goal by Mossy Riordan set Cork in the ascendant. Out of the clouds, Terry Leahy took a ball and the clever Urlingford-Faughs man crashed it into the net. In a flash, C. Murphy, of Bride Rovers, balanced with a deadly shot, but Leahy was back to hit another bullet of a ball for a green flag. Langton and Walton gathered rapid points. Kilkenny's blood was up and the score read: Cork 19; Kilkenny 17 — the huge crowd roaring encouragement from every angle.

Then came a rapid exchange of short and sharp goals — C. Murphy (Cork), P. O'Brien (Kilkenny). Cork still had a lot in reserve. Their midfield — Lynch and Cottrell — took control; the half-line where Alan Lotty shone through the hour, was firm — Donovan and Young held through a hard hour. "Din Joe" Buckley was game as a pebble, and Tom Mulcahy cool as ever under pressure.

Cork's tall young forwards would not be denied, with such a man as Christy Ring to feed them. Mossy Riordan goaled, Ring pointed, and Cork were all over Kilkenny's staggering backline when sprint champion, Joe Kelly, though well controlled by that stout Kilkenny City back, Paddy Grace, finished the story with a goal of lightning pace. Cork had won well, and scenes of excitement as Christy Ring was "chaired" reminded us of old-time Gaelic festival glamour at Tailteann, Tara and Loch Gorman. All finished in great good humour.

THRILLING 1947 FINAL

SUCH a packing of vivid incident into ten lurid minutes was rarely seen at any sporting venue. Last Sunday's grand game, which marked Kilkenny's fifth "one-point" final will be numbered amongst the great ones for that ten minutes alone.

For up to the fiftieth minute, it was just a good, tense hard game, with very little to rouse the pulses or open the lungs of loud-voiced followers, who lend such sound-colour to our big finals. There was far too much loose and ill-timed shooting by Cork's forwards and though Kilkenny backs had tightened and strengthened their weak links, they were far from comparing in brilliancy or stroke-range with their defenders of the past.

The brightest patches of play came from Cork's grand half-line — Paddy Donovan, Alan Lotty, Jim Young — and from those rippling Kilkenny forwards, who darted at the ball like arrows from the archer's bow, and at the slightest opening showed perfect ball-control in the placing of their shots. Con Murphy, Cork's full-back, made a good job of the problem of keeping young Cahill off the ball. The other Kilkenny five — Leahy, Langton, Walton, Reidy and Downey in that order — were up to the highest standard of Kilkenny attacking forwards. All were fast off their mark, of terrier-like tenacity and full of that zest for the ball which is so necessary to win championships in any code.

Somehow or other I think Cork's long train of successive finals had taken the edge off this essential zest for possession. They were cool and polished as usual. From Tom Mulcahy out, I cannot find much fault with their backs, just slowing down a bit, and often half-a-yard behind in the race to the ball. Yet, their inner skill and experience kept their goal lines clear. Jack Lynch was livelier than he had been for some time, and his physique and brains made all the difference when he went up to the forty-mark, where he helped to frame one of those dramatic goals that roused the sixty-two thousand crowd to frenzy. Sean Condon was the best of the others. Connie Murphy, Christy Ring, the O'Riordans and Joe Kelly were far from impressive for threequarters of the hour. They shot for goals against deadly ground block-hurlers such as Grace, Hayden, Donegan and Marnell. Seven wides in the first-half were all the outcome of loose hitting. Meanwhile Langton and Co. never put a ball astray. Kilkenny sought their golden road to victory by the clean avenue of points and found it a steadily progressive one. The Cork forwards — Kelly and Gerry

O'Riordan in particular — shot at Donegan, whose wizardry was dazzling, and found the non-spectacular Grace and Hayden stone-wall defenders.

Hats off to those lion-hearted Kilkenny men, who refused to be beaten when, twice near the end, Cork's dramatic late goals seemed to rob them of victory. They came back like an alley-cracker off a cement wall, laid in granite, and recovered with flashing, sparkling points, which robbed a gallantly battling Cork side of their seventeenth title, as referee Phil Purcell, of Tipperary fame, was glancing repeatedly at his wristlet watch for full time. Had he been less conscientious, Phil could have made a draw of it twice by calling it a day. But I am glad he played the full six-and-a-half minutes of broken time, for on the run of the hour, these scintillating Noreside hurlers of the sabre-like, sharp swings of ash thoroughly deserved their thundering, if slender, victory, which sent their followers wild. As Lory Meagher and Dick Grace said "It takes the two teams to make a final."

Rain fell heavily all morning from the September dawn to Masstime — when the clouds broke over the hills and the blue appeared. Such a procession of cars of all manner of shapes and sizes, of youth and old-age pensioners, such discrepancy never was seen in the five main avenues concentrating on Dublin from the four shores of Erin. The trains brought ten thousand. The bus strike cost the G.A.A. coffers a cool thousand pounds. Dublin suburban and outlying thousands stayed at home to listen in. The morning rain only served to give that lovely spring to Croke Park's verdant turf and that lift to the ball which true-born hurlers glory in. Artane Boy's Band kept the waiting thousands in good humour. Sidelines were packed by 12.30 p.m. When the senior game started, the stands and terraces were fully peopled by expectant throngs.

We had Dr. Kinnane, of Cashel, successor to Dr. Croke of Thurles and Mallow, to throw in the ball. He had seen his stalwart Tipperary minors play a sweeping hour, and beat a rather hesitant Galway side to the overwhelming crescendo of eight clear goals. Stewarding arrangements were good, though the queue system before the main gates broke down, and there was much confusion and congestion with anxious crowds who had come long distances by train and car.

Kilkenny broke away like the live-wire bundles of concentrated energy they were. In Walsh's absence, through injury, Kilkenny selectors made three wise changes in their line-out. Young Marnell came back to W. Walsh's corner, Mulcahy found his best position in Marnell's place at left-half and Heffernan came on again to partner the long-hitting Kilkenny Captain, Dan Kennedy at centre-field. Prendergast hit a strong, firm grounder to Tom Walton's range and the Tullaroan man, name to conjure with, promptly trapped and his polished swing pointed for Kilkenny inside thirty seconds from the breakaway. Ring dazzled through from the puck out, Lotty wided a "seventy" but collared the return, and placed speed merchant Joe Kelly for the equaliser.

Kilkenny forwards are ready and skilful; Langton, well-held by Pat Donovan flashed to centre in ten minutes of ranging movements, sent across three of his typical points. Mulcahy hit a seventy all the way, a grand ball, and Kilkenny seemed sailing to victory on the ready brilliance of their 40 yards line. But Cork were not duplicate hurling champions without reason. Long sweeping drives sent them upfield. Sean Condon had two grand points. Downey and Terry Leahy raised white flags with perfectly hit drives, well above Tom Mulcahy's reach. Cork hurled back. They stormed in on Donegan's goal. He saved point blank shots from Gerry Riordan and Kelly. Hayden was a stone wall; Grace and Marshall flanked him well. Condon shot a 21 yards free for a goal instead of taking his certain point — an error of judgment for which Cork paid dearly when the stirring hour was out.

Changing their tactics as the minutes sped, Cork went for points. Lynch and Condon got a brace to narrow the gap. Prendergast had his instructions to keep Christy Ring in check, and too well he did it, sticking to the Glensman like a limpet to a rock. Jimmy Kelly seemed too crafty for Connie Murphy and Kilkenny turned over with wind and sun to aid them and a useful lead of 7 points to 5.

Then Big Jim Hurley said wisely — "Cork will play as well against the wind as with it." Cork, hitting long and low, tore into wind and sun. Only Donegan's brilliancy in Kilkenny's goal foiled them, but Condon's point narrowed the gap to a minimum.

Then we enjoyed some terrific clashes around Kilkenny's goal area, which was so securely held. Jimmy Kelly broke away. Reidy flashed up the wing; Terry Leahy trapped his centre, a graceful swing over the bar restored Kilkenny's 2 points lead, 8 - 6. Cork were now playing strongly. Donegan saved another shot; Kilkenny were forced to drive to the sideline. Christy Ring had swopped with Condon; Lynch soon exchanged positions with Cork's captain and the switch paid rich dividends. Christy Ring cut in from the sideline and the ball sailed above Donegan's hurley for a point. Jimmy Kelly countered with a point for Kilkenny all the way.

Drama succeeded. Cork's best hurling was roused. Jim Young put a sideline cut to Con Murphy, who doubled. Cork's tall forwards stormed in and Mossie Riordan tore through for a goal and the first-time lead. Pandemonium reigned. The huge crowds swayed with excitement. Back came Kilkenny's rubber ball men. The game bubbled up and sparkled like a fountain. Walton balanced; Terry Leahy, now at his glorious best, crashed two points home. Kilkenny's immense following were roaring and rattling and waving. Hats waltzed in the air from the top of Hill 16.

Cork were undaunted. Up they flashed; Connie Murphy's drive to the square was timely and accurate; flyer Joe Kelly was on it, and he flicked the ball to the net as his forwards crowded in. Lost time was being played. Then came Terry Leahy's great hour (or minute). Coolly he took a free from 30 yards and split the crossbar — inches above its centre. A draw! Phil Purcell, glancing at his watch. Cork tear up for the last time. Grace clears. Leahy traps it and shoots a point with rifle accuracy for Kilkenny's greatest triumph!

THE 1949 FINALS

I THINK that it was a thunder-shower battering on my window-pane that brought me half awake on Monday morning. Weary from a long and rather disappointing five hours sitting at Croke Park and the hurling finals I had slept for six hours solid — not bad for an old wayfarer! The shower ceased, and then, faintly over the dusky September dawn came sounds of a convent bell on the stroke of five.

This little bell is very musical and only reaches my ear when the wind is at a certain point west of south. It is, I think, the bell of the Poor Clares of Donnybrook calling the Sisters to prayers. Suddenly it gathered strength, as if the freshening dawn wind swept it to me. I was now three-quarters awake and this convent bell struck what seemed an unusually glad note. It is not a swinging bell, but an outlaid fixture, hit by a gong (by one of the devout lay sisters, I presume). With Tipperary cheers still ringing in my awakening ears, the bell gladly said: "Tipp. Tipp. Tipp." in three chords and then, a long, rapid sequence — "Up Tipp., Up Tipp., Up Tipp!" My imagination hinted that the bell operator was a Tipperary woman who had been listening in to the Croke Park broadcast the previous evening! When the joyous little bell died away in the fitful breeze a blackbird broke covert in the lightening dusk and his merry call said, in a deep, low voice, full of gladness: "Up Tipp., Up Tipp." Soon I was fully awake as the early morning milk-cars trotted in from the farms beyond; the lorry laden with milk bottles rattled cheerily when the Angelus bells from the churches, designed for sleepy ears, greeted the dim, cloud-rimmed sun as I pulled the curtain aside.

Truly last Sunday was a great day for Tipperary and they celebrated it right royally in town and country. They had won the coveted senior and minor All-Ireland finals in the same afternoon.

Dublin City was thronged with "Final" enthusiasts from Saturday afternoon on; Munster and Ulster accents were more in evidence in the crowded thoroughfares converging on O'Connell Street's gracious width and splendid length. The Leinster sporting populace, nearer at hand awaited the morning trains. We had a real All-Ireland atmosphere about the Irish Capital, brisk and kindly, and the Church Masses over-flowed to the roadways.

Soon the drift of people tended towards Croke Park in strengthening streams of traffic; but so efficient were the Central Council G.A.A. arrangements that there was no discomfort and little crowding through the whole afternoon. A huge attendance, approaching 70,000 was handled very capably and, had the senior hurling final proved up to expectations, it would be my pleasure to record a memorable evening's sport. The senior game, however, was one of the poorest finals of many years; the Laoighis team after a very promising opening, failed inexplicably in the second half to reproduce the sparkling form which won them much praise throughout the 1949 Hurling Championship season. Nor were Tipperary without blemish, there was far too much mistiming and mishitting for class hurlers.

Yet when Sean Kenny and Pat Shanahan — a resolute and powerful pair of mid-fielders — got the measure of Styles and Bohane at the end of the first quarter, they proceeded to give a splendid service to Tipperary's quicksilver forwards, who, though not without weak links, finished the hour with real Tipperary fire.

Tommy Doyle, the Thurles pocket Hercules, played masterly hurling throughout and well earned his third All-Ireland medal, for he had figured prominently on the 1937 and 1945 winning sides. Whether at wing half early on, or centre after Flor Coffey retired injured, Tommy Doyle gave a delightful exhibition of clean, crisp striking, always showing precision, speed and judgment. He was well flanked by Pat Stakelum, the Holycross Captain, and John Ryan, who came down to left-wing half in the second quarter. Tony Reddan, of Lorrha, gave as fine a display of cool, confident goalkeeping as I have seen for many a day, saving shots of all kinds, from all angles, with not a shade of blemish in the hour. Covering him, Anthony Brennan, of Knockavilla, held Forde in a vice, whilst John Doyle, the Holycross minor, though not coming much into the limelight, never left an opening for the Laoighis corner man, Lalor, who shone in Leinster tests.

When all is said and done, however, it was the strong, resolute work and lengthy, accurate hitting of Sean Kenny and Pat Shanahan at mid-field that laid the foundation of Tipperary's overwhelming victory. Through the first quarter we saw several of those deft touches, passes and polished strokes which made Styles' big name in Leinster. But soon the Tipperary pair measured up to Styles and Bohane, beating them to falling balls and outstaying them.

Tipperary forwards were quick and ready, but by no means superlative hurlers. Murray, best Laoighis defender, held Jimmy Kennedy safe; Tommy Ryan, quicksilver in movement, sent many wides across, as did big, bustling Sonny Maher as spearhead. The other Ryans played their part, and I thought Seamus Bannon was at his best — a good earnest Tipperary team who do not quite measure up to their 1945 and 1937 forebears.

It is difficult to explain the Laoighis collapse in the second half. So closely did they hold Tipperary in the first session that the Munster champions wanted that vital goal, scored by the ex-minor star, Pat Kenny, who came on as a sub. and enhanced his name. Up to then neither side shone. Jim Kennedy out-manoeuvred Murray for one, centred to Tommy Ryan, who shot at goal. Fitzpatrick, a grand goalie throughout, stopped it dead, but Paddy Kenny flashed in and netted with a fast left-hander.

Nearing the end of the first half, Sean Kenny and Pat Shanahan were confidently outplaying Bohane and Styles at mid-field; this supremacy was more marked as the hour wore on.

Laoighis may have trained over-hard; the big occasion may have obsessed them. Ever familiar with the slower, red leather ball, this new white flyer of Johny McAuliffe's so attractive to watch, may have upset the Leinster champions. But for one reason or another they were completely overshadowed by the heavier and more aggressive Tipperary men in the closing session. It was heart-breaking on the tall Laoighis front-line to meet such a staunch defence, when they worked through on occasion it was heartbreaking, too, to have every manner of shot from all distances coolly covered and brilliantly cleared by Reddan.

It was a wise move by Tipperary's sideline control to shift Jimmy Kennedy (who had been in the wars) to right corner, for his nimble brain found the few openings which his genius sought. Showing pace and judgment, he flicked two balls outside Fitzpatrick's reach for clinching goals. The tall U.C.D. man, though lacking aggression in the close, is a master hurler whose glut of goals and points this year outdistances the great scoring men of the past, from Mikie Maher to Martin Kennedy whose North Tipperary territory figured so prominently in Tipperary's fourteenth title. .

I really relished the minor game — a delightfully clean exhibition. Kilkenny had quite as much of the game as the Tipperary boys for a long way, but their shooting close to goal was faulty. Tipperary, far taller and heavier, wore them down, the Moloneys, Finn, Ryan, Maher, Perkins and McDonnell playing in best Tipp. tradition. Outstanding, however, was O'Grady, the Tipp. goalkeeper and captain, who saved his side time and again, driving out the new ball in surpassing lengths. Live wire in Tipp's midfield and attack was Larry Keane, a tireless rover, good solo runner and deadly shot.

With O'Neill, Kilkenny's star as a schoolboy, well held by Finn, Kilkenny lacked direction in attack, where Larry Ryan stood out and contributed to their fine rally. Murphy (goal), Shaughnessy, Walton and Fitzgerald played well against a rangy and long-hitting Tipperary side who won well and meant it that way.

THE 1950 FINALS

I RECKON that thousands of rural workers decided to remain away from the All-Ireland hurling final to rescue the threatened corn and hay crop. Even so we had a splendid attendance of close on 70,000 at Croke Park to watch Tipperary and Kilkenny minors and seniors contest their ninth All-Ireland Final. Croke Park pitch and arrangements were at their great best. These Gaelic Athletic Association's annual All-Ireland Finals have become the greatest spectacles of the Irish sporting year.

In a long uphill fight against heavy odds, the G.A.A. administration have triumphed. Some greyheads like myself who have watched the uplift of the native games and pastimes for longer years than we care to name, cannot help feeling a thrill of pride on the occasion of these All-Ireland Finals. Watching the contrast between now and then — 1950 and 1900 — one cannot help throwing deserved bouquets at the feet of the men who, by life-long devotion, have made the games and the Association the influence for health and well-being which the G.A.A. commands in the land to-day. "Fools that came to scoff remain to pray," wrote Oliver Goldsmith.

Church and State were at Croke Park on that afternoon and all was smooth and bright and worthy of the occasion, though the thrills in the senior final were, for some unaccountable reason, absent. The senior hurlers who had made careful preparation cannot say that they had not a good example from their minors. These young lads from Kilkenny and Tipperary were a treat to watch. Tipperary looked an unbeatable lot of boys in all their southern games. But they met their masters in an hour's hurling, equal to seniors in skilful ashwork; close fearless tackling and fast masterly striking as you would wish to see in a day's walk. Kilkenny won 3-4 to 1-5.

Did I say — equal to seniors! Far surpassing them, we said as the afternoon's sport developed. I should like to write the 1950 senior final as such a great game as I had anticipated. It fell far below my expectations, for if we except the closing minutes and alternate goals — lightning goals at either end as the sands of the hour-glass were almost run out — there was very little to enthuse about.

Perhaps it was because we expected too much from these counties that have writ their names so deeply on hurling's roll of fame. Calmly thinking of the game afterwards, I remembered more than a few incidents of great skill and daring and that dramatic brace of goals in "broken time" compensated for much drab hurling reminiscent of a Church-Aid tournament match rather than an All-Ireland hurling final between Tipperary and Kilkenny.

Tipperary had a bad first half. They looked slow to race to the ball: they were hesitant. One wondered whether they were over-cautious under the keen eye of Mr. Con Murphy, our sharpest hurling referee. Kilkenny in the first half played with shrewd judgment, placing each ball low into the wind and accurate. Langton, ever elusive and deadly accurate, had six of Kilkenny's seven points in the first half, against Tipperary's five — S. Kenny, Bannon, Kennedy (2) and Mick Ryan's flying grounder, which sailed up from forty-five yards.

At this stage, with a strong wind and a lowering sun against them from the Canal goal, Tipperary looked in a bit of a spot. But once again that undaunted courage under a threat of defeat, that never-say-die spirit which won them so many finals in the past, came to their rescue. Their dressingroom mentors made very wise positional changes, and their greatest brainwave was to put Sean Kenny, the Tipperary Captain, into the middle of things to mark Prendergast, who played ducks and drakes with Tipperary's attacks in the first half. Sean Kenny's restless energy had room to let off steam there, and he proceeded to inspire his side to victory. Tipperary hurled steadily at first, and then opened their shoulders against the wind. They retained their title in that third quarter, when the best of Kilkenny's assaults broke on Tipperary's granite cliff of defence that broke many greater sides.

Kilkenny did not get a score in that third quarter, with the wind to aid. And they can blame themselves. Langton could have landed three easy points to win the match but, probably playing to orders, he went for goals, and went in vain, for Brennan and Reddan and Doyle and Stakelum and Byrne were firm and secure as the rock of Cashel.

Dan Kennedy, who had a right game in Kilkenny's midfield, broke Kilkenny's scoreless spell when he landed a point in the 52nd minute. Back came Tipperary after Langton had gone for the inner of the upright with a free from 21 yards, and knocked the whitewash off the outside of it a foot from the ground.

Tipperary smelt victory as war-horses do the blood of battle and tore up-field with the Kennys rampant. Ned Ryan pulled full-blooded and Ramie Dowling brought off a great save. In a flash, Pat Kenny fastened on the crossing ball and crashed it to the net behind Dowling. Then the blue and gold flags flew; hats and caps too. The game looked over, but from Dowling's puck Jim Kelly, the 1938 match winner, let fly a long sailing one dead on the crossbar. Before Reddan could cover it, Mulcahy followed the ball in like a terrier, and crashed Reddan in the act of clearing. The ball was in the net and the long whistle sounded. Kilkenny were, to my mind, the keener and more uniform through the field and threw the game away when shooting for goals with points at their mercy to win the day. To Tipperary I must give credit for their vastly improved hurling in the second half. Here we saw a glimpse of the real Tipperary. They opened their shoulders and set about winning their game. Pat Stakelum put in some great hurling near the end, and to hold Kilkenny's forwards scoreless for twenty-two minutes against the wind and sun is a great tribute to every back in Tipp's lines from Reddan out. Tipperary's strong finish earned their narrow victory (1-9 to 1-8) but they had nothing to spare.

FINALS OF 1952

SEPTEMBER of the sheaves had come in quietly; it had stolen upon us gently like a silent visitor at dusk. Just a few brown leaves on the garden path and a rustling of trees with the myriads of green berries on the holly showing a darkening shade as evening steals in closer, borrowing longer minutes daily from late August evenings. I hurried home from Saturday evening rural rambles amongst the rowan berries and lanes of russet crab-trees — hurried to see the "sights of town" on the eve of an All-Ireland hurling final.

We had two Dublin teams at the peak stage this year, and this thinned the gaiety of the O'Connell Street crowds. The red-capped and red-and-white buttoned Corkmen were here in hundreds — if possible more buoyant than ever; buoyant as the corky line of a salmon net bobbing on the crest of a wave on the Lee estuary when a spring tide brought its haul to the Blackrock salmon fishers, who once made salmon fishing their hobby and hurling their serious occupation. Tipperary minors had their enthusiastic bands of young followers wearing handsome blue-and-gold favours — all in the best of good humour.

Twelve morning trains brought many thousands of hurling enthusiasts from all four provinces; this time as often before, Munster sent the bumper contingents. Dublin's blue favours gathered strength on the leading thoroughfares of the capital as a bright noon passed. On the steps of the Gresham Hotel two score of unmistakable Irish-Americans watched the trek to Croke Park — heartening spectacle of peaceful pleasures at their best.

We are now so accustomed to clock-like smoothness in Croke Park arrangements on big occasions that we are liable to overlook the master's hand behind it all — Mr Padraig O'Keeffe and his staffs had worked long and hard to achieve such smooth perfection. The pitch itself was a joy to see. Those who were not in their seats early missed the best session of minor hurling I have ever watched. Dublin's native school boys held Tipperary's tall, rangy lads score for score. After the Munster youths crashed a few scores home above and below the bar, Dublin replied in kind, and there was only one point in it at half-time.

The Tipperary boys, however, must have held a lot in reserve, for the second half had no sooner opened up than we were roused by some galvanic hurling from these youths in the blue-and-gold. Reminding me of Tipperary senior hurling at its noble best, Wall, the Quinns, Hayes,

McGrath, Devanny, Butler, Brown and Cleary, most of all, seemed to take possession of the pitch. Hitting off left and right hand, overhead and on the sod, back and midfield gave the front lines abundant service, and soon the goal flags were shooting up in a procession. Cleary was elusive and incisive. Dublin's staggered backs were outmanoeuvred, and the big Tipp score mounted rapidly. I would write down this Tipperary minor team as amongst the best ever. Tipperary need have no doubts about their future senior strength with these boys sailing along to greatness. They won 9-9 to 2-3 and were worth every goal of it.

Waiting moments at Croke Park were attractively filled in by Artane's fine boys' band and massed pipers. For the first time ever, community singing was a success — the Traleeman's (Michael O'Duinn) fine voice was well heard and chorus with his fine singing of "The Banks of My Own Lovely Lee" and "Twenty Men from Dublin Town." It was all very inspiring, and the autumn sun shone across the well-filled new terraces on the city side as the seniors paraded. The teams were very evenly balanced in height and build; many of the Corkmen were new to Croke Park, as their early timid hurling showed; later they seemed to swell to their work. Dublin were playing on their home pitch, familiar with every blade of grass and every line of territory. No sooner had His Grace, Dr. Kinnane, Archbishop of Cashel, thrown in the ball than fit bodies crashed and the snow-white ball was speeding. The issue was set.

My earliest impression was the speed and readiness of the Dublin hurlers — a level blend of Dublin City-born men and players from hurling counties who had made their name in Dublin hurling circles. Following that opening point of Ring's from a free (which I thought should have gone the other way), Dublin played back with fine abandon. Con Murphy, from the half-way line, sent a perfect Dublin ball sailing over the bar for the balancing point, and Dublin's forwards tore in. Creedon was tested severely in Cork's goal; Herbert and McCarthy crashed fast balls at the Glenman, and he saved gallantly, a great beginning to a great game by a son of the famous Micus Creedon of another athletic generation.

Dublin were getting the upper hand and their followers were jubilant. Beneath the bar Creedon pulled down a bullet-like "70" by Con Murphy; Cork backs rallied but G. Kelly's free for a point gave Dublin the lead in the tenth hectic minute. Then came a lightning raid by Cork, rather against the run of the play. Christy Ring eluded Ferguson for the first time and worried himself into sleek possession at the main gate corner — a masterful cross-shot sharply across the goal line, and Dowling whipped it to the Dublin net — a staggering shot giving Matthews no chance. Teams were level at the 20th minute when Norman Allen, from a free, supplemented a fine point by McCarthy for Dublin.

Prior was hurling powerfully for Dublin, and his team were often around Cork's goal, but the Leeside backs were adamant. Another Cork raid and a sailing point by Captain Barry from a sharp angle. Back came Dublin with a flourish for G. Kelly to clinch a determined attack with a point.

Close on half-time Cork's team seemed to me to settle down to smoothe confident hurling; they were finding their feet after their usual slow opening — we remember this characteristic from Thurles and Limerick this year. Mattie Fouhy was now opening his shoulders to fine purpose; he placed Griffin (sound recruit) who sent a grand point across. Gerald Murphy cut in fast to Joe Twomey, who scarcely looked at the post as he let fly — a perfect ball from 60 yards crossed high above the bar to give Cork a clear goal lead at half-time (1-5 to 0-5). Cork were in the half-time lead but Dublin had the balance of play; their forwards failed repeatedly from good ground.

Cork were a transformed side on the resumption. Within a minute Ring was away and smashed a sizzling shot at Matthews, who brought it down with a grand effort — the Dublin goalie went prone to save his net for a "70." Then came an exchange of points — Daly and Murphy. Ring put Cork four points up, and Willie John soloed through with a Mick Mackey run to swing another Cork point. Joe Twomey, Christy Ring and Barry ran Cork's point score to 12, and Cork were in complete command. Matthews saved a rasper from Daly, but Ring switch-backed his way to drive to the square where Dowling headed a Cork rush and found the net for Cork's second goal as broken time was reached. Dublin's attack was rendered completely impotent by Matt Fouhy and his colleagues; a point by Allen was the loser's only contribution, whilst Cork sailed clean away to stretch their big lead by points from the now irrepressible Christy Ring and Captain Pat Barry of Sarsfields.

It was a one-sided Cork triumph in the end. Dublin had struggled manfully but were subdued after 40 minutes. Thence forward Cork, well served in every part, waltzed away to easy victory, and head Tipperary once more in a race for championship honours. Cork's sound bedrock hurling in the second half, their positioning and backing were very secure. They hurled their best game of the year. With a change or two in attack, the Leemen will set out on fresh fields next season with rosy prospects.

GALWAY LOSE

MUCH hurried harvest work was rushed into the early cloudy days of September; many reapers worked on, heedless of scattered showers. High south and west winds swept the grain lands, and only very late-ripening corn remained in the ear.

Then on Saturday, September 5th, the skies lifted; clouds got thinner and more kindly; by the afternoon the sun was out, and the great trek from every airt and part of the Thirty-Two Counties had begun. Glad crowds they were, with Croke Park and the 1953 All-Ireland hurling final their objective. A joyous annual invasion this, which seems to grow stronger and more happy as the years roll by. Forecasts of record crowds were justified.

Dublin folk are glad to welcome those American "Flights of the Gaels" which have become regularly associated with our big sporting finals at Croke Park. Here they were, some one hundred and ten of them in their light-coloured clothes and huge hats, headed by the popular Paddy Grimes himself, who once captained the American team of Tailteann hurlers. On Saturday night, the early railway specials brought crowds of Gaelic enthusiasts from the extreme South and West. O'Connell Street's wide footpaths were crowded, and when the theatres emptied, the good-humoured throngs spilled onto the roadway. Some of the paper-capped young men and maids found their way to Moore Street, a crowded shopping centre hard by the G.P.O. There were street musicians there and soon Galwaymen and Corkmen intermingled in dancing eight and four-hand reels on the roadway. It was a glad sight indeed.

Sunday morning broke bright and fair. City churches were thronged and from 10 o'clock onwards people were heading off past the Parnell Monument to Drumcondra and Croke Park. I joined them about noon, and was one of the first into the high vantage point of the Cusack Stand. This tribute to the dynamic Clareman who founded the Gaelic Athletic Association, looks so solidly and wisely constructed as if it were intended to rival the Roman Colosseum in future antiquity. Soon the crowds were streaming into the unbooked sideline seats and vantage points. The pitch looked a picture — one of the greenest and smoothest in this or any other country. Arrangements and stewarding were perfect — all was smooth and orderly under Mr. Padraig O'Caoimh's able directorship.

Early arrivals watched a really worthwhile minor hurling title game between the youths of Dublin and Tipperary — both well-tried fifteens on the road to the final. Tipperary were the taller and heavier bunch of boys; Dublin slightly faster and more nippy. Early scores were exchanged but soon the lengthy and well-controlled drives of the Munster youths told their tale, and rapid points and goals from Devaney, McLoughlin, Murphy, Stapleton and Connolly gave Tipperary a sound lead. Dublin boys attacked with great vigour in the third quarter. Rapid scores by Feely and Bell heralded a recovery, but back came Tipperary with a flourish.

The Munster champions have a grand set of forwards — all six are good; McLoughlin, Devaney, Murphy, Corcoran, Stapleton and Connolly — McLoughlin being the most prolific scorer. McCormack held a good goal for Dublin; Boothman and the Feely pair, and Bell gave good service. Bohane and Bracket also played well. Tipperary played delightful hurling in the last quarter and won well by five clear goals. Dublin fought hard to the end.

President Sean T. O'Kelly and Mrs. O'Kelly had a hearty and dignified welcome; all present stood to attention whilst the President's salute was played by the Artane Band; Mr Sean Og O'Callaghan announced over the field broadcast service that both the senior teams were unchanged. Every nook and vantage point was filled by this time and though some 72,000 broke all hurling records, as the teams marched round, there was ample room for all. The brilliant September sun beat down on the emerald pitch. The whole hearty scene reminded one of what we have read of hurling at Tara in the days of Ireland's ancient glory — no evidence of racial decay or decadence here.

Galway had a slight breeze to aid them when they backed the Railway goal but the sun was a handicap to their defenders. The pace was fast and the hurling open. Salmon and Duffy were on their toes at centrefield, and J. Duggan whipped Galway's first point across. Cork balanced when Barry finished a Ring movement. Sean Duggan had to save a rasping shot from Hartnett and grand hurling by Galway sent Duffy away to point from long range.

Cork's ground hurling told. O'Sullivan crossed a fast ball to Barry who shot hard and fair. Duggan blocked it back, only for Josie Hartnett to tear in at full speed and meet the return with a cracking shot to the Galway net. Cork were now moving well and Ring, though capably marked by Burke, the Western captain, drove a glorious shot from sixty yards out — dead on the crossbar. Duggan covered it but Cork's front forwards followed the ball in, and the ball went to the net. Galway rallied and got great length into their drives. Molloy, from seventy-five yards out drove a sailing drive all the way for Galway's third minor. Cork led 2-1 to 0-3 at half-time, but the game was far from over.

O'Flaherty came on for Nolan (injured) and held close to Gerry Riordan who had hurled through the first half as he never did before — he had grand assistance from J. Lyons and A. O'Shaughnessy. When the story of Cork's All-Ireland victory in 1953 is told, highest honours must go to that great and unbeatable line of defence — O'Riordan, Lyons, O'Shaughnessy and Creedon in goal holding watch and ward.

Galway reopened with a flourish. Gallagher cut in a corner-flag puck with a screw on it and the ball curled over the Cork bar. Duffy's point from a 65 yards' free got minor no. 2. Molloy's accurate "70" landed well over the bar and beyond for Galway's third. Excitement grew, the record crowd were roaring encouragement to Galway and there was a tornado of cheering when big, burly Hugh Gordon drove a perfect ball across to set the scores level and twenty minutes to play.

Cork had their backs to the wall and were under heavy pressure. But they were staunch backs — again and again O'Riordan, Lyons, Creedon and O'Shaughnessy beat these eager Galwegians back, rendering their front line impotent. Christy Ring was now at midfield and his presence steadied that sector. Burke followed him like a shadow. Long exchanges followed. The tropical sun was taking toll. There were frequent stoppages, more from exhaustion than injuries. Tired men were inclined to use their hurleys over much.

At the threequarter hour Ring got a valuable Cork point. Willie John Daly discarded his boots and thenceforward showed the speed and stamina of a trotting pony. Cork backs were adamant: Vincent Twomey and Matt Fouhy were finishing fast; Willie John went away on one of his solo runs and swung a heartening point across, setting the score 9 points to 7 as we entered the final stages.

Galway fought on desperately and Killeen swung a point from the left. Only a point in it — 9 to 8. Stoppages slowed down the pace, but Cork had something left for broken time. Cork backs sent their front lines away in a rapid ground movement started by Derry Hayes; Hartnett was immense as he bustled his big shoulders through. Galway's imminent goal for victory failed to materialise and it was Cork's forwards that clicked. Young O'Sullivan of Buttevant had the last say as he doubled a perfect grounder past Duggan. Cork had won, 3 goals 3 points (12 points) to Galway's 8 points. Not a great game by any means but a solid test of men and a searching one. Christy Ring got his seventh All-Ireland medal to tie with the select Kilkenny four — Drug Walsh, Jack Rochford, Dick Doyle and Sim Walton. What price Christy for No. 8!

WEXFORD'S YEAR

OUR 1956 hurling final is over and gone. No regrets from Cork. The better team won and the mighty men of Loch Gorman are once more honoured and worthy champions! But one cheer here for the losers!!

For Christy Ring was as near as not to matter to doing at Croke Park, what he did at Thurles against Limerick. Cork had been playing like Trojans for ten minutes round the three-quarter hour. Ring's awakening had roused them all. They had wiped out a seven points lead; Christy's flecked ball over the bar put them in front! The champions rallied; cheers were deafening. Nicky Rackard broke out field and two accurate frees once more recovered the lead. Then Ring got a chance at the other end and slipped Bobby Rackard. The Glen Rovers man had proved that his eye was in, by a bullet-goal from a 21 yards free. Every Corkman on the field then moved upfield like a regiment of soldiers.

Ring waltzed around Rackard and raced through in confident possession. His pace was startling and gave him time to steady himself. Three minutes to go and Cork two points behind!! Then to make assurance doubly sure Ringey crossed in straight in front of goal and with a smooth right-handed swing drove strong and fair from 20 yards out. So fast was he moving that he was almost on the goal-line as soon as the ball. But Art Foley was lynx-eyed and cool. He grabbed that bullet ball and cleared to safety. The great game was won and lost!

For Wexford pounced on the return drive, full of battle and full of hurling. Then Ring did a noble thing. He walked up to Art Foley, the Wexford goalie, and shook his hand in appreciation of a wonderful save! Ring's name will long be remembered for that incident. He knew how truly hit and hard was that ball. And when Nick Rackard's glorious final goal clinched the game in Wexford's favour at the last minute of the hour, and thousands of joyous Wexfordmen rushed in to the pitch to cheer their champions, two of the greatest of the winning team — Bob Rackard and Nick O'Donnell, took hold of protesting Ringey and shouldered him towards the dressing rooms. Lasting friendship and mutual esteem have been sealed between the Gaels of Cork and Wexford by last Sunday's great game.

This 1956 final between Wexford and Cork was amongst the greatest triumphs of organisation in the 72 years' history of the Association. The near-record crowd of 83,000 and a few hundred to spare was smoothly handled by the stewards. Rumours and scares led many people to think that the attendance would be down thousands on last year. Instead of this, attendance and gate receipts were thousands up. Hurling's popularity is now widespread and shows no signs of waning; Mr. Padriag O'Caoimh, chief executive of the G.A.A., is at present deeply occupied with the engineering problems of vastly increased accommodation for Croke Park. Many of the nation's leaders of Church, State and industry were in the Hogan Stand. Mr. P.J. Grimes was there with his growing group of American Gaels, here specially for the finals.

An exciting game and a strenuous one was expected by Wexfordmen and Corkmen alike. Nor were spectators disappointed. It was a most satisfying final with the second half brimful of exciting passages with a share of dramatic developments.

I have been asked by many hurling critics whether I considered the standard of hurling high, and I have been asked to compare the 1956 final with the great games of the past. It's hard to satisfy hurling fans nowadays. And if there were slack passages in the first half there were plenty of thrills and excitement galore in the second. In a sentence, I put this high in the list of finals without being quite up to half-a-dozen finals which I can recall in hurling standards. The middle game of 1931 (between Cork and Kilkenny) with the final scores 2-5 each was, to my mind, the greatest final of them all. But this latest match will be high in my list of great finals. Cork's great recovery (led by Ring) at the three-quarter hour, and Wexford's gallant final rally were memorable and worthy of real champions.

Wexford's fifteen have been playing so long together that they were into their stride like the crack of a whip! Cork, a newly-strung side, took a long time to settle down and rapid scores by Flood and Padge Kehoe gave the champions a great send-off with a point and a goal in startling fashion. Steadily the big commanding Leinstermen continued to slip away into a sound lead of 1 goal 5 points to 2 points near half-time and worth every point of it.

Ringey got his points then O'Regan and Goulding helped and the game was dead open on a windless day when the half-time score read 1 goal and 6 points to 5 points in Wexford's favour.

For the first ten minutes of the second half, Wexford continued to show the better-balanced and more sustained hurling. The Rackards (Billie and Nick) and Codd stretched Wexford's lead from frees, beautifully hit, and just then when Cork looked badly placed, our old friend Christy Ring thought it time to take a hand.

He was weaving his way in, forced a free and at the three-quarter hour crashed the ball to the net. Cork were soon a transformed team. Christy smoothly swung a beauty home, just above the bar. The fur flew. Though

Padge Kehoe had a glorious point, Cork were back with Paddy Barry in his best storming mood. The Sarsfield's man whipped a point in and then a goal to balance, amongst wild Leeside cheers. When Christy's handball "palm" above the bar gave Cork the lead — 14 to 13 — the crowd were swaying with excitement. Only eight minutes were left to play and Cork seemed to be well on the way for victory. Then came Wexford's gallant recovery. It was "certain and sure" sign of a real champion side. And Nick Rackard, outplayed until now by the tenacity of John Lyons, decided to forage for play outfield and he got it. Deadly accurate points sailed across from play and angle frees. Wexford were again rampant. Then young fair-haired Philpott (playing a gallant hour) sent a long daisy-trimmer to Ring who wheeled and rewheeled in possession and proceeded to have that vital crack at goal which I have detailed above. It was a gambler's throw and Art Foley won. The closing moments saw Tom Ryan place Nicky for a picture goal and Dixon's final point. Wexford's last rally won through.

I consider Wexford a truly great and enduring side. Their stick work is vastly improved, they combine well and are well balanced all over. Foley had a heroic hour. The Rackards were immense. So was M. Morrissey, O'Donnell and Jim English (after a weak opening). Hearne and Wheeler made a grand centre. Wexford's forwards were better than I have ever seen them. Tim Flood never had a better hour; Martin Codd was a wise selection on the 40 and was too big and strong for W.J. Daly. Padge Kehoe was good on the loose. I thought Tom Ryan a good help for Nicky in making openings. Rackard senior, like Ring, was there when most wanted and Dixon was generally in close company.

Cork can be built up into a grand side by next year. Cashman had a good game and John Lyons gave his last ounce of energy in successfully keeping the big Wexford forwards from Mount Leinster at bay. Lyons was "all-in" at the finish. O'Shaughnessy was sound, so was sub Vincent Twomey. Brohan is a great back in the making. I was disappointed with Cork's half-line where Philpott alone outplayed his man. Fouhy and Daly hit some good balls but they were generally outplayed by Tim Flood and Martin Codd. Goulding and Dowling are solid triers of promise! Outside Ring, Barry and O'Shea, I thought Cork forwards lacked consistency. O'Regan, Hartnett and Kelly were only good in spots. Trainer Jim Barry got through his work well but I am told from a reliable source that he had more trouble than usual with this 1956 Cork side! This question of the allocation of stand tickets still awaits a successful solution.

Where do all Tipperary's brilliant minors go? Here they are again with a grand champion side. And they will have another ready next year. They were altogether too good for Kilkenny's lighter boys.

KILKENNY'S 1957 WIN

PRECIOUS as gold were the sunny hours that blessed the "grain gatherers." Power machinery worked in relays in all four provinces and my unobstrusive train of newsbearers tell me that the bulk of the corn crop is saved, and well saved. The busy tillers are, as they say, "very thankful" to the yield. In the north and west of the country much work remains to be done, particularly in regions where oats is the principal grain crop. In Munster, Leinster and in most parts of Ulster and the Midlands, the main harvest is safe. In Kilkenny and Waterford the thousands of rural workers who joined the throngs on Sunday heading for Croke Park by road and rail left home with the happy knowledge that their harvest was secure.

By road and rail they came, these good-humoured enthusiasts, sporting the black and amber of Kilkenny and the blue and white of Waterford. They mixed harmoniously and indiscriminately in Dublin streets with everyone "in great good humour" as the storytellers say. Many of the "white and blue" groups of both sexes, spoke the beautiful sibilant Gaelic of the Decies coasts from Youghal and Ardmore to Ring and from Helvic Head to the Comeragh mountains. There was no inferiority complex amongst those joyous enthusiastic Waterford folk. Their hurlers had beaten Limerick, Cork and Galway in convincing fashion. Kilkenny's great record with thirteen All-Ireland finals to their credit, as against Waterford's solitary, troubled those new and sprightly Munster champions not at all.

Tipperary and Kilkenny minors were very well matched and served up a most satisfactory hour's hurling. This was no pit-pat tapping game; the young hurlers played with the courage and determination of seniors and there was not a dull moment in the whole hour. Though Butler opened with a Tipperary point, Lennon whipped in a ripping shot for a Kilkenny goal and thenceforward it was a case of "Jack was as good as his master." Though Tipperary had almost "farmed" the minor championship in recent years they found Kilkenny hurling hip-high with them. Jimmy Doyle, the rambler, soon was showing his hand, and Butler's goal for Tipperary gave them a lead which was often challenged but never lost. Dunne had Kilkenny's second goal and there were only a few points in it at halftime.

Jimmy Doyle and his brother Pat had a big share in Tipperary's strong period after half-time when Tipp. built up a two goal lead.

We saw some very fine hurling — fast and earnest. Kilkenny lads finished with rare dash and spirit; they whipped home one well-built goal by Dunne and were searching for the balancing goal in a fast closure. Keher and Dunne were prominent for Kilkenny; best for the winners were the Doyles, Lonergan, Reynolds, Murphy, Kennedy and Butler.

Rumours of the doubtful fitness of Sean Clohessy of Kilkenny and of Johny O'Connor of Waterford were busy before the game, but reassurance came when Sean Og O'Ceallachain announced "full teams" on the field broadcasting system. When Clohessy joined his team mates, however, it was seen that he was limping slightly and he was limping to the end. Johny O'Connor looked more sprightly but his injured thumb was the trouble and he was, like Clohessy, suffering from his period of inaction.

From the very first ball Waterford looked the faster and more eager side. They were winning every race for possession and swinging the ash with some purpose. John Kiely came outfield and turned a perfect point in without turning a hair, grey or otherwise. Phil Grimes gave us a taste of his perfect hurling technique when putting point number 2 over the bar for Waterford. Eight minutes had gone before Kilkenny made their first impression; Mick Kenny of the National Army was on the mark with a placed ball for a point just after Kilkenny's goal had a narrow escape when the upright was hit, with Ollie Walsh out of position.

Kilkenny seemed to awake to vigorous action; that flying right winger, young Heaslip, hit a sharp crossing pass to Mick Kenny, who promptly drove straight as a die to the Waterford net. Heaslip and Kenny added minors in a fertile Kilkenny patch round the quarter, but Waterford were full of battle. Clohessy hit his first ball and Kenny hit a Kilkenny point, but Waterford were giving as much as they got through the field. Grimes and Kiely swung good points for Waterford; Clohessy hit a beauty for Kilkenny's No. 5 in points. Undaunted and fearless, Waterford tore in and there was a rumpus in Walsh's goal as the whistle went as the ball crossed the goal-line. Free to Waterford pointed ref. Gleeson and Phil Grimes, from 21 yards, hit another beauty — it gave Walsh no chance and bulged the net. Teams were level at 1-5 each and the crowd roaring. Just as the referee was looking at his watch for half-time, F. Walsh drove a neat cross to Whelan and the big Waterford corner man took it as it came and lofted over the bar for Waterford's half-time lead — 1-6 to 1-5.

The game was as open as a barn door, but Kilkenny were now facing a low sun and whatever wayward wind there was it was against them. Early in the second half Ollie Walsh was tested twice in the Kilkenny goal. He cleared smoothly. Slowly and steadily Waterford forced the pace. Mick O'Connor, now at centre, was a force in all positions; a long drive of his reached Whelan, who crashed the ball to the net. Grimes' point put the Munster men five points ahead, but Kilkenny were hurling shrewdly and with a set plan. Mick Kelly placed O'Dwyer, who doubled home Kilkenny's second goal. Within two minutes Waterford were back and Kiely gave a shrewd pass to Whelan, who again proved his worth with a stinging shot and a goal.

In a pulsating game Kenny and Whelan swopped points and, when Cheasty, the endless trier, had Waterford's tenth point, Waterford were six points clear. At that stage Waterford were hurling so well and so confidently that I felt convinced they would win through — two goals clear, 12 minutes to go and hurling well. Kilkenny forwards were switched now and Clohessy came out from the corner; quickly he flicked a ground ball to O'Dwyer, who pounced on it and netted — Kilkenny only a goal behind. Grimes, deadly accurate, added to the points score; Kenny was equally good with placed shots and the critical score came. Eight minutes from the end "Ollie" saved a rasper; he drove upfield and Kelly tapped it into his loose man — Mick Kenny; the Callan drove a bullet shot to the net for Kilkenny's fourth goal — Kilkenny only a point behind.

Kilkenny men were now moving with new briskness and Clohessy round the 40 mark trapped a ball and with a smoothe swing drove it above the bar — teams level. Then came a glorious drive off Kilkenny's left wing. Aptly enough it was their captain hit it — from 60 yards out on the wing it sailed dead true high over Roche's head — the winning point for the Noremen. Waterford never lost heart and they stormed Kilkenny lines; the backs were rocklike; Grimes lost one chance, but the Walshs and Maher cleared to safety and victory.

Kilkenny's recovery was reminiscent of many other finals won by a point — five of them were from Cork and the Noremen were the winners, Waterford have never hurled a better game than this. They had never faltered and their splendid exhibition surprised and pleased us all. My opinion is that a draw would be a true verdict.

WATERFORD SHINE

MY heartiest congratulations to as fine a hurling team as ever won an All-Ireland final. And what a final it was. For the first time in 75 years, more than 150,000 paid for admission to see the drawn game and the decisive one. And not a soul went away disappointed with the fare presented.

Hurling was keen, clever, speedy and sustained in the first game on September 6. Everyone was absorbed with the speed and clean beauty of it all and were glad that both teams lived to fight another day. On Sunday last, all Gaeldom, at home and overseas responded generously to the "call of the ash." The high attendance of the opening day was surpassed and a decisive issue, fast and furious as before kept 78,000 enthralled in the exhilarating spectacle of thirty superb athletes battling on with grim resolve to bring honour to the little village.

Waterford won and won well. They had learnt much from the memorable drawn game and used that lesson well. Kilkenny opened brilliantly and crashed home those early goals so skilfully and crisply into the wind that the prophets who told us to expect a Waterford debacle were clapping their hands for joy.

Not so those who had seen the whole-hearted spirit with which Waterford hurled right through this year's Munster championships. They had smothered the Oireachtas Cup winners from Galway, they had astonished the All-Ireland champions of 1958, the mighty Tipperary men, and they were definitely the superior side in the Munster final against the Leemen at Thurles.

I "walked" the Croke Park pitch shortly after noon and found it bone-hard. There was a slight covering of grass after the long drought. Yet these looked very fit finalists both junior and senior. Sean Clohessy, the Tullaroan and Kilkenny captain won the toss for Kilkenny, but as usual the Black and Amber men decided to play against the sun and wind — into the city goal. "It helps our lads to steady their early shots," I was told by a wise Kilkenny veteran once. It has worked well for the Noremen and seemed lucky for the first quarter.

After Waterford drove two wild shots over the endline, Kilkenny came back; Mick Walsh hit a beauty of a point off a free (65), Billie Dwyer shoved another over the bar, and then Denis Heaslip flashed in like a kingfisher over a stream; as he ran he swung — with great accuracy the ball sped to the net.

Kilkenny were hurling confidently, Frankie Walsh opened for Waterford and soon the blue and white men were sparkling. Points came steadily and then that double shuffle approach and awkward, poked strokes brought shock goals to Waterford in the second quarter.

Cheasty was the puzzle man but he built scores and Waterford were a goal clear at half way (14 to 11) — not much of a lead and a bright lively breeze against them in the second half.

Waterford found their feet in a flash and played just as well into the wind in the third quarter as Kilkenny did in the opening session. As I looked down field every man in the Waterford side seemed to me to be on the move. And they moved at a sparkling rate. They never dallied with the ball. John Keane and Charlie Ware had schooled them well. Where I thought Waterford superior was in the speed and security with which they hit ground balls from all angles. With smooth, easy swings, they smacked that ball surprising distances and with great confidence and accuracy of direction.

Another feature of Waterford hurlers was their fearless tackling; they were not in the least awed by Kilkenny's great name. The blue and white clad backs showed surprising improvement on the drawn game. Austin Flynn, Barron and Harney kept well clear of Joe Power, who kept an impeccable goal from end to end. He saved quite as many shots and had as sound a record for the run of the hour than his better-known vis-a-vis, Ollie Walsh.

Frankie Walsh, the Decies captain, hit his most dazzling form in that winning second half. His left hand was meticulously accurate; he hit frees with rare accuracy from all ranges and angles; his play through the field was inspiring. Cheasty fitted in beautifully, whilst Flannelly hit some bullet-straight shots goalwards. I thought Guinan and Kiely best of the others — grand forwards.

As a team, the winners looked an efficiently schooled lot and obedient too. In a word, they played model hurling on Sunday, particularly near the end, when every man co-ordinated. Waterford won comfortably and will be a championship force for years to come. They must nurse their schoolboys. It was the Christian Brothers and National schools of Waterford that built up that glorious side which has built up a great hurling name.

Let us make no mistake about it — Kilkenny are still a grand lot of hurlers. They opened brightly and often forced Waterford backs on to their lines. Sean Clohessy played a captain's part — some of his shots carried lightning speed. Ollie Walsh saved a few hot ones and missed a few from short range. The Walshs, Maher and Buggy fought bravely; O'Dwyer, Heaslip, Fleming put in some spirited hurling, but young O'Connell was outplayed this time by Harney.

WEXFORD'S 1960 WIN

IN MY opinion the broken weather and precarious position of the 1960 harvest hit the All-Ireland hurling attendances at Croke Park. Mr. Padraig O'Caoimh, the busy General Secretary, anticipated an 80,000 crowd at the attractive Tipperary-Wexford game. The attendance was well under 70,000. As usual, the Wexford folk travelled in big numbers to support their men. Even so, I am reliably informed by Slaneymen that many stayed behind to help save their precarious corn. The same is true of Tipperary — their special trains and road services were not so crowded as usual. But it was the neutral counties that remained at home to listen in and save the corn before and after. There were almost as many at the Down-Offaly football semi-final as there were at the hurling final — an unusual position.

There was no lack of glamour or colour in and around Dublin over the week-end. The blue and gold of Tipperary, the purple and gold of Wexford, looked very much alike and blended well. The O'Connell Street crowds on Saturday night were good-humoured and cheerful as ever. Hotels, clubs and inns were full, and the bright moonlit night was a good portent for Sunday's weather.

Wexford looked the heavier team as they marched around and I noticed that there was a bit of a lift on the well-kept pitch which looked conducive to first-class hurling and there was much glorious hurling in that stirring senior hour; but it was the Wexford men that shone!

Rarely have I seen a team so abundantly fit and brimful of life and energy as these "purple and gold" men of Slaneyside. They left their mark like Olympic sprinters, went into every clash with a zest that swept the field, and they surprised us all by the adept skill with which they used these nicely turned Randall hurleys. I knew that the average weight of these hurleys was nearer to 22 ounces than 21. Yet they used them as if they were paper weight. And they were no paper-weight, but solid ash wielded by powerful arms which drove accurate balls fine distances, both on ground and overhead.

Somehow I got the impression near the three-quarter hour that Tipperary were neither as fit nor eager as they were against Cork, at Thurles. They looked more complacent — a dangerous state of mind with big hurling issues on the scales. Tipperary were but a shadow of their Munster greatness. I was very much taken aback.

Wexford were on their toes from the break of the ball. Padge Kehoe, a youthful and thrustful veteran, crashed one at Moloney in Tipp's goal, and he brought it down and cleared; Oliver McGrath was on it and whipped a point across in half-a-minute. Jimmy Doyle's free balanced — his only score for a whole hour of frustration and ill-luck.

Padge Kehoe cracked a free, of Nick Rackard pattern, and it glanced off a defender's ash to fly to the net. And so did Wexford take the initiative, and hold it from end to end of a truly remarkable and memorable game.

Wexford's skill and power continued to surprise me, but approaching the half-hour, Tipperary hit a patch of true hurling — short and sharp and neat. Their points swung in — Tom Ryan (2), Tony Wall and two by Liam Devaney. And so Tipperary's recovery sent Munster hopes soaring at half-time, with the score 1-7 for Wexford against 8 points for Tipp. The game looked wide open.

The second half left one dominant impression on my mind — that Wexford were a super-team or else that Tipperary lacked something in their training — over-confidence, perhaps sub-conscious. Wexford were deerlike in the speed and elasticity of their movements. Pat Nolan kept a peerless goal and saved many scoring shots; Nick O'Donnell, full-back, graced his 35th birthday by playing brilliant hurling, overhead and on the ground. He was capably backed by Mitchell and Neville. Wexford's half-back line excelled. Led by Willie Rackard's inspiration and early drives, Jim English,like a prancing pony, showed a return to his best, and newcomer John Nolan of Oylgate performed wonders in rendering Tipperary's most prolific scoring star in subjection for the run of the hour. John Nolan's skill in keen swerving, tackling and long reach in blocking kept the elusive Thurles man at bay — a great achievement.

Upfield, the Wexford men were as good as their backs; Jim Morrissey, a class hurler, was at his peak and Ned Wheeler's long ground drives were of surpassing length. On the "forty" Padge Kehoe was a hurling dynamo. His crashing shots from frees and from play were very valuable and he finished like a war-horse. Tim Flood signalised his re-entry into the team by a splendid hour's contribution; Seamus Quaid, Jim O'Brien, John Harding and McGrath fitted in like a glove. The further the game went the more definite was Wexford's superiority.

The best that I can say of Tipperary is that they had a subnormal game. They seemed surprised at first and then stunned by the unexpected speed and skill of the Wexford men. One could not blame Moloney in goal, for he saved some scorching shots. Tony Wall and John Doyle were the best of an uneven back-line. Theo English and Tom Ryan were good in spots and again were uneven in their work. Tipperary's great 40 yards line — Jimmy Doyle, Liam Devaney, and Donie Nealon were "held" as they never were before. They met a grand half-back bulwark that knew all the answers. Tipperary's front range of forwards dissipated many scoring chances, and O'Donnell was a stone wall. I again attribute Tipperary's failure to over-confidence and under-training.

My heartiest congratulations to a very fine Kilkenny minor team. For a long way I thought the tall Tipperary youths would win through. But when Tom Barry, Freyne, Walsh, Nyhan and company settled down, they bored holes through Tipp's defence. Kilkenny came from behind and finished like champions. Tipperary teams had almost monopolised these competitions in recent years. Last Sunday was an unlucky day, but Tipperary will glitter again.

FINAL OF 1961

AS USUAL, on the eve of an All-Ireland Final, I make it my business to stroll down the streets of Dublin and see the crowds sauntering along. This year I expected a smaller crowd than usual, for only one "county" team was in the final. But these blue and gold men and women of Tipperary were a host in themselves — a glad, good-humoured host of hurling lovers. And to keep them company were thousands of young Dubliners with merry quip and happy confidence — they had beaten the Wexford champions and Wexford had beaten Tipperary just twelve months ago. Dublin stock was buoyant of recent days; their men had reported 100 per cent fit. Tipperary were still worrying a little about their key-men — Jimmy Doyle, Kieran Carey and Tony Wall, but I was told that all three were in good shape and taking the field. So we looked forward eagerly to one grand game. Instead of that we had two of the best — with superb minor hurling.

The throngs were heading away for Croke Park from early morning but there was no crowding or confusion. Mr. Padraig O'Caoimh's arrangements, carefully planned in every detail, worked smoothly as ever; Croke Park was of velvet texture and the attendance, approaching 70,000 were placed in comfort.

Teams looked very well matched as they marched round — Tipperary looked the more seasoned lot, Dublin looked younger and swifter. From the throw-in by that much revered Killenaule gentleman, Dr. T. Morris, Archbishop of Cashel, Tipperary burst away and whipped three points in masterly fashion — one by Mackey McKenna and two by Jimmy Doyle. For a brief moment it looked as if Tipperary were in complete control.

But Dublin's speed was soon in evidence and they struck back. Billy Jackson opened their point score from the left corner and a free gave Lar Shannon another point and the great game was set. I must say that the hurling was fast and keen without being exciting. It reminded me more of a first-class league game than of a championship final. Tom Moloughney and Achill Boothman exchanged flying points. Des Foley and Matt O'Gara were always in the midfield picture, but it was Tipperary's forwards that got the scores. Whilst Dublin forwards battled for goals and failed before Tipperary's peerless backs, Tipperary forwards — Doyle, O'Gara, Nealon kept the points flag busy with long sailing shots. Bernie Boothman and Shannon had isolated Dublin points, but Tipperary's soaring minors were very useful. On the whole Tipperary were worth their four points (10 - 6) lead at half-time.

Dublin had been in attack for longer periods than Tipperary in that rather quiet and subdued first half; Dublin's good approach and undoubted speed deserved better fortune; they didn't appear to translate attacks into scores. They were soon to prove to us how premature they were. The third quarter was electric. A diagonal Dublin approach of accurate ground shots, finished in Billy Jackson's left top corner. The New Ireland Assurance star set himself and shot home a perfectly timed shot to the net for the only goal of the match. That score set the teams aflame. We saw some thrilling hurling, gloriously played by two fine sides determined on victory. A flashing Dublin point by Achill Boothman set the teams level and a neatly hit ball from Lar Shannon sailed over the bar for the lead to Dublin — first time in the course of the game.

Thenceforward it was man for man, in every corner of the field and every man on his mettle. The shouts and cheers of the crowd were continuous. Points came freely and the lead changed with heart-throbbing frequency. Achill Boothman was deadly accurate on Dublin's right; Billy Jackson had a useful minor. Dublin again in the lead. Back comes Jimmy Doyle with a brace — level again.

In a breathless finish, Donie Nealon and Jimmy Doyle sent two flying balls above the bar with rifle accuracy — Tipperary two points in front but not safe. Both sets of backs were herioc and never a goal was scored — O'Brien and Gray were equally staunch. Achill Boothman finished a great hour's hurling with a curling point. Amidst fierce excitement, well controlled, the final whistle sounded and Tipperary had won their eighteenth title in grand style. Dublin had played so well that they would not have been flattered with a draw. They were rather unlucky with some close shots. But so consistent and tenacious were Tipperary's defence and attack that they deserved their hard-earned victory.

Early arrivals at Croke Park enjoyed a delightful minor game. Teams hurled level for three-quarters of the hour. Then a splendid run of accurate scores by Kilkenny's front lines brought ready victory. This made up a splendid pair of finals and the fine, though overcast weather lent its aid. There was no wind, the light at Croke Park was good throughout and the sod perfect — an afternoon to be remembered by homefolk and overseas visitors.

Football Favourites

1941 FOOTBALL FINAL

KERRY are head of the list of football champions. Ever since the Dublin Young Irelands captured three titles in the '90's the Capital had led the van. At one time they led Kerry by fourteen titles to five. That was in 1923. To have captured ten All-Irelands since then, in a competition where 32 counties are entered, is an achievement which establishes Kerry's claim to undisputed leadership. When it comes to championship football — and "final" football in particular — Kerry are in a class apart. There appears to be some umplumbed depths of energy and resource in their physical and mental make-up, which heave into a tidal wave overwhelming all barriers at the end of a championship game.

Last Sunday it was the same old story. Kerry were out-manoeuvred by Galway's grand team for fully twenty minutes of the first half and it was a miracle that Galway weren't goals in front. On change of goals the Tribesmen slashed two points home and Western cheers rang high. Then Kerry seemed to awake in one huge upheaval, like a giant who had overslept himself. Their midfield was roused. Then came O'Connor's mighty goal and Kerry rampant. It was one tremendous finish where hard knocks were taken as they came and the thud of men's eager bodies left many prone again and again as herculean athletes heaved their weight and unbeaten spirit into the mighty fray. And there were bouts of grand football in a thundering game of real championship mettle.

The Harvest Moon, which shone unbroken and round during a whole week, had looked down on many a plan to reach Croke Park when each heavy harvest day was done. And it was a record harvest week in garnered grain for which the Irish people must thank a bounteous Providence. The heart of the people was uplifted in succeeding suns. The harvest was safe in settled weather and all roads led to Croke Park. Despite shortage of petrol and coal, "love had found a way." We had a fine hearty gathering of Irish humanity at Croke Park — we had the wheat of the land.

These Gaeltacht counties that had toured America together and became fast friends, have appeared in three All-Irelands within four years. Up to yesterday honours ran even. Mutual respect bred high endeavour. On the way to the final, both teams had their anxious moments. Both counties rose to great occasions and so widespread was the interest and keen the rivalry, that all attendance records would have been broken had transport been normal. Instead of forty train specials of

1938 we only had three last Sunday. The petrol, too, was scarce, but never before was there such a biking parade to the Liffeyside. Cyclists lined the roads in one continuous stream. The trek which opened early in the week ended at 3 p.m. on Sabbath day, though a few stragglers with tyre troubles wheeled dusty cycles in, sweating and very weary, round the half-time whistle.

Ulster had sent packed trains, and I met many bronzed men of the North on the Cusack Stand. Galway men had come in thousands by every manner of transport. The maroon and white favours altogether outnumbered Kerry's green and gold badges. I heard Connemara and Dingle Gaelic blend sweetly in O'Connell Street. For the Gaeltacht outposts had many stalwart players in action — and right well did they play their part.

It was the Dingle peninsula that sent the strongest individual contingent. A nest of fisher houses at the head of Dingle Quay is known as The Colony. It is very much akin to The Claddagh of Galway. And the Colony men and women are proud of their modest hero, Paddy Bawn Brosnan, captain of fishing smack "Rory" that had won a rich harvest from the sea in recent months. And so the Colony was there in all their glory. Men, women and children had travelled on week-end trains — wholesome buoyant folk, for Dingle are champions of Kerry and champions of Ireland. The Kerry Captain, Willie Dillon, lives just round the corner from The Colony, and Sean Brosnan, a previous Captain, was reared on the head of the Creek where the boats ride at anchor. At the head of the town overlooking the harbour lives Tom O'Connor ("Gegga") who clinched the winning goal and added two fine points to his fame.

Three miles due east of Dingle there is a comfortable farm-house by the roadside — the home of Willie Casey, Kerry's cool centre-half. And a few miles beyond that, Annascaul (River of Shadows) boasts of Paddy Kennedy of the Guards. Over the hill we find the home of Charlie O'Sullivan hard by Castlegregory, and deep in the Western Gaeltacht young Kavanagh, of Galway University, saw the light — his brilliant opening passages for his adopted county almost took our breath away. No wonder that Dingle peninsula is proud of her football sons, with Falvey of Dingle town and Seamus O'Dowd of Ballydavid, still shining for Dublin.

Galway supporters, who patronised the greyhound racing at Shelbourne Park on Saturday night, were bounding with confidence. Brendan Nestor said "we'll win" with such assurance that I began to fear for Kerry — until I met Con Brosnan of six-title fame. Con looks fine and his judicious handling of the Kerrymen in their Tralee preparation put them on the high road to victory. "The lads are in great form," says the North Kerryman, "and they won't lose." So we waited the momentous hour.

Croke Park never looked such a picture. The carpet was emerald — a darker green over the spot near Hill Sixteen where Hogan fell. From the heights of Cusack Stand, the Artane Band and Pipers looked midget. They kept a grand line. There was a happy blend of colour in the crowd. Summer weather brought blues and purples and reds and saffrons in happy harmony. Padraig McNamee was there to throw the ball in with the tall graceful Central Secretary, Padraig O'Keeffe in easy control of detail and procedure. A fine orderly presentation of a significant day in the national year.

I thought Kerry had filled in a lot since last year. Eddie Walsh and Tadg Healy had thickened around the shoulders and hips. Keohane's tall shoulders towered over all except the beautifully moulded athlete, Duggan, of Galway University. These Galway men looked bronzed, fit and well. An ever muscular lot with the weight in the right place. If anything more rugged than the rangy Kerry backs, amongst whom Captain Bill Dillon looked small despite his 5ft. 11ins. Two champion teams representing historic provinces of the Gael. Resurgent Ireland was here in unmistakable strength which these thirty athletes typified.

Galway were the first away and so ready were their midfield men that they were soon plying balls galore to fast forwards. Kerry backs were soon busy. Their close tackling alone saved their lines and rushed Galway's front lines to shoot wide when scores should have come. Kerry broke the virgin score board. Paddy Bawn, with safest of hands, parted perfectly to O'Gorman, who had ranged in to take his chance and swing the opening point across. Then we saw Galway at their best. Their fielding, anticipation and reactions were all a shade in front in Kerry. Mulholland, Burke and John Dunne gave Galway a lead that was not reversed for three-quarters of the hour. O'Connor swung Kerry's number two high above the rigging and a powerful run by Paddy Bawn brought a glorious point to balance. Galway again forced the pace in grand combined movements. They did everything but score goals. Connolly and Burke made wild shots from good scoring ground, before the Clare star turned a lovely point to resume the lead. The Walshs and O'Connor were tearing in for Kerry now and O'Connor's balancing point close to half-time was a grand spot of work. Galway were unlucky and had the better of the half.

When the eager maroon men raced away in beautifully combined movements at change of ends, Galway were in the ascendant. Burke and Dunne had flashing minor scores to lead 6 to 4. But strong work by Myers and Dillon gave O'Gorman a side-stepping chance and he narrowed the gap. Kerry were still in arrears when Brosnan and Kennedy started to soar high for balls round midfield. Kerry forced the pace. They seemed all alive now; forcing a free, S. Brosnan swung it out to the right where Walsh placed O'Connor. That "ball-of-a-man" whirled right and left and then made an opening. He raced right in and at the vital instant let fly a whale of a ball hard and low. It was a grand rising shot that tore straight to the net for the decisive score and the only goal in a strenuous hour.

Kerry were blooded now, like beagles on a mountain. They stormed through. Pat Kennedy hit a remarkable point over his head and Kerry were a goal clear. Next came a grand Galway rally. John Dunne had a typical point after dummying his way in and crashed one great ball for the net that only one goalie in Ireland could save. That man was Danno Keeffe. He held it and kicked clear, cheered to the echo. Murt Kelly's brace of points from frees clinched the great game. McGauran and his backs played heroically and Kerry's goal had more than one escape; Keohane, Dillon, Casey and Healy all lending a hand. Galway had played a grand game and only failed by a narrow margin. Kerry's traditional rally and inspired finish brought them their all important and 15th title — one of the Kingdom's greatest triumphs. And Danno Keeffe can break all football records in winning seven All-Irelands — if he can stop at that. For Kerry are still a young team of balance and skill.

ROSCOMMON WIN FOOTBALL FINAL

NEVER was there a train from Castlemaine to Annascaul in Kerry, nor from Annascaul to Castlemaine for that matter — mountains and sea preclude it. But facts are no hindrance to Kerry buoyancy; not even defeat by Roscommon! And so here were those tired, but happy, young folk from the peninsulas of the South-West heading off for their return trains in joyous mood, still singing their droll, whimsical, lively choruses:-

> "Are you the man that drives the train,
> From Annascaul to Castlemaine?
> Are you the man that killed our ducks —
> On the lonesome road to Dingle?"

Thirty foot-weary travellers had slept on the stairs of a private boarding house in the Southern suburbs of Dublin City on Saturday night and were glad of the privilege. This was typical of the position all over Dublin, in the townships and convenient seaside resorts as far away as Arklow and Skerries. Never was there such sporting invasion since Finn McCool and his Robin Hood merry men from the Hill of Allen in Kildare crossed the Liffey to the Aonach of Loch Garman, 1,700 years ago.

How the tens of thousands of enthusiasts came is a "ghostly" mystery. Some mystic headless coaches of their old fairyworld must have wafted them hither. But here they were over the week-end to receive Dublin's kindly welcome. Despite broken, late harvest weather, the central thoroughfares of the city were thronged to the idle tram tracks on Saturday night. Every welcoming hostel was thronged to headsroom only. Restaurants, private hotels were crowded out where I passed. Yet the best of good humour prevailed.

The harvest was safe; the bulk of it sold for "fair-good prices," they told me. These men and maids from the provinces had the sun and the wind and the soft rain written on their pleasant faces — carefree enthusiasts of Kerry and Roscommon. But the West and North predominated; Amiens Street and Westland Row areas were congested even on Sunday forenoon. All were heading for Croke Park in smooth, ever-growing dark streams of humanity.

I reached the Cusack Stand's huge airy fastnesses an hour before the game to watch the swelling throngs. Sideline seats were already full, even behind the goals. Over every converging road and avenue they poured. Every vantage point was occupied. Roscommon's blue and gold colours seemed to be most in favour. They had won last year's All-Ireland, but these men of the fertile western plains felt that the biggest feather in their cap and the culminating point of their ambitions would be to beat Kerry of the fifteen titles in a Croke Park final.

All were snug and serene in the Western dressing rooms. Trainer Kehoe reported a clean bill of health. Last year's winning team was almost intact, and weak links rewelded. Kerry had twenty-nine men ready; yet one sensed from the furrowed brows of the selectors that they had not yet fully decided. Their men were so uniform that they decided to hold fast to their first selection, keeping these eager substitutes still on a close leash.

Paddy Bawn Brosnan, fishing boat owner, of Dingle was captain — a rugged, gnarled, oak-trunk of a man who played on in pain with a twisted ankle for fifty minutes of the hour. Seven men of this southern side were six feet or over — rangy limber men. The most striking of the newcomers were the sunny-haired Lyne brothers of Killarney. Lieutenant Joe Keohane towered above them all.

Roscommon paraded better. Their step was precise and military. Thirteen of the side were uniformly muscular, wide-shouldered, sturdy, youthful men, clean limbed and lean-faced. Brimful of confidence, Kerry's might held no terrors for Jimmy Murray's men. That popular business man from Knockcroghery village is the idol of the West. He has opened the road to victory in a score of recent games — the inspiration of Roscommon's attack; the brainy pivot on which all their winning attacking movements hinge.

When I reached the lofty heights of the Cusack Stand again, every vantage point was occupied and the booked seats were filling rapidly. A gusty wind and slanting, thin showers crossed the pitch — looking well despite recent rains.

The band parade and musical programmes filled the interval. By the time they were under way, fully 70,000 people were inside the pitch and still they came in thousands over the Canal bridge. By that time 100 venturous souls were astride the railway wall and even the roof of the long stand held 50 plucky climbers, who laughed at the showers.

The game was more earnest than brilliant. Marking was close; fit men, who knew every trick in the trade, struggled in close company. Roscommon were faster, Kerry the more far-seeing. First one and then the other led. Jimmy Murray sparkled and fed his wings with shrewd passes. Roscommon deserved their half-time lead of two points. They stretched it when, ranging upfield, Gilmartin put them three points clear. Kerry were roused. Kennedy first and then Dunne raised flags and Kerry were in front on a winning vein that promised change of title.

Roscommon followers in the stands were subdued for a session. But not for long. They looked to me to be the better trained, more uniform side. They showed pace, cohesion and skill. Keenan, tall, dark, U.C.D. man, was deadly accurate on frees, and Kinlough swung over the winning point from far out on the right wing. Keenan supplemented. The referee's whistle came before we expected it. Roscommon were again champions.

Such scenes of good-humoured enthusiasm were never seen at Croke Park. I even saw Roscommon players embracing their famous opponents, who caressed their shoulders firmly in appreciation of a great win. And so the heather hills of Connaught will blaze from hill to hill.

FOOTBALL FINAL 1945

THIRTY-FOUR years — half a lifetime — since Cork won a football All-Ireland! That explains why I laughed and defied the fierce 'nor'-wester' shower that swept Croke Park as the immense good-humoured throng were smoothing away after as exciting an hour's football as you could wish to see. A West Cork relative, who had travelled 230 miles, then stuck a red-and-white goose quill in my hat as I mounted my trusty bike; sane people were wondering who was the wild "mountaineer" with the raking red goose quill out of his hat and rising a *strouncawn* of Land League days:-

> One evening of late as I happened to stray
> Bound for Clonakilty from sweet Timoleague,
> 'Twas at Ballinscarthy some time I delayed,
>   I wetted my whistle with porter
> I kindled my pipe and I spat on my stick,
> I kept the Coach road, like a deer I did trip,
> I cared for no Bailiff, Landlord or Old Nick —
>   I sang like a lark in the morning.

There were nine Clonakilty men amongst the team and subs of the 1945 All-Ireland football champions.

The Southern invasion reminded me of old times. The driver of one train must have had a bet on the match, for he made the journey from Glanmire to Kingsbridge in 4½ hours. Danny Hobbs kept another well-ful of the boys in roars of laughter. The Hogan Stand was streaked with red and white favours. Genial Mickey Roche shouted at me when I stood up in my Press seat, "Sit down ou're that, Paddy M-." His usual sporting crowd of Cork eminents were with him, of course — old Cork footballers of the 1904 to 1911 brilliant patch, Billie Mackesy, Ned Buckley, John McCarthy, who all captained the Lee inter-county sides, John Buckley, and the All-Ireland hurler, Tom Barry, who captained London Hibernians in their palmiest days. The other Tom Barry of more recent fame was down in the body of the stand, and Sean Collins hard by; the Lord Mayor of Cork (Mr. Sheehan) had a special Southern cheer as he crossed the pitch with athletic steps after wishing those hearty red jerseys the "best of luck."

And they wanted it, for Cavan rose to unexpected heights against the wind in the second half when they tore in in waves, and shook Cork backs to their foundations. These defence lines of the Corkonians were as firm and defiant as the "cliffs of sweet Dunowen" where the Cork goalkeeper, Mike O'Driscoll, was bred and born.

Cavan were at Croke Park in full force. The Northern lines, with ample coal, brought anything from 15,000 to 18,000 eager Gaelic enthusiasts. They would not hear of Cavan's defeat, though Mick Higgins' injury was a serious handicap. These Breffni followers know Croke Park well and though beaten, their team covered themselves with glory in that grand rally which could not have failed to succeed against less determined do-or-die defenders.

Trainer Jim Barry reported a clean bill of health, although Eamonn Young paid two visits to a doctor for a slight neck trouble. Jim, breezy as ever, showed great respect for Cavan football, but knew the rock-bottom timbre of his own fifteen. The other Jim — most famous of Clonakilty Gaels, Jim Hurley, inter-county and multiple All-Ireland man in both codes, who had thrown all his abundant life and fire into the footballers' uphill fight, was there in all his gushing confidence. Croke Park pitch was a picture of deep emerald. Good order, stewarding and efficient control of the master artist, Paddy O'Keeffe, was apparent everywhere; affable Gardai lent a strong hand, and 70,000 were pretty comfortably situated before the gates were closed.

A gusty north-west swept the ground; the showers held off as Dublin boys proved too smart for the taller Leitrim minors. Real good football demands a still day, and the swinging, shifting wind accounted for much misfielding and faulty kicking. From a football point of view, the game did not reach the Cork-Galway semi final. But what it lacked in brilliancy of movement, was balanced by full-hearted endeavour where the scores ran alternately, and thirty fully fit and full blooded men battled out their final with abundant fire and resolution with never an unmanly or depressing incident to mar the great day.

Cork were quickly away, but Big Tom O'Reilly was as safe as he is huge. He sent his mid-field away, and in a brief space, T.P. O'Reilly handled on the right, and swung the opening point for Cavan within four minutes. Murphy, Crowley and Cronin then beat back telling drives. Soon Young was dummying his way up-field, Donovan covering well; Beckett received and doubled in. With fine anticipation and pace, Lieut. Tubridy raced across from the right to meet the centre and a thundering, rising shot hit the lower edge of the crossbar before glancing to the net for Cork's lead that they never lost.

Cavan pressure again tested Cork's tall and powerful backs — they all figured — O'Driscoll, Murphy, Crone, Magnier, Cronin, Crowley and O'Connor. Points out of their reach came from Tighe (a dangerous ranger) and Stafford, but Beckett pointed a free and H. O'Neill drove a grand straight point for Cork from long range. Tubridy and T.P. O'Reilly exchanged minors before half-time (Cork 1-4; Cavan 5 points).

Referee John Dunne of Galway, All-Ireland note, had little difficulty with the teams. He whistled for half-time with Eamonn Young in possession. Eamonn dropped the ball and Deignan raced in to shoot to the net — the whistle had gone and O'Driscoll made no attempt to stop the ball. The green flag waved but the goal was cancelled.

Derry Beckett was very adept in adding a Cork point on change of ends, and the game waxed fast and furious as both goals were visited. Cavan had a grand half-back line — Wilson, John Joe O'Reilly (brother of Tom's) and Paddy Smith. Stafford pointed a free for the North and Cavan were playing back. Cork's brace of wings — Tubridy and Casey — showed pace and ball control, yet the O'Reillys and Tighe swung the game round to the canal goal. For fully ten minutes Cork backs were under pressure. O'Driscoll was immensely cool and resourceful and his net never fell for the run of the hour, though he had to give a few fifties away under heavy storming attacks by the eager Cavan forwards, who seemed to have found a second life in defying wind and sun.

Tighe, a tall, rangy boy and T.P. O'Reilly were ever dangerous; Murphy was in his element — he took high and low in his stride and nailed O'Donoghue to the sod more than once. Crone and Magnier were little behind the Beara man during this testing period and Tadg Crowley often was found defending his own goalmouth. Cork's goal had many narrow escapes, but somehow or other they blocked, rooted, parried and bored a way out of danger.

"Togher" Casey, playing rattling football was now involved in a full-blooded charge and went down and out. He was taken to the lines and Jim "O'Brien" of Clon came on. Casey had recovered when I went to enquire behind the scenes after the match. Game as a pebble, he sang sweetly at the Corkmen's sing-song later in the evening.

Cavan again weaved in; Tighe was all but through. O'Donoghue, with an open goal in front, was clung to the ground by a super-effort of "Weesh" Murphy — a free and a point but worth it all at that stage of the game. At the other end, Young and O'Donovan got a move on — Young put in some beautiful runs, and Jim "O'Brien" was almost through for a Cork goal when pulled down. The free went wide. Once again Young and Tubridy ranged in with Lynch now busy outfield. Lynch and Young managed to bear the ball out to Derry Beckett — watchful as a cat, he fielded safe, slipped nimbly round Cully, steadied himself and let fly — a grand rising ball to the net corner for a goal that clinched the issue. Then such a scene there was, my countrymen. Staid men and maids went wild — hats, sticks, coats, flags were thrown into the air. Red flags waved everywhere and bells rattled all round us. It was a score "worth a ransom," as Jim Hurley says. Cavan struggled gallantly, but Cork were irrepressible now and were forcing the pace at the final whistle.

Without being a star game, this was a satisfying one, and Cavan's tenacity won many new friends. Remarkable that after 34 years the two sons of two men who helped to win Cork's last All-Ireland — Jerry Beckett and Jack Young — should have shone out so clearly last Sunday. Both Derry Beckett and Eamonn Young played a major part in Cork's great win — sturdy branches of the parent tree; sons of the old stock.

Says The Man With The Velour Hat

"YOU can't keep de Corkmen down, I'm telling yeh! Push him down and drive him down or squeeze him down — you might as well be idle, me sonny boy! He'll always come to de top, like de cork in de water."

He blew the froth off his pint. Clearly a character; I tried to place that battered brown hat of real Australian velour, wondering how many hands it passed through on the way down. The felt had worn clear of fur in patches where many hands had handled it, perhaps for generations. But he was a gay, old soul, cheery-cheeked and happy.

"Whot's day you said, me sonny boy! Cavan were de best team! Yerra gwane witcha. Shut your mout' and don't open it 'till yeh go home to yer supper.

"What Cavan man could score dat goal of Derry Beckett an' he not de size uv a sod o' turf, wit big Tom Riley and Barney Cully tryin' to drive him down tru de groun'. An' what about Weeshy Murphy of Beare Island — me sonny boy, de Cork full back dat pulled de whole side of a boat agin four strong men in Bantry Bay Regatta, an' I know what I'm talking about for I'm a Covey man from de Cove uv Cork. De best Riley I ivir knew was Barrelo Riley of de Redmonds dat hurled for Cork. An' didn't we win four hurling titles in a row, until we were ashamed uv winning them, and dis year made a present uv it to Tipp! In de're own town uv Turliss! An' now we comes to flake hell out uv Tipperary, Kerry, Galway an' Cavan. Dey said Cork could play no football. Dat in me eye for a yarn."

All of a sudden I remembered I had to go to the office to write a report of Croke Park and the 1945 All-Ireland Final. I thought it a good hard game, in all seriousness. Same huge crowds and billiard table pitch; band parades "mixed" like the weather, in scope and quality. Marching teams around the field looked fine but a little too near a gladiator display in Ancient Rome or a parade of artists before a music hall show.

Dublin youths were a lot too artful and nimble for the taller Leitrim minors who seemed moonstruck by the immensity of the occasion after their long seclusion in the Arigna Hills.

The Senior game was no kidglove affair. Both teams fought like Trojans to the final whistle. Cork forwards seemed to make better use of their chances — Beckett and Tubridy in particular. The crossing wind put perfect football out of the question; there was much misfielding and wild shooting for a classic game, and the high light from a spectator's view point was that stern passage near the three-quarter way when Cavan forced the pace and stormed in on Cork's tall backs in one of the finest rallies of many years.

Cork's pair of goals were skilfully manoeuvred and Beckett shared in both; though he didn't do a lot for the hour his majors were worth a ransom to this County. For the surest sign of strength through the field was the number of times the respective goalkeepers were tested, and O'Driscoll, guarding Cork's net, saved three times as many shots as the Ulster goalie encountered in the hour.

Cavan's half-back line was superb — Wilson, John Joe O'Reilly and Paddy Smith played with fine precision and confidence. Tighe, a rangy schoolboy of 19, was, with T.P. O'Reilly, the brain-wave of Cavan's attack, who only woke up when the sands were running out. Stafford's screwkick for a point from the touchline at an impossible angle was a delightful effort. Lt. Tubridy's pace on Cork's right wing and Lt. Eamonn Young's dummy swerve at midfield gave Cork's front line the chances they wanted.

When Cavan forwards stepped on the gas they searched every hole and cranny in Cork's defensive armour, which seemed to be made of Damascus steel. Again and again these boys in blue from Lough Rombar and Virginia, from Cootehill, Mulnahorna and Cornafean tore on in multiple hosts. Cork's goal was stormed like a Bastille. But the Home Guards stood firm as the Mizen Head when storms break on it. Yet, a lucky score would have forced a replay at level scoring near the end, and, had a draw been the verdict, not a man in the field would quarrel at the ending.

Unless, indeed, that slightly boisterous and somewhat provocative batch of Corkonians in the Cusack Stand. They must have had the four-leaf shamrock to get eight seats in a block — and didn't they make their presence felt, as they called on "Micko" Crowley and "Weeshy" Murphy (who is 6 foot 1 in his socks); on "Togher" Casey, who was knocked out stone cold in a battering ram charge and carried off senseless; on "Moll" Driscoll, their goalie.

The troop of buoyant souls on the Cusack Stand had come well prepared and brooked no denial. A spacious suitcase carried half-a-dozen five-naggin bottles of Cork malt and a dozen flagons of Munster cider; that malt would fetch the price of a tidy Cork farm in Piccadilly or on Broadway. Every man had a glass, with a few to spare in case of damage. They wouldn't hear of defeat, and sang "The Banks" and their rallying song:-

"Some of them came from Kerry,
Some from County Clare,
From Galway, Dublin, Donegal and
Some from old Kildare,
Some from a land beyond the sea
From Boston and New York
But the boys that licked the Black and Tans
Were the boys from the County Cork".

Remonstrating with them was useless; they were here to enjoy themselves and did to their hearts' content.

Cavan followers were meek and unobtrusive in comparison. Yet Cavan had a huge following on stand and line, as the deep roar that greeted their gallant uphill struggle demonstrated. They took their beating with good-humoured gravity. "We're coming back again next year," they told me outside Amiens Street Station in pleasant Northern accents, slightly clipped.

One more view I had of the battered velour hat, that looked as if a dose of D.D.T. would do it good. Its owner slightly the worse for wear as he headed across O'Connell Bridge for the down train. But he was ironically humorous as ever as he gave the parting shot to his Dublin butties of the day:-

"What mather same if me mudder sold pigs' crubbens in de Coal-quay. Shure dey were dat sweet dat you'd lick yer fingers after dem; sa'long me sonny boya; Up Beckett; Up de Barrs!"

KERRY -V- ANTRIM AT CROKE PARK 1946

ALL along the slopes of the hills reapers and binders were going full blast towards the end of last week, and I was really surprised to see such a big proportion of the golden grain standing up well after the storm and downpour of the previous week-end. Four or five dry cool days helped and some good work was done in these neighbouring parishes, where help was plentiful, though expensive, close to the city.

Strange to say it was in the sheltered belts between the trees in the hollow that the greatest storm damage was done. It seemed to me that the straw was softest top heavy. Much of it was flattened and a lot tossed beyond a reaper and binder's capacity. Through the provinces, too, much promising corn has been tossed and lodged too grievously to rise again. Here the mowing machine and old-fashioned scythe must be requisitioned. Whatever the weather, double labour is involved in saving what promised to be a record harvest. On the east coast Friday and Saturday proved to be great gathering days — much heavy corn was stooked and capped. The sky was lifting and those myriads of yachts within and outside Dun Laoghaire Harbour had flapping sails in the stillness of the evening. The last of the ocean-going yachts at the end of their long reach from behind Land's End were becalmed within reach of home — between Bri Head and Ben Edar.

Even then the glass-in-the-hall was dropping slowly; wireless news of more floods and storms in Britain was ominous, and sure enough back we swung to rain overnight, just when hopes of recovery seemed brightest. To those born on the land, who understand how valuable every cloudless sunny day is at this stage of the year and the harvest, this menacing rain is depressing. We want sun galore in the next few weeks — as one wise man said: "We don't want a drop of rain 'til Christmas." Following the grain, comes the potatoes and roots harvesting. The sky is overcast as I write but there is not a breath of wind to rustle the leaves. The barometer stirs slowly upward and with "hope springing eternal" we hope the shanachie was a true prophet when he said more as a prayer than a prophecy, "God never sent a good harvest but He gave us weather to save it."

And just as I watched the rain-clouds gathering in the south-west after Mass on Sunday I made another rather disappointing discovery. In the grove in front, favoured by my friends the blackbirds and thrushes, robins, linnets and finches of all descriptions that wake the morning and glad the sunset from December to June, there are many songbirds' nests

194

which I have tried assiduously to protect by voice and advice — vigorous or otherwise, directed to two-footed and four-footed marauders — cats are most active in the latter category.

About five years ago the "baby" of the house rushed in from his play in The Square with the news: "Daddy, there's a white blackbird in The Square." "All white, boy," said I eagerly. "Well nearly white — he has white wings on him, anyhow."

True enough. Yellow bill was there amongst the close lower branches of the shrubbery — half his wings and breast were white. He became a great favourite and we kept a supply of snails, worms and breadcrumbs near his haunts. He sang rather timidly, as if ashamed of those white feathers that seemed to outlaw him from his tribe. Yet he was a real "londuv" in every characteristic even in his morning chuckle as he broke covert. Betrayed by his white feathers perhaps, he was pounced on by an ambush cat and his body rather mangled, but intact, was lying there before me on the way home from early devotions. I buried him in the dark moist earth beneath his favourite tree.

Then the rain teemed for three solid hours, so I had to rake out an old pre-war pair of pull-ups and a battered hat and overcoat as I faced the weather on a trusty little cycle on my way to Croke Park, consoled by telephone message from Rineanna Meteorological Office that the afternoon may not be too bad.

They were right. Thirty thousand filed in; the streets of the capital, glistening with rain, carried streams of defiant folk, sporting "green and gold" (Kerry) and white and saffron (Antrim) favours. The Ulster supporters were in an immense majority — specials on the Northern line, almost a dozen of them, had trooped into Amiens Street Station packed to the buffers. They would not hear of Antrim's defeat.

Yet I knew in my heart that this was "Kerry" weather. And there were many glad troops of stalwart young men and earnest maids from the south-west; they looked cheery — I then learned that they had travelled from Tralee and beyond through the night. Croke Park again played well and defied the weather. American priests with extreme south-west and north-east accents in sharp contrast, were all round us, flags and favours everywhere.

The game opened at an astonishing pace. Fast firm open football. Antrim were first away, giving us a taste of their weaving hand-passing movements. Willie Casey halted Kevin Armstrong in his flight. Soon Kerry were upfield.

A mis-kick free gave Kennedy and O'Donnell a chance. They passed and repassed, Antrim fashion. Janc Lyne rounded his man and Willy O'Donnell, racing through took Lyne's pass in his long stride and crashed a grand ground ball to the net corner — ninety seconds of play and Kerry one goal up.

Then Antrim played back. Gallagher and O'Neill outfielded Dowling and Cremin, the young North Kerrymen — Amstrong and Co. were away in lightning runs. Points from Gallagher and McCorry (2) balanced scores and a good shot of O'Hara's brought them ahead in a grand first quarter.

'Twas the best part of the hour, Antrim's short passing and swerving methods were hampered by the weather, the greasy-topped sod and a slippery ball. Willie O'Donnell played fine football to recover the Kerry lead; Watterson drove a long one home for the equaliser near half-time. Level scoring 1-2 to 0-5, and Kerry happy with the wind and drizzle on their backs.

The second half was not near so good. Antrim's huge following roared hoarsely as their forwards broke away — Gibson had a dodging run before shooting a point. Playing sound solid football now, gripping every ball confidently and driving well, Kerry attacked. O'Donnell balanced. Antrim's movements broke down on Kerry's stonewall defence. O'Keeffe and his six backs in front were determined not to let those flashing speed merchants through.

Pat Kennedy, playing masterly football, swung a grand ball from forty-five yards for Kerry's lead. The green and gold men took control; even Dowling and Cremin held Gallagher and O'Neill to level terms. Young E. O'Connor, Willie Casey and G. Teehan held the Gibson, Armstrong and McCorry line in a vice. Kerry forwards showed slim accuracy — O'Donnell had two minors; Dan Kavanagh number three and Kerry had a clear four points lead.

As Armstrong was swerving away on a solo run, Casey had him down; O'Neill rushed in and there was a brief "ruggy" — over in a flash, but Casey and O'Neill were marched off. Casey's loss at this stage almost cost Kerry the game.

Released from a stranglehold, Armstrong got a free leg and fed his wings, McCorry a powerful winger, had two points, well hit frees; Watterson, best of a moderate back line, had another and Antrim were only a point behind. Kerry backs, particularly Walshe, Lyne and E. O'Connor, gripped every ball and never lost one; Keohane was cool and safe. Pat Kennedy, of Annascaul, ranged downfield and Lyne got it; O'Donnell and Burke took a hand. It all happened in ten seconds. Batt Garvey came up the left from nowhere and before Antrim backs knew what was happening the Dingle man flicked the ball to the net.

Antrim again rallied gallantly and Kevin Armstrong tore through on his own to kick Antrim's last point. Antrim died game, but there was no mistaking Kerry's all-round proficiency in skilful, orthodox Gaelic football of the very best kind. Their handling was secure as ever and they had gathered a bunch of forwards of the true Kerry pattern — cool, calculating men, who rarely put a ball astray even when harassed by close attention. Whether Roscommon or Laoighis win next Sunday we shall have a good final.

ROSCOMMON -V- LAOIGHIS

THE Roscommon-Laoighis game attracted another record crowd to Croke Park — 51,000 is a staggering figure for a semi-final — further evidence that our native games go from strength to strength, and that our people are in good heart despite broken harvest weather. The game itself was a stirring affair, particularly in the second half, when Laoighis rallied to such purpose that only the stonewall defence of the Connaught champions saved the day.

The Western team opened very brightly, with Jimmy Murray, Captain, in his happiest mood. His opening points were masterpieces of a "40 yards" man's art — anticipation, swerving and shooting whenever he could give the posts a chance. Goals from Fallon and McQuillan gave the Men of the West an 8 points to nil lead at the end of the first quarter. Then Laoighis woke up. The Delaneys figured in a rapid exchange between Willie and Morgan Delaney. A brilliant screw kick of Tommy Murphy's from the left corner for a point was cheered to the echo, and Willie Delaney, shrewd, strong and elusive as ever, drove a high ball to the posts. As two Roscommon defenders crashed in going for it, the ball found the net. Yet Roscommon well deserved their five points lead at half-time.

Laoighis came back to the arena like lions refreshed. They took the game to Connaught lines, Murphy and Haughney fed their front lines and the huge crowd were roused when Murphy placed Connolly to shoot a first-time ground ball of tremendous pace to the Roscommon net. His point balanced scores before the threequarter hour, and hundreds of Laoighis banners of blue and white were waving wildly on the crowded terraces and packed side-lines, whose gates were locked half-an-hour before the games.

The Murray pair, Phelim and Captain Jim again got moving. Jimmy dummied, shrewdly drawing the opposition; O'Beirne crashed the ball across the goal. Laoighis backs were caught on the wrong foot and fumbled their clearance, leaving the door open for Donal Keenan to shoot left-legged to the net for a decisive and staggering goal. Yet Laoighis never eased off. Murphy forced ball after ball in. He pointed a free. But 'twas then that Roscommon's backs rose to their greatest heights. They refused to let Laoighis attackers through — head, neck and heels they went into the earnest battle. Lynch, Phelim Murray, Casserly and Jackson were sound as bell-metal under pressure. 'Twas a tremendous struggle. Hughes of Laoighis tore in and drove a fierce ground ball just inside the upright. Dolan threw himself at it and brought off the save of the hour, as he rolled clean with the ball in his arms — Roscommon were in the final against their greatest rivals, Kerry, whose clever young forwards will be well matched by this trojan Roscommon defence. Once again it was — so near and yet so far with Laoighis — most unlucky and plucky of teams.

CAVAN AND MAYO

NOT since the Eucharistic Congress of 1932 had Dublin such an invasion. For once in a way Munster was not represented in the final; the North and West sent thousands by all manner of transport. Dublin's main thoroughfares were thronged from Friday evening when the first contingents came by car, bus and rail — hardy, wiry men of the West, the salt of the sea in their weather-brown faces. Much Gaelic was spoken — these fine hearty folk of Bangor Erris and Connemara — a soft, tender Gaelic with accentuations on the slender vowels and sibilant consonants. It was late on Saturday evening and in the early hours of Sunday morning that the big Ulster contingent trooped in to pack all Liffeyside.

Cavan were dominant in this Northern contingent. The broad highway through Virginia, Oldcastle, Kells, Navan and Dunboyne carried a constant stream of traffic from early morn. All approach roads to Dublin had parked cars and special buses stretching out for miles. The centre of the city hummed with happy, murmuring voices as the trek to Croke Park developed after early Masses which were thronged on to the public streets in every parish.

Despite recent rains, the Croke Park pitch looked its emerald best. Mr. Padraig O'Keeffe's staffs were at their posts from 9 a.m. and they had a heavy day as every turnstile clicked merrily. Serpent-like queues developed on the approach routes. The sideline seats were closed at noon and the minor game (1.30) between Dublin and Tyrone was not long under way before every vantage point was packed. The doors were all closed to thousands of folk who had travelled long distances. From the top of the packed Cusack Stand, I could see more people than ever before in the environment of Croke Park. Mr. O'Keeffe wisely decided, when 75,000 were within the grounds, to take no risks of over-crushing in the congested areas. There were still some corners at the canal side of the Cusack and of the long covered stand where spectators told me they were so comfortable that they could sit down on the steps at half-time in the senior game and enjoy their sandwiches.

No wonder that this All-Ireland Football Final has come to be accepted as the greatest outdoor pageant of Ireland's sporting year. They were a singularly well-ordered and good-humoured gathering. Rival supporters swopped their challenging slogans. The entrance of Tyrone and Dublin minor finalists brought cheers and counter-cheers. A particularly hearty welcome awaited these young Gaels from our severed counties — from the land of the O'Neill whose red hand they sported on their white jerseys — happy contrast to Dublin's royal blue. This was a most promising curtain-raiser.

Tyrone, a stalwart lot of boys, drawn mainly from secondary schools prominent in the Ulster College Championships, played grand football throughout. They held Dublin to a level three points each at half-time, and looked all over winners with a sweeping wind behind them. The Dublin boys played with abundant pluck and determination through a fine, bright second half. The reach and strength of Devlin, McGrath and Dargan gave the O'Neill boys a substantial lead. Ferguson's final goal for Dublin made a lively finish, 1-5 (8) to 11 points. Tyrone worthy winners.

Three tall stately men — standing to attention whilst the "Faith of Our Fathers" was played — marched to centre. His Grace, Dr. Walsh, of Tuam had Mr. T. McNamara, President of the G.A.A. of America, at his right; Mr. Dan O'Rourke, G.A.A. President, on his left. Behind the banners of Ireland and America marched P.J. Grimes of Tailteann fame who organised the "Flight of the Gaels" tours. The green and red Mayo jerseys contrasted well with Cavan's (holders) dark blue, as thirty fit men marched past — 'twas an inspiring sight as all stood to attention for the Soldiers Song and the great game was under way, dead on time, when Archbishop Walsh threw the ball between them. Cavan had won the toss and John Joe O'Reilly decided to play with the wind whilst the gusts from the city were strong. They were in attack at once — Tighe and Sherlock driving two wides. Big Peter Donoghue, Cavan's full forward, kicked two frees for accurate points, but for fifteen minutes close marking by Mayo backs kept those hard-working Cavan forwards out.

The second quarter was all Cavan. Those swinging forwards wove their way in, and Tony Tighe on Cavan's right wing, kept fielding difficult crossing balls in vice-like grip, to swerve like a whalebone, give and take return passes as he slipped through to shoot first a left and then a right shot well out of Byrne's reach. Tom was holding a brave goal and went down to forwards fearlessly. Mayo backs were hesitant. Brady and Sherlock, huge men, had too much reach and weight for Carney and Mongey in that brief session of Cavan supremacy. Again it was Tighe, ever elusive, that crossed to centre and placed Sherlock. Taking the pass in his stride, Sherlock bored his way right through to shoot a picture goal before half-time. Acton and Solan had missed good Mayo openings, and the men of the West were scoreless at half-time against Cavan's 3-2 (11).

This looked a sound lead. The high wind, gusty at times, put "class" football at a premium and there were patches of scrappy football throughout where the half-gale curled the ball. Marking continued close as Mayo backed the breeze. Gilvarry brothers shone now, and Joe placed

Mulderrig for Mayo's opening point. The Western clans had been reticent so far; that first white flag for them raised a surge of encouraging calls "Come on Muigheo." Carney and Mongey were now matching Brady and Sherlock in hip-to-hip struggles. The cool and clever Western midfield pair began to give their front lines shrewdly placed service. Carney put a fast-driven free to Benson's hands under the Cavan bar. He saved, but didn't clear, and Solan was on the ball like chained lightning to net Mayo's first goal.

Cavan's sound experience and field craft again told. Keeping the ball on the floor, these clever sweeping forwards bored their way into the wind. Donoghue pointed his third free from well out and Garda Mick Higgins, well held by 6 foot 4 McAndrew, now came into his own. He saw a slender opening and grasped it. McGovern, who had come on for John Joe Reilly, who had been in the wars, put a careful ball into Higgin's hands and he was away with a thrilling run goalwards. He caught Mayo's backs unsettled and crashed home a fine ground goal as he tore in. Sherlock's point gave Cavan a formidable 12 points lead at the three-quarter hour and the game looked over.

Gerald Courell of Ballina, Mayo's mentor, now whipped his fit but rather inexperienced men to new endeavour by voice and gesture. In a respite, he gave fresh encouragement — he knew there was more in the men who had beaten Kerry and asked them for it. They rallied in a gallant way. Mayo tore downfield to the goalmouth; Smith of Cavan, hard pressed, caught and passed to Doonan who erred in turning to the left to clear — Acton was on him in a flash to bustle the ball past Benson just inside the post.

Mayo were roused now, these Western forwards swarmed in. John Gilvarry fed his front line and in a scrambling charge, Acton was the last to receive and flick the ball to the net — 16 to 10. Mayo bubbling over with newly-roused ambition kept the 1947 champions close to the posts. Joe Gilvarry and Mulderrig, on Mayo's left were nippy and eel-like. Tearing into the square, a Mayo forward was pulled down, and Padraig Carney (U.C.D.) hit a perfect shot at cannon pace out of Benson's reach — the score 4-1 to 4-4 and Mayo full of vigour.

Cavan's backs held on grimly, but Carney and Mulderrig narrowed the margin to one point, 4-4 to 4-3. Sideline fans were standing up now roaring orders. The grim battle went on. Then Eamonn Mongey of Mayo's centre, an old-looking young man, fastened on a fast-travelling ball and swung it safe above the cross-bar for a Mayo point, setting the score at 4-4 to 4-4 at the 25th minute and the crowd roaring.

Cavan threw all their craft into a last throw. Higgins, trojan-like, now tore in to Carolan, who was pulled down. Coolly Peter Donoghue walked in to a tricky free — a grand shot lifted the ball over the bar for what proved to be Cavan's winning point in the 29th minute. Mayo came back swift as the wind, and forced a free. Cavan manned their goal — Carney drove low and Higgins, who had ranged himself on the line, blocked the ball, and in two kicks the game was over. It was a grim, rugged battle between fit, determined men. Mayo's day may arrive in 1949!

THE 1949 FOOTBALL FINALS

TIME was when only Kerry could pack Croke Park in an All-Ireland final. So popular have Gaelic games become that two next-door neighbours — Meath and Cavan — not alone packed the ground to the walls, but drew 10,000 hopeful visitors who arrived after the gates were locked to the tune of "full house." Disappointed but not dismayed they returned from Croke Park to the centre of the city where loud speakers telling the story of the game were convenient; or heading for their suburban homes to spend the afternoon in the sun before the open windows where a wireless set was operating.

We had all the "final" atmosphere in Dublin City over the week-end. Kerry ran a well-filled midnight train from Tralee, arriving in time for early Mass on Sunday morning; many of them hoped to bring home minor football honours once again with their tall youths who had put paid to the accounts of Cork and Dublin. Many of those on the Kerry ghost train, however, were tried and hardy annuals who never miss an All-Ireland football final whatever the counties involved.

One group of Donegal enthusiasts had chartered a private plane and flew to Dublin for the game. On Saturday night I sauntered down the centre of the city to watch the gay happy crowds enjoying this wondrous autumn balm in the air which lives on unbroken. Even the stragglers can save their late corn in comfort this year. I hope the remarkable season does not give the lazy ones a bad habit. Ulster accents told that the North were down following Cavan and Armagh to a man. Cork City sent the usual contingent of Gaelic football lovers; the soft sibilant accents of the West were not absent, though they lacked their usual volume.

The Cavan-Kerry double was forecast by the wise football critics. In two fast, clean games which gave a hearty and gripping afternoon's sport to all, those football critics were confounded for both Cavan senior and Kerry minors were beaten — and well beaten!

I was particularly interested in the American contingent who had flown over for the final; I sought them out at their hotel on Sunday before noon, renewing acquaintance with many old friends. A happy lot of young Irishmen (and a few not so young) whose industry and ability had succeeded in their different avocations.

The Irish-American party were in charge of an old friend, Mr. P.J. Grimes of Offaly, a rip-roaring young hurler with the U.S.A. when they tested Ireland's best at the Tailteann Games. Pat Grimes flies over regularly to our big G.A.A. games here, his interests are rather in hurling than in football.

I was very glad to meet Mr. Miah Ahearne of Kilbrittain, once more. I first met him under the shadows of the famous Kilbrittain Castle many years ago. All four brothers of the Ahearnes were useful hurlers; they played their part in the national struggles before emigrating. Miah Ahearne is prominent in G.A.A. and national circles in New York. He left Dublin to visit his old home in West Cork this week.

Mr. Tommy Armitage, of Tipperary, one of the greatest Gaelic footballers ever that the G.A.A. in America has seen, looks bigger and better than ever. I met him last when he captained the U.S.A. Gaelic footballers who made such a big impression in the Tailteann games. He played first-class football for 20 years in America. Now he is teaching his eldest son the elements of the art. For some years, too, I have been anxious to meet John ("Kerry") O'Donnell, native of Camp, Co. Kerry — a great tall rangy player of 20 years back, now owner, builder, manager of Gaelic Sports Park, New York, called New York Croke Park, where all the U.S.A. inter-county games are played. John Kerry O'Donnell, typical of the great county that claims him, is brother to that fine clean All-Ireland player for Kerry, Mr. Tim O'Donnell — a player of true Kerry polish who shone with the best of the Garda Dublin great teams. What a fine reception this Irish-American "Flight of the Gaels" got from the crowds heading for Croke Park when they appeared near the Parnell statue headed with their beautifully fringed banners — the Tricolour and the Stars and Stripes, brought over specially by plane for the occasion.

The Kerry-Armagh minor final was delightful entertainment for the football lover. Both sides had shown convincing form on the way up. Kerry were taller and heavier, but Armagh had a grand lot of boys. Not so confident or cool in their fielding as were Kerry, these Ulster boys can place a ball to the best possible purpose. I noticed when the Ulster boys fielded a ball even in defence they did not lash out for length — they invariably punted the ball to either wing, where a colleague was awaiting it. Armagh scored a point quickly (Blayney) but Kerry went into the lead when Sheehy (son of a famous Kerry Captain, John Joe Sheehy) swerved past and swung a beautiful centre; the goalie got to it but Galvin charged in and the return was charged to the net. A grand swaying game continued, Kerry keeping their lead well into the second-half. Then came a brilliant Armagh goal by Blayney from a neat passing movement. Thenceforward it was a game of alternate scores. Two points behind in the last quarter, Kerry threw all their weight into attack; they threw a few chances away but could make no impression on the stolid Northern backs, who held their posts secure in a sparkling finish.

Entrance gates were locked before the senior game opened. Packed thousands of eager faces made a colourful frame for the emerald texture of Croke Park, which never looked so well. Both camps reported a clean bill of health and confidence, and we settled down for a fast bright game. Meath were on their toes from the breakaway and made every post a winning one, making up their mind that Cavan would get neither time nor leisure to develop those smooth, weaving passing movements in attack that have so often swung the Breffni men to victory.

Cavan men themselves will acknowledge that Meath have always been their bogey team, particularly in League games. They proved real giant-killers on this occasion. Earlier in the week. a surprise decision was reached — to bring back Jim Kearney from retirement to their training camp; that sturdy man had shone as left-half-back away back in 1939, when Meath narrowly lost to Kerry. Kearney shone in club games and concentrated training. His partnership of O'Connell in Meath's midfield last Sunday was a trump card, for the pair stood shoulder to shoulder with Cavan's unbeaten pair (Brady and Sherlock). And from the first falling ball, Brady and Sherlock were held and often beaten in every phase of this vital sector.

Every man on the Meath side threw himself into the game with whole-hearted zeal, and, true to tell, they never looked like losing. Hand, Dixon and Heery held the famous Tighe, Higgins, Cassidy line of half-forwards and big Paddy O'Brien never gave Peter O'Donoghue an opening. The game developed into a battle royal between Cavan's craft and experience against a rampant and willing Meath side who ran early into a lead and built it up so securely that Cavan were always struggling.

Meath's front lines — particularly Byrne, Meegan, Smith and McDermott — showed speed, zest and purpose. Even Donohoe's six points from frees broke their unison. Then came Donohoe's low shot for a goal. It was cleared at the posts; the ball reached the tireless Cristo Hand, who drove across to Meegan — a fast swerving run thrilled the crowd. Meegan sent a grounder in swerving; Morris scooped it out, but Halpenny made amends for earlier errors and whipped the ball in the net! Meath were five points clear.

Cavan made more than one gallant rally, and new life was infused into the game when a glorious passing movement which Brady built up saw Carolan punch to centre; Cassidy had a share in it; Mick Higgins caught and swerved to shoot a glorious Cavan goal. But Meath came back like giants refreshed and drove home convincing winning points from Byrne and McConnell. What the game lost in classy football it made up in clean, hearty, honest-to-goodness, purposeful work. Meath had crowned their long persevering endeavour with a well-deserved and popular victory.

THE FOOTBALL FINAL 1950

MAYO and Louth came dancing on to the field amidst tumultuous flag-waving. Louth's red and white outnumbered Mayo's red and green by 8 to 1. Every man, woman and child in Louth seemed to be here.

Captain Sean Flanagan won the toss for the Men of the West and decided to play against the gusty wind blowing from the City. After Roe pointed for Louth from the breakaway, Mayo took strong control, forcing the game in determined fashion. Carney and Mongey were busy, and soon Mayo balanced to tear into the lead with five points by Mongey, Mulderrig and Gilvarry, clinched by a brilliant goal by Solan — a cleverly placed ground shot out of Thornton's reach in the net corner. Back came Louth with a will. Markey shone time and again; Sean Flanagan gave a masterly display in Mayo's defence, but Louth stole up. Roe had a slick point and then rounded John Forde to shoot a grand Louth goal.

McDonnell and Roe had points to set the score 1-3 each and close on half-time the elusive Ardee man, Roe, gave them the turnover lead 1-4 to 1-3.

Both goals had narrow escapes on resumption, but Louth dictated play in a vigorous third quarter, where Willie Kenny was unlucky to get a fractured leg. Mayo were shaken; Roe and Mongey exchanged minors, and Roe's point from a free set the score at 1-6 to 1-4 in Louth's favour. They looked like holding it with Markey, McArdle, Regan, Boyle and Reid all playing strong football.

But Mayo were abundantly fit. Racing downfield towards the railway goal, they were countered by Condon and Byrne. Then Sean Boyle trapped a fast one; he tried to dribble, but Langan, now outfield, was on him and took possession in a lightning forward movement. At a critical moment the tall, dark-haired Garda parted out to M. Flanagan, who was racing in at ten yards per second. Taking the ball as he sped, he swerved round Louth backs and raced goalwards. He rounded Thornton, who came out of goal, and Flanagan tapped the ball to the net — a staggering and decisive Mayo goal.

Mayo were set alight by this sudden swing of fortune's wheel, Mongey was always in the right place and fed Mulderrig. The red-haired boy handled perfectly and drove a lovely ball over the shoulder for a clinching Mayo point. Both sides finished all-out, but backs beat forwards in a breath-taking finish. Louth had tried hard and lost nobly.

Their big day is to come. The game was no classic; there were too many minor stoppages for frees and accidents. Yet this 1950 final had tensity and drama galore, played in a grand spirit between two gallant teams.

FOOTBALL FINAL 1951

G.A.A. luck held for the football final. Right through what must be considered a broken, showery summer and autumn all our big championship matches were blessed with splendid weather and that Sunday a glorious sun came out to gild the brilliant spectacle. All that was best in Irish life was at Croke Park that Sunday when Mayo won their second All-Ireland in succession and their third in all. And after Langan's goal in the tenth minute, these nimble men of the West left no doubt whatever of their superiority. At times they were really brilliant and in the second half often made Meath look a mediocre side. So much so that their final winning margin of five points hardly represented their marked superiority in every department of the game — defence, midfield and attack.

Meath played very steady, finished football throughout the first half and their forwards rarely put a ball astray; every one of their eight points was well earned. But there was no mistaking the flashing sparkle of Mayo's forwards against the wind. And that dynamic brace of goals by Langan and Gilvarry paved the way for a Western triumph.

Through the second half, Meath were forever struggling and rocking in vain efffort to match the scintillating movements of Mayo and only the herioc work of Mick O'Brien, Kevin McConnell and Kevin Smyth (goal) saved Meath from heavier disaster.

Meath forwards played headline football in that first ten minutes with a smart breeze to aid their flights towards the Railway goal. Christo Hand swung a powerful "lofter" from underneath the Hogan Stand. The ball soared high between the posts for Meath's first point in the opening minutes. In the fifth minute O'Reilly doubled the lead and when young Mattie McDonnell rattled up No. 3 from Hand's free, the Royal County were sailing smoothly along with a fair wind and a flowing sea.

Mayo were not perturbed. Driving low, straight punts into the wind around the tenth minute, the ball reached Joe Gilvarry, a swerving genius, who came out of his corner to pounce on the white sphere and crack it across to Garda Tom Langan, who, too, had raced out to take it. A double swerve and a deadly left-footed shot from 21 yards pasted the ball high up in the corner of the net. Mayo were level and lines and terraces were tasselled with widely waving green-red flags.

Carney's point from a free put them in front, but Taaffe levelled in the fifteenth minute. Mongey, elusive as a swallow, sent a neat ball above Smyth's head but inside a minute Paddy Meegan (Meath's best forward) had the levelling point from forty yards out — a model of long range accuracy. Byrne and Carney exchanged minors in a uniform game of attractive open football, but Meath's slender lead was crashed in broken time when the ball sped — Carney to Mulderrig and across the Meath goal to Joe Gilvarry who swerved around eel-like to drive a great ball well out of Smyth's compass — Mayo's second and convincing goal which told us that Meath's staunch defence was indeed vulnerable with Christo Hand — the iron man, carried off after a crashing charge in possession. Peter McDermott had Meath's eighth point before the short whistle called a respite — Mayo were just in front against the wind and their prospects bright indeed.

Meath's huge following were anxious but had not lost faith in their great-hearted, rock-bottom team, that had so often in the past recovered from seeming disaster and crashed their way to victory from behind. In the past, Meath were like Kerry Blue terriers, they could fight best on their backs.

But it was Mayo who rose to the great occasion. Slowly and firmly they took over control. Their fine backs breasted every ball with secure hands. Headed by veteran Harry Dixon (centre back) they tied the Meath forwards into a black knot and indeed played them to a standstill. Sean Flanagan never let the elusive Brian Smyth stray from his side where strength won. Prendergast, Fr. Quinn, Staunton and Dixon were safe as the Rock of Cashel. Padraig Carney now at midfield, was tireless in energy and rampaging around for loose balls which he punted boldly goalwards. He pointed a free, Irwin had another, and Mayo were three points clear, and flashing movements came between dour and rather crude bouts of play.

Mick Flanagan, well covered by McConnell now tore away in swerving solo runs. Twice Meath's goal seemed at his mercy until Heery and Smyth came around to grass him on the five yards line. Then Hand's return was cheered. Meath, though outsped and outplayed, rallied for a moment or two but their hopes were dashed when Carney drove a forty yards free safe above the bar. Frankie Byrne's point from a free did not disturb Mayo who were now all over their men.

Carney passed out to Gilvarry who finished a grand bit of work with Mayo's seventh point, and Carney lobbed another free across as if for good measure. It was idle to deny that Meath had a disappointing second half. All their collected craft, born of three years of gallantry vanished before the scintillating football of the men of the Heather, who finished as fresh as they began — a great Western triumph 2-8 to 0-9.

We had a delightful game of minor football between the nimble youth of Kerry and Armagh. Kerry's backs were so efficient in the first half that they held a fast-moving lot of Armagh forwards to a point margin at the recess — two points to one. Then the Green and the Gold boys went steadily ahead to lead six points to three at the three-quarter hour. Then came a great race through by Armagh and a great Hanratty goal to balance. Late in the hour McAuliffe's point seemed to make Kerry secure. Dead on time, after eight minutes' broken time was played, Armagh again flashed right through for McArdle to crash a great goal home and snatch dramatic victory. Kerry were unlucky losers, but Armagh's success was the result of well executed opportunity. A team deserves its luck and the Kerry boys took their unexpected defeat like sportsmen. A grand satisfying game for lovers of the Gaelic football at its best.

FOOTBALL FINAL 1952

IRISH-IRELAND was dominant in Dublin City and its environment through the week; the opening of the Oireachtas Festival was colourful; its competitions and musical and dramatic functions were all splendidly presented, and the public rallied behind the promoters with a whole-heartedness that suggests another wave of Gaelic resurgence. The big Gaelic League Festival coincided with the replay of the All-Ireland senior football final at Croke Park and the long Gaelic week will have to wind up on Sunday with the final of the Oireachtas hurling cup between Galway and Wexford.

Entries in all branches of Oireachtas competitions showed a decided step-up on last year's figures. The Choral, Dramatic and Art sectors were particularly successful. Mr. M.V. O'Donoghue of Waterford, President of the G.A.A. was forceful and eloquent in his opening address. Aindreas O'Muinneachain's beautiful Ballyvourney Gaelic was heard to good purpose. Old and young showed old-world enthusiasm for native vogues. At the stands in Croke Park the Gaelic tongue was general.

Winning competitors in traditional singing were widely scattered between the provinces with Sligo prominent — Cork, Dublin, Tirconnell, Kerry all did well. Eighteen counties took part in these branches, and widespread interest is apparent. An t-Oireachtas is coming back rapidly to the position it occupied in the nation's life around the border centuries. So rapidly has the Festival developed of recent years that it will be necessary to have separate paid staff appointed for its efficient management and promotion. This is a healthy sign; hitherto all the work was voluntary.

Heavy rain fell over Ireland on early Sunday morning and the outlook for the replay All-Ireland final between Cavan and Meath did not look too healthy from a weather viewpoint. Yet the thoroughfares of Dublin were just as thronged as they were before the drawn game. The menacing south-eastern sky which sent us torrents of rain all through the early morning, broke slowly and rain held off during the afternoon, though the sky became overcast and threatening towards the end of the senior game.

From a purely football viewpoint, the spectators who were in their places early got the bigger treat. For the minor final between Galway and Cavan was one of the best ever played. Those splendid young athletes, product of the secondary schools and colleges, defied the weather and made light of the greasy ball and heavy pitch. From the very outset the catching, kicking and passing were high-grade, reminding one of Kerry-Kildare skill of a generation back.

Cavan were just as skilful as Galway, and were rather unlucky to be in arrears at half-way. The heavy going, however, told more on Cavan's lighter team, and soon the height and reach of the maroon-clad Galway youth told their tale. And then Galway had Tom Brosnan, a Tuam boy, with a Kerry father and apparently with Kerry football instinct. Tom is a cool, speedy youth who flashes out of nowhere to capture the ball and drive dead and true for the posts. Kyne, full-back, Hoban, Kirwan, Dunleavy and Kelly (midfield) were other Galway stalwarts. Cavan battled on gallantly to a sparkling finish. The Ulster champions were best served by Frawley (goal) and the Farrellys, Smith and McKenna — a great game.

Some 60,000 were present when the senior teams from Meath and Cavan lined out under Mr. Sean Hayes (Tipperary). The rain had ceased, and if we except an occasional drizzle, held off for the afternoon. It is difficult to assess the senior game, for it was so tense and earnest with close and effective marking by man on man that we had little brilliant passages. The greasy ball and turf led to many miskicks, some mis-fields and an abundance of slips and falls in possession. Once again the teams were very well matched and the low scoring of the first half — 3 points to 2 in Cavan's favour — is sufficient evidence of the close, hard marking struggle between the teams that knew every move in each opponent's game. It was a game of missed frees by Meath and prolific frees by Cavan with the Breffni Captain, Mick Higgins, the hero of the piece. Impressions left in my mind are rather dull, with the immaculate place-kicking of Higgins shining out like a lighthouse in the gloom. Seven points from seven frees at all distances and at all angles, is something of a record in All-Ireland football finals. From play, Cavan scored two points only, but it must be remembered that every free given against Meath from which the vital points were scored, was conceded by Meath backs under pressure. Higgins, cool and unconcerned, as if he were taking practice kicks, landed them dead and true above the crossbar, to win the Championship for Cavan in a most unusual way.

In dramatic contrast came the Meath Captain's failure under similar circumstances. Meegan is a model of accuracy with his frees as a rule. He has won big matches for Meath by his place-kicking alone. Last Sunday he could do nothing right. He kicked four placed balls wide from safe angles in the first half and Meath never recovered from the disheartening sequence of points thrown away. There was not a whole lot of difference between the teams through the field, but Meath's forty-yards line — Meegan, Smyth and Brennan (promoted junior) — could make no impression on Cavan's fine half-back formation — Pat Carolan, Leo Maguire and Brian O'Reilly. There the match was lost and won, though Cavan all the time gave the impression of being the superior team.

Higgins had Cavan two points up from frees and exchanges through the field were even. Meegan's unexpected wides shocked Meath. Then Mattie McDonnell pointed for them before a glorious run by Tony Tighe ended in a flying Cavan point. Meath were lucky to turn over only a point behind — O'Reilly pointed a rebound before half-time — two points to three in Cavan's favour.

When Peter McDermott balanced scores in the eight minute, Meath looked on top, for Paddy O'Brien and his backs were playing right well. Once again it was a case of lost opportunity. Cusack, a promising recruit, brought Cavan's lead and then followed Higgins' charmed boot to kick that greasy ball four times over the crossbar with easy accuracy and confidence. McDermott made a great opening close on time and, with only the Cavan goalie to beat, drove the ball harmlessly wide of Morris' goal. Taaffe's free for Meath brought the last score of the game, where Cavan were worthy winners — the reward of two hours' stern football under most difficult conditions.

FOOTBALL FINAL 1953

DUBLIN'S great dignified central thoroughfare stretching in a straight Irish mile from St. Stephens Green via Grafton Street, O'Connell Bridge and Statue, past the G.P.O. (of memory) and the Parnell Statue to "Leavey's Corner" takes on a new and refreshing holiday air on the eve of an All-Ireland Final. And this latest was the greatest occasion of all. By 9 o'clock on Saturday night, the usual week-end "saunterers" were augmented by joyous young folk sporting rosettes and paper caps of gay colours. But when the cinemas and theatres, the inns and restaurants emptied themselves as the midnight hour approached; as the late special trains swelled the throng, the scene was really animated. One noticed that the saffron and white favours of the young Armagh folk fully outnumbered the green and gold of Kerry by five to one. They were a joyous crowd, their banter was all kindly and good-humoured, without a trace of rancour or the bitterness of rivalry. Orange and green mingled as easily as good old Irish whiskey accepts crystal water from the wayside spring. That spirit of goodwill prevailed all through the football week-end in Ireland's capital. Kerryfolk are habitually good-humoured and well behaved. But the buoyant Armagh contingents were not a whit behind them in decorum and self-restraint. Banter galore and all in "great good humour" as the traditional writers tell of the ancient football game of *Caid* played in the long ago on the strands of Kerry.

I do not think I ever saw so many motor cars in Dublin — not even in Eucharistic Congress year. When I crossed the city on Sunday after Mass the lanes of cars crowded both sides far out into the suburbs. All Ulster seemed to be here; "saffron and white" favours still dominated. The Gaels from the hotbed of bitterness — Portadown — had an outstanding banner and the groups of young men carrying raucous rattles were the highest spirited of the early arrivals at Croke Park, where the gates were opened at 10.30. The Portadown contingent took up a prominent place in the now limited side-line, which promptly filled. The entrance gate to these inner seats was closed at 12 noon, as the Angelus bell rang.

Artane's Boy's Band, a centre-piece of All-Ireland preliminaries, were soon augmented by the massed pipers and as we watched the streams of people gathering weight and momentum, the quarter hours passed quickly. In no time at all the officials in control of the minor game between Clare and Mayo took the field. By 1.30 every point of vantage in the unbooked sections were well manned, and still the streams poured in from all directions as I watched them from different corners high up in the

215

Cusack Stand. The grounds were packed to capacity before the minor game finished, and "still they came" across the bridges from the city. Results were inevitable when 85,000 were inside, some gates gave way under pressure. Thousands returned to the city to listen-in. Though a few hundred burst through to the side-line, the breach was quickly and effectively sealed off by the very efficient Gardai under Chief O'Neill and the G.A.A. officials. A really threatening situation passed, and the people who were crushed through the inside barrier, never gave a moment's trouble. What President O'Donoghue called "the Greatest Sporting Day in the sixty-nine years' history of the Gaelic Athletic Association" left nothing behind but pleasant memories.

Following their very fine football against Louth minors in the semi-final I felt that the Clare youths would win the Championship even against such a polished lot of young footballers as Mayo. The Banner County boys never settled down, and failed signally, to reproduce their recent form. Somewhat heavier than Mayo, the Clare boys fumbled a lot with the ball. Well as McCarthy, Griffin, and Mangan played in defence, Mayo's skilful handling of the ball and their accurate work near goal quickly got control. The Stewart pair, the Keanes, Treacy, McDonnell and Kilcullen played grand attacking football for Mayo. Drury and Comer were the best of Clare's forwards. Mayo played with all the swerving skill of their seniors and their ball control proved too much for Clare — a robust, plucky lot of boys who will improve rapidly with experience.

Shortly after 3 o'clock Kerry came quickly on to the field at full selected strength, led by "Jass" Murphy, their captain for the day. They had a big reception from the 90,000 people who were now within the ground, but it was nothing to the rapturous cheers that greet saffron-jerseyed Armagh as they came on to the pitch: they reminded me of March hares in moonlight when Spring is in, or movie pictures of sprightly antelopes at play in a tropical reservation.

His Lordship, Dr. Moynihan, Bishop of Kerry, was even taller than the G.A.A. President, Mr. M.V. O'Donoghue of Waterford, as they marched to greet the teams to the solemn air of "Faith of our Fathers." Then we had Peadar Kearney's "Soldier Song" — Kerry facing the wind and backing the Railway goal. Armagh, coolest of the cool against Roscommon, were obviously keyed-up now for they missed and fumbled a lot in the opening passages.

Kerry took due advantage with their forwards moving smoothly. Jim Brosnan, busy as an Irish terrier in a hunt, was on the mark with a point; "Con's son" made an opening for Tom Ashe for another, and it was only the cool skill of McMahon in Armagh's goal that saved his net as he covered and held a rasping shot by Sean Kelly.

Soon Armagh's composure was recovered, and they proceeded to play twenty minutes of as sound and constructive football as we have enjoyed at Croke Park in a decade. There was none of the fancy work as we have come to associate with "Ulster" style. Here was good, honest-to-goodness Gaelic football matching Kerry man for man and ball for ball. Gerry O'Neill, master of place kicks, kicked a jittery first "21" and sent the ball wide. He found range next time and set the score 0-1 and 0-2. Then came McEvoy's great Northern goal. The tall, long-kicking teacher burst away and lashed a drop-kick which carried deceptive pace — dead on the mark. Roche got his fingers to it and blinded Foley — the ball flashed to the Kerry net, and Armagh were ahead. Kerry recovered well and Tadhg Lyne scored the first of the five points to balance scores. Gerry O'Neill pointed a 14 yards free and McEvoy's raking shot put Ulster two points up in a game of magnificent football. Sheehan, playing with cool skill, then finished off lovely work by Kerry to place the ball to Jim Brosnan, who pointed pronto. Half time: Armagh 1-3; Kerry 0-5.

Brosnan's third minor set the teams level but McEvoy again broke the "sound barrier" as he wove in and lashed a point across. The great game swung from goal to goal. Sean Murphy was switched across on Mal McEvoy and proceeded to quickly seal off that grave danger to Kerry's seventeenth title. The Camp teacher played a great second half and McEvoy rather faded from the scene. Hannafin was replaced by Gerald O'Sullivan. Kerry were working smoothly now. The Murphys, Roche, Cronin, Kenneally and Palmer were filling the bill in defence, and Kerry's midfield and attack were playing typical Kerry football. Tadhg Lyne had three points in a row, and Kerry were again on top, but Armagh were still there with a battling chance. They forced their way upfield, and McEvoy sent a deceptive ball to the Kerry goal. Foley made his first mistake of the hour — nearly a fatal one. He fumbled with the dropping ball and had to back almost over his own goal line. As he swerved to avoid the Armagh charge, he dropped the ball to the ground, gathered it and managed to clear. There was an Armagh protest to the goal umpire. Referee Peter McDermott consulted both umpires and promptly awarded a penalty kick — "all out but Foley."

McCorry was entrusted with the shot which would have put the Ulster Champions in front. Groans arose from the Armagh crowds around me as the ball flashed a yard wide. Armagh's glorious chance was gone, and time was now short.

One other point they got — Seeley's point. They seemed to sag a little under that penalty blow, and Kerry finished the hour on the crest of the wave. We saw the old Kerry in these closing minutes, with Sean Murphy, the Lynes and Brosnan in their happiest mood, and J.J. Sheehan, the lively and constructive pivot on the vital "40" mark. He had two points kicked with cool precision. Jackie Lyne flashed Kerry's twelfth minor across and a final salute from Sheehan clinched the issue — 13 points to 1 goal and 6 points.

Armagh were splendid in defeat — "'tis not in mortals to command success but we'll do more, Horatio, we'll deserve it," said the immortal Liam. As for Kerry — spectators have come to the conviction that when their minds are set, they are invincible. At Castleisland Fair I once heard a tinker shouting in tinker's tongue: "You can't best Kerry!" It could be a slogan.

FOOTBALL FINAL 1954

HOW are the mighty fallen! That is what I felt for the thousands of Kerrymen heading for railway stations and other rendezvous last Sunday evening. Yet, were they downhearted? No! Somehow I always feel sorry for fallen champions. And the general public are very fickle in their allegiance. I recall that the script writers like myself were extolling the Kerry champions after a wonderful rallying victory over Armagh, just twelve months ago. This year the same team with one little change or two were lauded to the skies by reason of their magnificent victory over Armagh. And even last Sunday, one desperate Kerry attack near the end saw the ball going into the goal upright and cannoning off it to be cleared by the busy Meath men. Had the ball passed inside the upright, Kerry could have led and Meath would have had little time to recover! 'Twas only a game after all and a decent manly game at that, though it did not quite please the football experts and advocates of whole-time training which was banned last April.

'Twas a great All-Ireland Day. I felt it in my bones that we should have a good but not a superlative match, for Kerry and Meath of 1954 were not the outstanding teams of vintage football years, and Gaelic football, like every other game, goes around in cycles. Nor did I believe that the old football record would be broken — 85,000 at Croke Park. I had an idea at the heel of my mind that some thousands would stay at home in the endeavour to succour the precarious crops on the land.

A brisk westerly wind swept the countryside and suburbs of the city where I travelled on Sunday morning. By noon some of the "Ghost Trains" from the far-off South West peninsulas were in the capital. I met Mr. P.J. Grimes, Terry Long, Jack Phelan and several more of the "Flight of the Gaels," with their marshalling party on Upper O'Connell Street. All was orderly and precise. There seemed to be no rush or hurry anywhere. When I reached Croke Park gates as the Angelus rang at noon, the church bell was a signal to prepare for opening gates and soon the gay young bloods could be seen as they climbed over the top of Hill 16 to get a right good vantage point. Internal stewarding in Croke Park was excellent.

What a disastrous day for Kerry well many thick and thin followers declare. One North Kerryman — Mr. Brian McMahon of Listowel — scored a single success with his Historical and Symbolic Pageant, Eire's Four Beautiful Fields. I noticed that there was a particularly hearty reception for the Province of Ulster, where the anti-Irish Law of Partition still prevails.

I must pause to devote a little space to the minor final between Kerry and Dublin. For I thought it the most remarkable game of the series with an abundance of good football and a dramatic ending which no one expected even late in the hour. Kerry boys took a long time to settle down and use that fine wind. Dublin youths, a hefty, sturdy lot, showed splendid judgment in keeping the ball low in the wind; their perfect understanding and crossing passes helped them goalwards. Their points began to come and when Bell, a live wire, burst through for a goal, Kerry were in sore straits. Near half-time Kerry rallied well, but they were only a point clear and now faced a half-gale.

It looked bad for Kerry but from the break of the ball at half-time, Kerry minors played transformed football. I don't think I have seen better Gaelic football (of the true Kerry pattern) than that played by Kerry in the second half. It seemed against such a really fine side as Dublin, that nothing short of a miracle could give the game to Kerry against the wind in the second half. But these youths — Curnane, Barrett, Dowling, O'Shea, Long, O'Leary, Culloty, O'Dowd and Foley caught and kicked sailing balls with the technique of masters. For full 20 minutes Dublin were mastered. Kerry boys seemed to relish the difficult wind, and seemed to have the match all to themselves with a 5 points lead — 1 goal 8 pts. to 1 goal 3 pts. when broken time was reached. Then Bell, the elusive, burst away like a streak, he operated the short kick at sprinter's pace and placed Farnan the fair, close in, to shoot a rasping ball to the Kerry net — only 2 points down now. Before losing possession Dublin forced a free and a neat flick to the goalmouth gave Kavanagh a chance and he tapped it the wrong way — away from Curnane's snatch — two goals in three minutes. A lead of five secure points was changed into a one-point arrear in three minutes. And Kerry with no time to recover. I think it was the most dramatic finish I have ever seen to a match. Hard luck Kerry!

Both senior teams were at full strength as listed, a fine uniform body of athletes they were, as they paraded round. I do not think there were many pounds or inches in their height and weight. Kerry had a very strong breeze from the City goal and Jim Brosnan was very slick with an early shot for a point — 2 minutes played and Kerry already on the board. But Meath were soon on their toes and Mattie McDonnell raced past to balance scores with a perfectly hit ball from 35 yards out. Kerry were not by any means outplaying Meath at this stage. The Royal County men were battling every inch of the road, wind or no wind. P. Meegan kicked a splendid point from a free and it took a great individual effort of Tadg

Lyne to land the equaliser across. Lyne's next minor from Paud Sheehy forced the lead. Meegan dominated play for ten minutes. He kicked two points from frees and one from play to put Meath followers jubilant.

Meath had one last crack into the wind and Moriarty, the student, landed two grand balls home, setting the score in Meath's favour — 7 points to 3 — wind and all. Kerry were roused at last and Paud Sheehy tore away to cross over for a chance ball, solo and drive to the goalmouth. McGearty flicked it but Sheehan was on him like a streak and goaled boldly. Kerry revived and two accurate shots (one free) brought Tadg Lyne two valuable points and helped Kerry to turn over a point ahead.

Kerry were a most heartbreaking team in the second half. I expected them to sail home on a winning wind, but with them everything went amiss on this disastrous day of days. Kerry backs were rooted to the ground, their midfieldmen were little better and all the football talent owned by their forwards were left at home. It is true that they fought on doggedly and flashed up a bit with occasional promise. But soon after they began to slip and fumble and miskick. It was Meath then that began to play really attractive football. Every man in the team appeared to be moving. It seems a wonder to me, looking back on the game, that Meath did not win by 10 points instead of 6. Soon Brian Smith, the old Meath Captain, began playing beautiful football, reminiscent of his palmy days. He pointed and fed McDermott for another. Meegan and Sheehan exchanged minors. McDermott swerved in and shot — O'Mahony saved well but Moriarty sped on him and drove his clearance to the net — a most vital score in the game.

Meath were in again and McDermott boxed a free from Meegan. Brosnan now did one of his pretty things and pointed but Brian Smith had the last say with a grand swerve and a sailing point, dead centre above the bar — it was the unlucky 13th for Kerry. Meath won well.

Lack of their usual collective training in camp hurt Kerry. Of that I have no doubt. Some restricted but more controlled training may be introduced. They were too bad to be true. Meath, in my opinion, played the best football in recent years — most deserving winners.

FOOTBALL FINAL 1956

BEATEN in three All-Ireland finals in a fortnight is the unique 1956 record of Cork's Athletic Gaeldom! Yet even in their most successful years, I don't think Corkmen had more reason to hold their heads high. They were splendid in defeat. Hurling final lost to Wexford on September the 23rd, Camogie final lost to Antrim a week later and defeat by a sparkling Galway side in the football final! The sequence is unprecedented in the whole G.A.A. history.

What makes this 1956 Autumn odyssey more memorable for Corkmen (and maids) is that on all three occasions when Cork looked well beaten, they rallied in most courageous fashion; threw fear to the winds, challenged the leaders and made the closing minutes of all three games a welter of healthy excitement. And all three games were finished in an exemplary spirit of high sportsmanship. I do not think Cork teams ever stood in higher esteem than they do now. All sportsmen love good losers and the dauntless rallies of Cork teams in weeks of the immediate past, will live in memory of supporters and rivals alike. Never before have I felt so comfortable about defeats — a sweet regret for chances lost is tinged with the pride of sportsmanship and the evidence of brotherhood as the six teams marched off the field shoulder to shoulder and hand in hand. This was something which the early and tireless workers in the Gaelic movement would dream of and not see fulfilled in such a sequence until now.

The 1956 Galway-Cork football final was a splendid exhibition of the code from end to end — a hearty exhilarating exhibition of a manly strenuous game. There were honest, shoulder to shoulder charges in plenty, but not a word or gesture from any man on either side to mar the great occasion — another triumph of organisation for Mr. Padraig O'Caoimh and his Council. There was ne'er a hitch in this smooth handling of another huge crowd.

As usual I sauntered over to the slopes of Drumcondra after early Mass and breakfast. I take a great delight in watching the crowds gathering from the heights of the Cusack Stand. The eternal Artane boys were here again in good trim. You heard the story about the youth who came to an All-Ireland final with his father when he was 10 and came again when his county was back in the final seven years later. He said to his father:

"What's wrong with these band boys, father, I saw them seven years ago and they haven't grown an inch."

Croke Park finals and Artane Boys' Band are familiar terms. The pitch was even greener than usual — resodded around the goals. Leitrim boys, a plucky lot of chaps, were out-manoeuvred by the slick Dublin lads who had six of last year's winning side in key positions. By three o'clock the dignatories of Church and State were in their seats in the Hogan Stand. Mr. Peter McDermott, the Meath scoring star was whistling the seniors in and they were soon here. In the usual march around I could not help remarking that the Galway men in their white (Connaught) jerseys looked the more military and uniform side. There was little between them in weight. Cork had more six-footers, but Galway were the more uniform and muscular side. His Grace Dr. Walsh, Archbishop of Tuam threw the ball in and the tornado broke.

I have often seen some sparkling openings but Galway were like greased lightning. Beating back Cork's first raid which Mangan cleared, Galway forwards got away and then we saw the wizard-like pair — Purcell and Stockwell blaze into action. These white-clad forwards seemed to be on wires; they flashed here and there; Purcell placed a diagonal pass in front of Kirwan and the Ballinasloe youth flashed it over the bar. Hot foot came 20-year-old Coyle racing on Galway's right wing; a swing to Stockwell who jinked in and shot point number 2. The Western forwards seemed to hold Cork's famed backs mesmerised. At the seventh minute Galway were 3 up when O'Neill placed dancing master Stockwell for another minor.

Cork woke to realities. Sean Moore set them going and Creedon placed Furlong who swung a beauty of a point for Cork. Eric Ryan pointed a free and the issue was set. Stockwell and Ryan, Purcell and Fitzgerald (2) swopped rapid points. Kelleher brightened Southern hopes with number 6 for Cork, but then Stockwell broke clear and goaled with a brilliant move. Alternate scoring kept the game alive and at the 25th minute the scoring sheet promised a close finish but Galway had a great scoring spasm before half-time. Another flashing goal by Stockwell and points by Kirwan and Purcell; these grand winning shots built a 2 goal lead at the short whistle — 2-6 to 0-6

Cork re-adjusted their defence — O'Driscoll was now centre half. Bernard on his left and Gould at right full. Cork hopes were fair enough but Galway tore away into the breeze to add two flying points by the ubiquitous Stockwell. It was then that Cork's real fighting heart was roused.

Eight points down and twenty minutes to play, they fought back with a will. Moore and Duggan started the fun and Niellie drove a grand ball in. Mangan fisted it out but Creedon nailed it and crashed past the Tuam man for Cork's first goal. Thenceforward the hills were aflame. Galway stormed back and landed two fast points by Coyle and Evers. But Duggan and Moore again got Cork forwards moving. Duggan drove to the air and Kelleher tore in after it to drive a terrific shot against the underside of the crossbar and beat Mangan all ends up. Coyle — a great recruit, put in a high point for Galway, but Cork were back like lions on the warpath. Kelleher went into a goalmouth ruck and the Millstreet man, now in the left corner, flashed one in which Mangan stopped but fumbled and it crossed the line for Cork's third goal. Ryan's point from a free set the score 17-16 — Galway one point up but the crowd roaring and Cork like bloodhounds on the trail.

One Cork shot grazed the high posts and looked good but 'twas flagged wide and back came Galway to save the precarious game. It was right that the two scoring heroes, Purcell and Stockwell should clinch the game — two grand points with time dead close gave the Sam Maguire Cup to Jack Mangan (hero number 3) amidst scenes of unprecedented enthusiasm. The Cork and Galway men marched away shoulder to shoulder in mutual esteem and perfect sportsmanship. It was one great match to live in memory at many a winter fire in glen and hill. Galway won well but Cork were gallant losers.

The game brought me more than one surprise. In the first place I never anticipated such polished and almost classic football from this recently sprung Galway side. They were all they looked on parade — fifteen cool, fit men, fully resolved. So uniform were they that it is hardly fair to name a man. The three Tuam pals — Mangan, Purcell and Stockwell, however, made a shining trinity. The Glanmire man, Willie O'Neill played a man's part and Mahon held an unerring centre back position. Coyle and Keely filled the bill; Kissane, Kirwan, Grealy — all were good.

My second surprise was the huge success of Cork's much abused forwards and the failure (comparative) of their lauded backs, who had served them so well in the past. For some reason or another, Denis Bernard, who had been indisposed was only a shadow of his past greatness; Harrington had the ball running badly for him and Donal O'Sullivan met just the type of forward that can beat him — the will-o'-the-wisp, waltzing, jinking Stockwell. Cork forwards were glorious at times when they ground their teeth near the end. Duggan, Kelleher and Furlong played fearless terrier-like football. They looked like having Galway backs crumbling six minutes from the end. I often saw Tyers more secure, but like O'Sullivan, he did not know where Stockwell would strike next. Ryan was very good in the first half, but so good was Moore from end to end I have no hesitation in naming him as the best man on the Cork fifteen. He almost won the match on his own. I missed one old friend on that great day, Mr. Jim Clarke, the Ballybunion sportsman, missed his first football final since 1887.

ALL-IRELAND FOOTBALL FINALS 1958

"SALVAGING the harvest" is the most apt description of the present farm activities and it is those nearest to the land who know how much agriculturalists have suffered in the wettest year in my rather long and tenacious memory. Heavy, the harvest loss has been in most places, and, whilst the incidence of moisture has varied a lot in different counties, the general picture is rather grim. This is particularly true of the Midlands and east coast counties. One farmer was bitter in his condemnation of some newspaper reports which were too optimistic, "and," he said, "they allow nothing at all for mental worry and wear and tear." He did look worried this poor man from Southern Louth, where tillage is skilful and concentrated. Yet he could also tell me that the G.A.A. writers were wrong when stating that Dublin and Derry never met before in an All-Ireland championship.

My friend, who is seventy years or more, said that Derry and Dublin played at Drogheda in the All-Ireland semi-final of 1902. Strange to say it was not in football that they met but in hurling.

It is not generally known that a form of hurling was played in many parts of Ulster at the time the G.A.A. was founded in 1884. The hurleys they used then were a narrow-bladed, wide-soled caman, particularly suited for ground hurling. Quite recently the President of the G.A.A., Dr. J.J. Stuart, in a public pronouncement, stated that there was a hurling club in every parish of Derry in the early days of the G.A.A.

This Dublin-Derry senior Gaelic Football championship final of 1958 carried all the old final-day glamour. Following a lovely morning — sun and breeze — clouds gathered about noon as I was heading north through Dublin's crowded city for Croke Park Mecca. I had hundreds of fellow pilgrims to accompany me even at that early hour.

On my return from early Mass I found welcome visitors from the south awaiting me — the visit was unexpected, for we were in the unusual position of not having a team from Munster either in the minor or senior football finals. But then big Jim Hurley and his fine sons never miss a final, whether Munster teams are in action or not. This great hurler and administrator was as happy and exhilarating as a breeze from the Fastnet Lighthouse, as we talked of old times and new.

Mr. Hurley, who played hurling and football for his native Cork and won four all-Ireland championships, has friends in every county of Ireland; in the Cusack Stand this seventeen stone, 6 feet 1 giant was the centre of an admiring crowd and I was away to my writing duties.

Three well-known and still sturdy all-Ireland folk from three different provinces halted as they passed my seat. This was early, before the crowd gathered and all seats in my area were rapidly being occupied. First that came was a great old friend and neighbour, whom I had not met for a long time — David Kelleher of Charleville — hurler, footballer, oarsman, golfer and coursing lover. Davy won three All-Ireland football medals with Kickhams and Geraldines of Dublin — 1906, 1907 and 1908. He was on the hurling final team of 1908 that drew against Tipperary and then lost — an athlete of wonderful endurance and skill.

Tom Burke of Drogheda, also looking wonderfully fit for his years, was in the great Louth sides of forty-five years ago and was one of a powerful defence that won the 1912 All-Ireland final for Louth following hard luck in earlier years. A six-foot man, Tom Burke was a tireless worker in the G.A.A. and all kindred national movements. Just behind him came one of the great Gaelic football family of Courell — Frank, another six-foot giant and a remarkably fine footballer with Mayo. Frank Courell shone in many positions, particularly in defence. His brother, Gerald Courell, was the most prolific goal-scorer of his period.

All we had heard about the big crowds expected for the football final was not mythical. The black streams of humanity filled every approaching road; the terraces were rapidly filled and every vantage point — even the roofs of the stands and the long railway wall had their patiently awaiting occupants. Doors and gates were all locked an hour before the senior game opened. It was estimated by Mr. Padraig O Caoimh and his officials that about 25,000 people were locked out — 73,371 passed the turnstiles. Skilful stewarding and good humoured crowds helped in the smooth running of a splendid afternoon's sport. Clouds gathered, but the rain held off, and football was good throughout.

Dublin and Mayo minors played splendidly skilled football for a long way. Mayo boys swopped scores right through a sparkling first half and it was around the three-quarter hour that two flashing Dublin goals clinched the game. Mayo were unlucky when good shots hit timber. The better side won, for the Dublin youths finished a grand hour with exuberant sparkle. The game of Gaelic football flourishes in the Dublin schools.

I have heard many thundering receptions for teams entering the playing pitch at Croke Park, but when these red and white clad athletes from Derry pranced in on Sunday, the roofs on the stands shook with the volume of cheering.

This was a tribute to the young men from the most historic of our severed Six Counties. This was Derry's first appearance at Croke Park in a senior championship and the sporting crowds rose to them. They were worthy of the acclaim for they treated the packed and swaying crowds to a sound exhibition of good Gaelic football. They handled high balls with the precision and confidence of a Kerry side and their midfield were masters of every branch of the Gaelic art and their forwards rivalled Dublin in the well-controlled, slick movements near goal.

Mr. Simon Deignan of Cavan's greatest All-Ireland sides is considered one of our very best referees and he never had any trouble with two sporting sides. Dublin won the toss and played into the Railway goal. There was a good, steady breeze from the city to aid them.

What first impressed me was the fine, confident fielding of the ball by the Derry backs and midfield. There was no hesitancy here, as was usual with Ulster sides in the past. Gribben, Doherty, McLarnan, Breen and Smith broke up many wind-borne Dublin drives, and I settled down to see a good game of Gaelic football.

Ollie Freaney's place-kicking was deadly accurate for Dublin and referee Deignan's extra-keen refereeing gave Ollie many extra opportunities. Dublin ran up five points in the first quarter to Derry's two, but there was no evidence yet of defeat or victory, for Derry were standing up in solid phalanx and giving Dublin's scoring machine few open paths to the goal. Sean O'Connell, a tall Derry school-teacher, was the most dangerous of Derry's attackers and he landed two good points in sharp exchange with Dublin's high-over-the-bar scores. With the wind to aid them in the second half Derry were by no means out of it at eight points to four.

We had a rattling third quarter. Derry's captain, Jim McKeever, hit one of his inspired periods and played havoc in and around midfield. He fielded at all angles and drove beautifully directed balls goalwards; he pointed one and forced a free later which Sean O'Connell pointed and the score read: Dublin 8, Derry 6, and the breeze freshening.

Dublin got busy then and Haughey's runs held the field; Ollie Freaney pointed (free) and Dublin were again a goal clear. Back came Derry with a rattle, and in swept her forwards. When Owney Gribben crashed a goal to balance the scores there was a solid roar from the excited Derry (and neutral) followers. Scores were level pegging 0-9 to 1-6.

We were brimful of incidents now, for Des Ferguson streaked away and swung one across to Farnan on Dublin's right wing — Doherty in checking slipped and Farnan raced through and drove a perfect grounder hard and straight to the net. That was the decisive score. Freaney's points off frees stretched the lead. O'Connell had a fine point for Derry. A beautiful Dublin movement saw Joyce crash Dublin's second goal through and the game was over.

Derry battled on unperturbed and two points to remind us that these Northmen finished undaunted, finished a solid, if not classic game. Derry will be back again.

FOOTBALL FINAL 1959

CROKE Park was more glamorous than ever. I've rarely seen a more orderly or more eagerly expectant crowd. The bright autumn sun shone down on a sea of colour — green and gold of Kerry and maroon and white of Galway.

The peaceful invasion of the country's capital began on Friday evening and continued in increasing streams right through Saturday, when thousands travelled by road, rail, sea and air. O'Connell Street, as usual on All-Ireland night, was a joyous looking place as the beflagged and hatted rivals mingled in great good humour and pleasant banter. Gaelic phrases were flung around between the groups — Dingle men and Carraroe men, Aran Islandmen and youths from Valentia and deep Iveragh.

By noon I was, as usual, heading my unobtrusive way to Croke Park. The city was full and the trek up towards Drumcondra road was bigger than ever I've seen at such an early hour. Mr. Padraig O'Caoimh seemed to have everything in smooth control and his genius for detail was evident on all sides — not a hitch, not a neglect in the masterly control of every possibility. I saw more overseas visitors at Croke Park than ever before — our games are commanding international interest. I counted half-a-dozen Bishops from home dioceses and from overseas. Leaders in Church and State were here and legislative bodies were strongly represented in different parts of the New Hogan Stand. There was one solid contingent from the Eastern American States who had flown across for the game on a specially chartered plane — an express, Saturday-to-Monday hop to see the long awaited final. Croke Park's famous playing pitch was back in its best emerald velvet texture.

We had a bright minor football final between Dublin (holders) and Cavan, the northern champions. Cavan had much the better of the opening session and Dublin seemed thrown off their game at first. Cavan led at half time (1-2 to 0-4) but Dublin's advisors gave them some helpful hints during the respite and we saw a different Dublin team on resumption. They went into the fray with fresh dash and were soon in front, to take full possession. Dublin kicked half-a-dozen good points across and Cavan youths faded away near the end. Dublin minor teams, changing every year, have won five of the last six finals.

The gates were closed and barred forty-five minutes before the senior game opened. Many late arrivals were disappointed but they were kept in touch with the position — "house full" by field announcements. The attendance of almost 86,000 is a near record. The gate figures are difficult to assess for there are thousands of seasonal tickets (10 year) which do not enter into the day's receipts. There appears no shrinkage in Croke Park's attendances and popularity. Too bad that space is confined.

As the teams bounced out of their dressing rooms, it was noted that they were well matched in height and weight. Six foot two Frank Evers in the maroon and white of Galway towered above colleagues and rivals. Galway looked more muscular; Kerry a bit more deerlike and sprightly. Here were two fine sides, sound friends and keenest of rivals, in this great game of the Gaels.

Exchanges were rapid; two very well-taken points by John Dowling in the first three minutes set Kerry followers jubilant. Galway were soon surging up and Evers sent Purcell away in a swerving run goalwards. Evers raced through on Purcell's right and took a shrewd pass as he sped — he rattled a drop to the net and the western champions were in front. Tackling was razor-keen yet as clean and upright as could be. Hard knocks, mostly in those shoulder to shoulder shocks which both Kerry and Galway adopt. So close was the charge and counter-charge that there was little spectacular football. Over-anxiety brought many wides. Yet there were some very fine bouts of football which the critics seem to have forgotten. Teams were level at half-way and the issue dead open.

What rather astonished me in that tough but honest first half was the ease with which Frank Evers and Mattie McDonagh mastered the Kerry midfield stars — Mick O'Connell and Seamus Murphy. Evers reached highest and got his hands on most of the falling balls. I had noticed frequently that the Valentia captain takes some time to settle down. He was "out of it" up to the time he got a severe knock on the muscles of his thigh. He was forced to retire later.

Then did Kerry technicians on the sideline show their football skill. They put the limping O'Connell on the "40" and put Tom Long on Evers at midfield. The switch worked wonders. Long always played centrefield for Erin's Hopes (St. Patrick's College) and for his native Dingle. His clever tactics in outsprinting Evers swung the game round in Kerry's favour and the success of Long brought further switches at the half-hour. McAuliffe and Geaney; O'Dwyer to the "40" when Mick O'Connell retired; John Dowling outfield and Seamus Murphy at full-forward.

Most likely that Dr. Eamonn O'Sullivan, John Joe Sheehy and Frank Sheehy were in the planning of these wise switches.

Every move worked. Kerry forwards got good service of the ball and the flashing moves of Dan McAuliffe got two shock goals that put Kerry on the high road of success. When Garry McMahon of Listowel came on as a sub. he raced in to a crossing ball and drove a rising shot against the far upright and flashed to the net. Galway were three goals in arrears, rocking.

Kerry were clearly the faster and fitter side during the closing and decisive stages of the game. Sean Purcell was well-covered by Kevin Coffey and Frank Stockwell got few openings from the vastly improved full-back, Niall Sheehy. Not a man in Kerry lost his sparkling form, but one man stood out from the lot — Sean Murphy, the U.C.D. medical student from Camp, in the Dingle peninsula. Sean Murphy has helped to win many a final for Kerry, but in this 1959 final against Galway he was "the man of the match." Behind the beaten midfield in the first half-hour, Sean Murphy did trojan work.

He flashed into every danger and showed considerable ball-control and speed. He was not beaten once in the hour and he kept up that sparkling form to the end of his finest hour. Tadhg Lyne made a brilliant return to the game. Paudie Sheehy was better than ever; his pace and football talent led up to many a Kerry score. Kerry were winning easily near the end and Culloty never erred. John Dowling, wherever set, put in grand strong work.

Jerome O'Shea, Mick O'Dwyer and Kevin (Beaufort) Coffey played their parts well, but Sean Murphy, Tim Lyons, John Dowling and Paud Sheehy were outstanding from end to end. Dr. Eamonn O'Sullivan's coaching skill had worked wonders on a side which looked moderate in their Munster Final against Cork at Killarney.

Galway had been chopping and changing their side a lot of late. It looked improved on paper but failed badly under pressure. It was a case of "diamond cut diamond" for a long time with one side helping to hold the other in check. I liked Meade, Greally, Mahon, Evers and in particular, liked Mattie McDonagh's dash and tenacity, even when in heavy arrears. Sean Purcell was always dangerous; Stockwell was well shadowed by Niall Sheehy; John Nallen was never playing like a fit man. Galway failed to keep the pace up against the ruthless fitness of Kerry who are again "on the crest of the wave."

DOWN'S GREAT VICTORY 1960

AND so the great day has come and gone! The historic Sam Maguire Cup has "crossed the Border" for the first time and the occasion brought enthusiasm and rejoicing unprecedented in the history of Croke Park Gaelic football. Never before were there such exuberant scenes of mass fervour on Croke Park's verdant sod — scene of many great rejoicings and great sorrows too — on one ill-fated November day, just forty years ago.

And the 1960 winning team was as gallant and sporting a bunch of Gaels as ever won an All-Ireland championship. They had no more sincere or hearty well-wishers than the fifteen Kerrymen who battled so hard and so honest to beat Down. The victorious Down team were no sooner landed at their dressing-rooms than Paudie Sheehy, the Kerry captain, sought them and congratulated them on their splendid display — sportsmen all on a great day for the Gaelic Athletic Association.

From the North-East and the South-West — from opposite ends of the one island came the glad-hearted thousands. What matter if some of their late-ripening corn was still in the fields! Didn't the weather look settled and one day's rest would do it no harm — tomorrow was another day. I wended my way down the long, broad, central streets of Dublin town. Already hundreds of enthusiastic men and maids were mingling their contrasting colours — the red and black of Down and green and gold of Kerry looked bright and gay. I heard the sharp Gaelic speech from Omeath and the Mournes, as well as the melodious cadences of Dingle and Ballinskelligs on the southwestern coast. Latest news from the respective camps told of the quiet assurance from Kerry and of the bubbling confidence of Down. I looked forward to a great final.

As usual I was outside Jones's Road entrances when the gates were opened and at once the turnstiles began to click merrily, never to cease until 87,768 people of all ages and occupations were enclosed. Mr. Padraig O'Caoimh, prince of organised detail, had all his plans well laid for a record crowd. Not one minute item was overlooked and during the whole glorious afternoon the busy stewards and Gardai were on duty. A few crowded corners threatened a break-through, but they were sealed off readily. The terraces were already packed comfortably when the minor footballers of Galway and Cork took the field. The waiting period had brought us bright national music from the ever-popular Artane Boy's Band and the Black Raven Pipers' Band. The Galway and Cork youths looked very well matched in weight and reach.

The Cork boys held their own right well up and down the field. They failed in one vital feature — their forwards were most inaccurate approaching goal. Wide after wide by these speedy Cork minors was heartbreaking to their supporters. Through the field Cork held sway for a long part of the hour. They were far more frequently in attack than the Galway youths. But when it came to shooting for scores, Galway were infinitely superior. Hardly a raid by these boys from the West was unrewarded and some of their scores were a treat to see. Galway were a beautifully balanced side, smooth in every part. Twelve Corkmen matched them man for man and kick for kick but the red-and-white stockinged lads had no scoring men worthy of the name. Cork never ceased to persevere and got a big cheer from the crowd as worthy losers. Galway, with a St. Jarlath foundation, made a great impression — stylish footballers from goal to goal. Some of their diagonal passes were delightful to watch as they developed.

In the parade around I thought that Down, led by Kevin Mussen, were the more spruce and livelier side. Some Kerrymen seemed heavier than in 1959 and their ex-captain, John Dowling was limping throughout and he limped until he retired injured midway through the second half. Referee John Dowling of Offaly had his men quickly under control and they were a very decent, though very keen and earnest lot of men. Four minutes of swaying play saw Kevin Mussen and George Lavery drive the ball towards the canal goal. Tony Hadden sprinted across to trap it and he promptly swung well above the crossbar for the opening score of the hour. Mick O'Connell was just as prompt as he drove long and high at McKay who cleared beneath the bar — level pegging. Lyne's free and Joe Lennon's punt brought neat points, and they were level after twelve minutes of play. Then came some really fine football by Down and their forwards finished right well — four points in a row — Pat Doherty, Sean O'Neill, Jim McCartan and Tony Hadden. At the sixteenth minute of play, Down led by six points to two, and had earned their lead.

Two picture frees by Tadgie Lyne made the board look better for Munster and alternate scores kept interest alive — Pat Doherty for Down and Tadhg Lyne for Kerry setting the score seven to five in Down's favour at half-time and the game dead open with little or no favouring wind.

Kerry must have made up their minds during the half-time respite that Down, the victors of Kerry in the 1959/60 League were "foemen worthy of their steel." For Mick O'Connell and company at once set about saving the game. O'Connell tore into every approaching ball and drove a perfect shot well above the crossbar. All Kerrymen on the field were moving forward when Seamus Murphy trapped a ball on Kerry's right wing; he swerved well and drove a good shot for the balancing point after 13 minutes of play.

At that point Kerry looked in a winning mood. Down's fairy godmother must have been flighting around Croke Park when Jim McCartan swung one of his long shots in. The ball travelled dead on but Johnie Culloty covered it with great confidence. The ball dropped just under the bar and Culloty put his hands to it. There were no Down attackers in, but by one of those accidents common in sport the ball dropped from his hands into the corner of the net. Down were one goal up and were doubly assured of victory. Their luck continued for Sean O'Neill raced through for a goal but was pulled down in the parallelogram. Referee Sean Dowling at once waved "all out" and red and green flags again waved. Pat Doherty drove the penalty kick safe home and Down were two goals up with 18 minutes to go.

Kerry battled on bravely and Jerdie O'Connor lashed their eighth point through. Down were now rampant and Pat Doherty, deadly accurate, drove three further Down points above the bar. Down won — 2-10 to 0-8 — a sound victory, earned by better all-round forward work. Kerry's front lines were disappointing.

Also published by Beaver Row Press

Ann Hartigan *Long Tongue*
Steve McDonogh *My Tribe*
Brendan Kennelly *Shelley in Dublin* (revised edition)
Brendan Kennelly *House that Jack didn't build*
Brendan Kennelly *Cromwell*
Wood-Martin *Lake Dwellings of Ireland* (re-issue)